# The Stratified Leadership Model
*of the* First-Century Christian Church

# The Stratified Leadership Model
## *of the* First-Century Christian Church

BARTON S. GARRATT EDSALL IV

WIPF & STOCK · Eugene, Oregon

THE STRATIFIED LEADERSHIP MODEL OF THE FIRST-CENTURY CHRISTIAN CHURCH

Copyright © 2025 Barton S. Garratt Edsall IV. All rights reserved. Except for brief quotations in critical publications or reviews, no part of this book may be reproduced in any manner without prior written permission from the publisher. Write: Permissions, Wipf and Stock Publishers, 199 W. 8th Ave., Suite 3, Eugene, OR 97401.

Wipf & Stock
An Imprint of Wipf and Stock Publishers
199 W. 8th Ave., Suite 3
Eugene, OR 97401

www.wipfandstock.com

PAPERBACK ISBN: 979-8-3852-3500-1
HARDCOVER ISBN: 979-8-3852-3501-8
EBOOK ISBN: 979-8-3852-3502-5

07/17/25

# Contents

| | |
|---|---|
| *Preface* | vii |
| *Acknowledgments* | ix |
| *Abbreviations* | xi |
| *Abstract* | xiii |
| CHAPTER 1 \| Introduction to the Stratified Leadership Model | 1 |
| CHAPTER 2 \| The State of the Research | 14 |
| CHAPTER 3 \| The Emergence of the First-Century Church | 31 |
| CHAPTER 4 \| The Stratification of Leadership | 62 |
| CHAPTER 5 \| The Perpetuation of the Church | 146 |
| CHAPTER 6 \| Conclusions | 188 |
| *Bibliography* | 203 |
| *Scripture Index* | 211 |

# Preface

To the reader who has opened the pages of this book, the following work is a faithful reproduction of my doctoral dissertation and the culmination of ten years of varied biblical studies and amassed research. I fully believe that Yehovah, the Lord God, laid upon me the desire to study in-depth the seven subjects that the apostle Paul declares explicitly in his epistles in the New Testament, of which believers should not be ignorant. When I was finishing my associate's degree, I conversed with my father concerning my goal to self-publish a second work, as he had supported my first publication three years prior. My first work tackled the subject of 1 Cor 12:1; I shared with him my intent to expound and explore Rom 1:13 and sent him my rough draft of the first three chapters. He commended my goal but instructed me to save it for some forthcoming paper and focus instead on my then-current studies.

In my final semester, my professor Dr. David Grant encouraged me to pursue further degrees that would equip me to become a collegiate professor so that I might teach others. Similar to how an associate's degree became a bachelor's degree, which in turn became a master's and then a doctorate, likewise, two years became five, which became ten, and I lost sight of the research I had begun until it came time to start work on a dissertation. As I reviewed possible topics to submit for my prospectus, the subject of *God's order for leadership among first-century believers* was brought back to the forefront of my consciousness. I realized that what seemed to be a collection of random essays, research works, and term papers over four years became an interconnected foundation for my final work for my doctorate submission, which I cannot take credit for having the forethought to have planned out so well in advance.

As this work becomes published to make its research available for the academic studies of others, I fully intend to produce a version that will be more readily received by those who may have only gone as far as a high school education because the lessons of the Holy Scriptures should be available to any that desire to know them. May God's love, grace, mercy, and blessings be imparted unto any who seek him, and the truths of his Holy Word enlighten all who read them.

Sincerely,
*Garratt Edsall*

# Acknowledgments

FIRST AND FOREMOST, ALL praises to Yehovah Yire, the LORD God, who sees and provides, with whom all things are possible, and without whom nothing is possible.

I would like to thank and praise my loving and supportive wife, Michelle, for accompanying me on this long and winding journey that has culminated in this dissertation and my collegiate success.

I would like to thank Dr. Benjamin Laird of Liberty University for serving as my mentor and guide for my dissertation. He continuously challenged me to delve deeper into the research topics within this work. I would also like to thank Dr. William Craig Price of Liberty University for his encouragement to research and present the subject matter contained herein.

I am grateful to Rev. Vern Edwards and his wife, Jill, for supporting my collegiate endeavors and sponsoring my enrollment at Liberty University.

A special heartfelt thanks to Rev. Gene Slavit, who aided me, graciously serving as my editor *pro bono* for over a year, checking and double-checking my understanding, interpretation, and utilization of the Greek language; your friendship and service are priceless.

I would like to dedicate this dissertation to my parents, Gail Malley and Bart Edsall. My father, Bart Edsall, aided me as a content and presentation editor. In addition, he has encouraged me and all his children to pursue excellence in any field of endeavor. To his credit, he had the vision for me to achieve a doctorate degree long before I could believe it was possible. My mother, Gail Malley, was my first Bible teacher, and it was she who implanted and fostered a love for God and his Word in my soul. She taught me how to search the Scriptures diligently as a youth and coached me through many biblical courses, stoking my passion for biblical research before I attained adulthood.

# Abbreviations

| | |
|---|---|
| *AJP* | *The American Journal of Philology* |
| *ACR* | *Australasian Catholic Record* |
| *BDBG* | *The New Brown-Driver-Briggs-Gesenius Hebrew and English Lexicon with appendix containing the Biblical Aramaic* |
| *BICS* | *Bulletin of the Institute of Classical Studies* |
| *BR* | *Biblical Research* |
| *BSac* | *Bibliotheca Sacra* |
| *BBR* | *Bulletin for Biblical Research* |
| *EvQ* | *The Evangelical Quarterly* |
| *ExpTim* | *The Expository Times* |
| Hec. Ab. | Hecataeus of Abdera |
| HR | History of Religions |
| *HvTSt* | *Hervormde Teologiese Studies* |
| ITS | Invitation to Theological Studies Series |
| *JBL* | *Journal of Biblical Literature* |
| *JETS* | *Journal of the Evangelical Theological Society* |
| *JHS* | *Journal of Hellenic Studies* |
| *JPT* | *Journal of Pentecostal Theology* |
| *JQR* | *Jewish Quarterly Review* |
| *JRS* | *Journal of Roman Studies* |
| *JTS* | *The Journal of Theological Studies* |

| | |
|---|---|
| L&N | Louw Johannes P., and Eugene A. Nida, *Greek-English Lexicon of the New Testament: Based on Semantic Domains*, 2nd ed., New York: United Bible Societies, 1989 |
| Neot | *Neotestamentica* |
| NTS | *New Testament Studies* |
| NovT | *Novum Testamentum* |
| Presb | *Presbyterion* |
| PIBA | Proceedings of the Irish Biblical Association |
| RevExp | *Review and Expositor* |
| RBPH | *Revue belge de philologie et d'histoire* |
| StBibLit | Studies in Biblical Literature |
| TS | *Theological Studies* |
| TynBul | *Tyndale Bulletin* |
| ZNW | *Zeitschrift für die neutestamentliche Wissenschaft und die Kunde der älteren Kirche* |

## BIBLES

| | |
|---|---|
| ESV | The Holy Bible, English Standard Version, 2016. |
| KJV | The King James Version of The Holy Bible, 1991. |
| Lamsa | *Holy Bible from Ancient Eastern Manuscripts . . . Translated from the Peshitta*, by George M. Lamsa, 1968. |
| NIV | The Holy Bible, New International Version, 1995. |

# Abstract

As Christianity enters its third millennium, it faces the sharpest decline in the number of people attending church congregations compared to the total population. In Rom 1:13, the apostle Paul states that God's people should not be ignorant that the purpose for leaders within the collective church body, beginning with himself as the example, is so the people's lives would be fruitful—spiritually enriched and productive. Logic dictates that if the lives of those who attended Christian churches in the twenty-first century experienced and displayed such spiritual quality, attendance would not be declining but contrarily on the rise. Regarding church clergy and their congregations, are the shepherds genuinely caring for and tending to the spiritual needs of their flocks if the people are departing?

This study proposes that modern Christian churches reform and realign their leadership structures according to the examples of the followers of Jesus Christ, as found in the book of Acts and the Pastoral Epistles. Most churches still follow their inherited traditions from past centuries and millennia and seem little inclined to question the possibility of a better format. This study argues that the Scriptures promote a more efficient archetype that has been forgotten and replaced in favor of traditions. This discourse aims to demonstrate from selected New Testament scriptures that God's leadership design of the early church was a stratified model, different and superior to the religious hierarchical models of the Second Temple era. The stratified leadership model of the first-century Christian church presented herein is a viable doctrinal and practical formula for modern churches to utilize as they carry out the Great Commission entrusted to them.

# CHAPTER 1

# Introduction to the Stratified Leadership Model

## THE PROBLEM: THE STATE OF MODERN CHRISTIANITY

THE FRATERNITY COMPRISED OF North American Christian churches is suffering under a growing epidemic—but not that of an infectious disease. Instead, the number of members within their congregations has severely declined. A Gallup poll conducted in 2002 recounted that approximately 36 percent of millennials claim not to belong to a church and that attachment to a religious institution is a concept that belongs to older generations of Americans.[1] In 2014, the Pew Research Center surveyed religious affiliation and attendance in the United States, revealing that mainline Protestant churches had endured the harshest decline in membership.[2] In 2019 the number of "the religiously unaffiliated share of the population" in the United States had risen to 26 percent.[3] In 2013, on the eve of the election of a new pope, Father Peter Daly criticized the Roman Catholic Church's organization, finery, and pomposity, claiming that Jesus Christ would not recognize them as the church he established.[4]

---

1. Bailey, "Church Membership in the U.S."
2. Pew Research Center, "America's Changing Religious Landscape."
3. Pew Research Center, "In U.S., Decline of Christianity Continues at Rapid Pace.".
4. Daly, "What Would Christ Say."

In Father Daly's beliefs, the Roman Catholic Church does not reflect the virtue of humility or the service vision that Jesus taught his people. In his dissertation, Louis A. Butcher Jr. probed this national problem, uncovering that those who had departed expressed a host of issues with their various churches.[5] These issues included disinterest in and detachment from bloated assemblies, dissent against traditional church practices and politics, and neglect by those in leadership.[6] Numerous studies have divulged many causes, but marginalization is the lowest common denominator expressed by those disaffected. Marginalization is the term best used to describe the experience people endure when they become a minority among a larger group and they and their issues are directly or indirectly removed from the focus and attention of those leading the body public and pushed to the periphery of attention, becoming ignored, devalued outliers. Those deserting their churches profess feeling ignored, brushed off to the sidelines, and left waiting in the shadows by their leaders, ministers, and clergy. Hence, this dissertation aims to provide a solution to the issue of the departing, detached, disassociated, and disenfranchised members of the Christian community.

"Sometimes you want to go where everybody knows your name," sung the theme song of the 1980s television show *Cheers*, and those lyrics expressed the desire for belonging intrinsic to each person.[7] Social media platforms such as Facebook, X (formerly Twitter), and others display that people crave personal attention, association, and recognition from others, which has also produced social gatherings. As a center for shared beliefs for social and ritual religious practices in the surrounding community, the church was once the locus for such meetings. However, should an individual feel they have become just a number, a face in the crowd, their positive sense of belonging in the community diminishes due to lack of personal attention. In his work *The Decline of Established Christianity in the Western World: Interpretations and Responses*, Paul Silas Peterson presents many views on the subject because, according to his assessment, the studies performed by various schools of scholarly interpretation have not formulated an agreed baseline for stable interaction. He states, "The decline of established Christianity in the Western world is being addressed in various interconnected historical, political, religious,

---

5. Butcher, "Decline in Church Attendance."
6. Butcher, "Decline in Church Attendance," 24–28.
7. *Cheers*, "Where Everybody Knows Your Name."

sociological and cultural discourses."[8] Peterson's statement expresses that the spectrum for debate on the subject is broad, and scholars present their meritorious theories without any consensus or solution. Concerning the relationships between church leadership and their disciplined followers, it is worth noting that the leaders must not be leading if the people are leaving.

This study advocates for searching the Scriptures, independent of religious dogma, for what they have to say or any examples they provide. Then, the Scriptures become the answer and the solution to repair and restore any church. People tend to go astray from the designs and doctrine of the Scriptures, so some reformation is necessary from time to time. Paul writes, "Now I would not have you ignorant, brethren, that oftentimes I purposed to come unto you, (but was let hitherto) that I might have some fruit among you also, even as among other Gentiles" (Rom 1:13).[9] In the introduction of the Epistle to the Romans, he had identified himself as Jesus Christ's servant, having the office of an apostle—one of the heads in authority in the church. Paul declared that his purpose for visiting the Roman believers was not to collect money or to build houses of worship but so that their lives might manifest spiritual fruit. Following that example, improving the spiritual quality of their people's lives should be the primary goal of Christian ministers. Church leaders have a symbiotic relationship with their congregations. Jesus detailed this in a most simple and eloquent metaphor when he stated, "I am the good shepherd: the good shepherd giveth his life for the sheep . . . I am the good shepherd, and know my sheep, and am known of mine" (John 10:11, 14). A shepherd without a flock is no shepherd, for the flock disbands, goes astray, and flounders without a shepherd who tends to their needs. The canonical Gospels record Jesus' teachings and, together with those of his apostles, serve as the contextual doctrine and instructions for the manner in which Christ's followers were to carry out his commission of "making disciples of all nations" (Matt 28:19). Jesus set the example with his own life for all who participate in the Great Commission: the responsibility for the congregation begins with the leaders.

---

8. Peterson, *Decline of Established Christianity in the Western World*, 33.

9. Unless otherwise noted, all biblical passages referenced are from the *King James Version* of the Holy Bible (Iowa Falls: World Bible Publishers, 1991).

## THE PROPOSED SOLUTION

After the events of Acts chapter two, there is a paradigm shift within the movement of the followers of the Lord Jesus Christ. Those followers, who are a significant focus of the research of this discourse, have many titles. This study often refers to them as the First-Century Church to separate them from other generations of Christians. Jesus called those followers his ἐκκλησία (ekklēsia), or more commonly in English, "church," but it means more than what the word "church" communicates for modernity (Matt 16:18). Ἐκκλησία (ekklēsia) may be defined more appropriately as:

> A gathering of citizens called out from their homes into some public place; an assembly; among the Greeks from Thucydides ... an assembly of the people convened at the public place of council for the purposes of deliberating: Acts 19:39; in the Sept. often equivalent to קָהָל, the assembly of Israelites ... especially when gathered for sacred purposes; an assembly of Christians gathered for worship: in the religious meeting; a company of Christians, or of those who, hoping for eternal salvation through Jesus Christ, observe their own religious rites, hold their own religious meetings, and manage their own affairs according to regulations prescribed for the body of order's sake (195-96).[10]

The followers of the Lord Jesus Christ, as led by his apostles after his ascension, formed a new church—*ekklēsia*, which this study labels and refers to as "First-Century Church." On the day of Pentecost, they experienced an evangelistic explosion that demanded changes and adaptations to minister effectively to those newly added to their numbers. The First-Century Church, those dedicated followers of Jesus Christ, gradually separated themselves from the temple hierarchy and organization in Jerusalem and the Jewish synagogues. Instead, according to the definition, they set up their own organizational structure, which served their spiritual needs and practices. That structure focused on smaller gatherings in the home and an increased number of individuals serving the smaller groups, increasing personal attention and overall followers.

There was nothing wrong per se with the temple-cult model of leadership or the format employed in Jewish synagogues, for both served godly purposes in their times until the day of Pentecost arrived and a new system born of Jesus' teachings took shape. Much like other fields of life, such as technology, when a system is improved, it is not logical to return

---

10. Thayer, "ἐκκλησία," 195–96.

to former operations despite tradition, familiarity, or comfort. However, the upheld belief is that the doctrine and arrangement of leaders that developed within the early church may have been overlooked and lost by the wayside of history in favor of established traditions. This study then offers the possibility of a more advanced model for leadership, which may prove more adept at ministering to Christians, especially those of modernity. The majority of this work will conduct a careful exegesis of selected passages from the New Testament, which focus on leadership through service and the varied forms that service occupied in the First-Century Church.

## Reformation is Necessary

This study proposes that the solution to the withering Christian congregations begins with reforming the leadership models found in modern Christian churches and formulating them according to the example of the First-Century Church in the book of Acts and the Pastoral Epistles. Unfortunately, the dominant leadership models of modernity still follow the inherited traditions from the temple-cult and synagogue formats established during the Second Temple period of Jewish society. In these formats, there was one leader or possibly a small group of individuals leading hundreds, thousands, or more followers who came seeking spiritual nourishment and guidance. The Roman and Greek religious structures operated similarly. However, when one individual attempts to serve a hundred or hundreds, people find themselves pushed aside into the figurative margins of the group and ignored. Such an occurrence is commonplace in the public-school systems of the United States, where a single teacher leads a classroom of thirty to fifty. Compare that to a single pastor leading a congregation of one hundred to two hundred (two hundred is considered a small church), and there should be no wonder about members deserting their churches. Yet many of the congregations found in North American churches have dwindled to less than one hundred.[11] Thom S. Rainer, C. Peter Wagner, and Elmer Towns co-authored a text devoted to aiding churches to grow their congregations beyond two hundred. They describe a trend in North America where people favor smaller groups due to the increased degree of personal attention

---

11. Butcher, "Decline in Church Attendance in Lancaster County," 95–96.

available.[12] Wagner states, "Without effective pastoral leadership scarcely any church could possibly pass the 200 barrier."[13] Yet the book of Acts recorded that the followers of Jesus' apostles left the hierarchy of the temple in favor of the more intimate household setting. If one looks at the examples from the book of Acts, they gauged success by increasing the number of disciples—disciplined, devoted followers (Acts 6:7) and the number of households won to the movement (Acts 20:20; Rom 16:5; 1 Cor 1:11; 16:15–19; Col 4:15). The spread of the gospel of Christ won new people to the early church, and effective ministering, leadership, and mentorship added to the ranks of disciples. More households of disciplined followers, in turn, meant more churches while remaining small in number within each church.

There is no substitute for power-filled Christian evangelism that brings the gospel of Christ to the lives of people desperate for salvation's wholeness. After new believers have been won, the leadership has the duty of teaching and raising those neophytes to become disciples. The people then manifest spiritual fruit in their lives and become the harvest Paul spoke of in Rom 1:13. In the first century, the temple proved unfit, and the immense congregation was not conducive to nurturing and raising people to become faithful disciples. Ministering to the spiritual deficits in people's lives requires more personal interactions than a large congregation will allow; leaders must become invested in their followers' lives, and both situations require a more intimate setting.

In the first century, the church in the home replaced the temple and the synagogue until the fourth century when, under Constantine's reign, Christian edifices were erected, replacing pagan ones. During his rule, the religious leaders—Constantine was the head—corralled the people back into a temple-like setting. Perhaps today, like in the first century, the larger congregation is not practical for meeting the spiritual needs of the individual believer, and ministers might be more effective in a smaller social environment. This study explores how the First-Century Church replaced the hierarchical setting of the temple, where members outnumbered the leadership by thousands, in favor of much smaller groups in more intimate settings, specifically the arrangement of their leadership.

---

12. Wagner, Towns, and Rainer, *Everychurch Guide to Growth*, 100–3.

13. Wagner, Towns, and Rainer, *Everychurch Guide to Growth*, 36.

## A Hierarchical Model Versus a Stratified Model

Temple cults, churches, governments, and even businesses of modernity are hierarchical, following a pyramid-like model, with one individual or a small body of people exercising managerial control and dominion over their subordinates and followers. The Greek words ἱερός (*hieros*), meaning "sacred," and ἀρχή (*archē*), meaning "the first, the leader, one who commences, principality, rule, or magistracy," combine to form the word "hierarchy."[14] The term "hierarchy" does not occur in the Scriptures, but illustrations of hierarchies do. For example, the high priest officiated the highest level of authority in the Jewish temple with descending ranks of subordinate leadership offices. The Jewish synagogues, which originated during the Second Temple period, also operated via a hierarchical arrangement with a ruler of the synagogue as its head, followed by those who served under him. Recognizing the source of exercised dominion and command is essential to identifying a hierarchical organization.

Yet, such was not the doctrine that Jesus or his apostles promoted, as displayed in the four canonical Gospels, the Acts of the Apostles, or the New Testament (NT) epistles. In the orchestration promoted by Jesus and his apostles, service unto others was the principal focus. Jesus illustrated the degree to which his disciples were to extend themselves in service when he culturally debased himself and washed their feet, a task usually delegated to a lowly household servant (John 13:3–10). In contrast, in Jewish society, the high priest's rule and dominion often rivaled the oligarchs of the day, as exemplified by Jonathan Maccabeus and Hyrcanus I (1 Macc 12:1–3; 16:1–23).[15] Those people society deemed of a lower value or caste served those who commanded power and demanded reverence. Instead, Jesus placed the godliest and most spiritual leader at the foundation, serving and supporting all others from beneath (Matt 11:28–29). At the top were the lowliest members needing the most attention, thus inverting the pyramid hierarchy (Mark 10:42–45). With this change in doctrinal standards, Jesus created what this study calls the stratified leadership model. The difference between a hierarchical and a stratified model is that in the stratified leadership model, the most outstanding leader with the most responsibility undertook the most selfless position as the bottommost member devoted to serving all others before God. The other leadership roles and functions were arranged in strata, like layers

---

14. Thayer, "ἀρχή"; "ἱερός," *Thayer's Greek-English Lexicon*, 76–77, 299.
15. Coogan, *New Oxford Annotated Bible*, 234, 243–44.

of the earth's crust or atmosphere, according to their developed maturity, degrees of responsibility, and service to the *ekklēsia*.

Since the late nineteenth century, academic research has referred to elders, deacons, and bishops as "offices" of the First-Century Church. More accurately, the position or function of a leader within the church was one of service unto others and not commanding like an officer within a military unit; therefore, this study prefers to refer to them not as offices but as positions, roles, and functions of authority within the church body. The crucial difference is that this study promotes that there were not two or three offices as has been handed down; instead, there were eight possible positions that operated in the early church. In a later chapter, this study will provide an overview of that academic research. This study theorizes that in NT Scriptures, the eight specific titles signify the positions that comprised the leadership body of Christ's devoted followers, the First-Century Church, formulating this author's proposed stratified leadership model.

In Acts 19:10, a phenomenon was recorded: during the two years and many months that Paul remained in Ephesus teaching from the school of Tyrannus, "all they which dwelt in Asia [Asia Minor] heard the word of the Lord Jesus, both Jews and Greeks." Of course, some scholars have claimed the Bible contains exaggerations, contradictions, half-truths, or outright falsifications. But even if the testimony of Acts 19:10 was an approximation or, at worst, an exaggeration, no evangelical movement experiences transnational success without trained, dedicated leadership and an organized network of people conditioned to their mission. The First-Century Church operated a network that stretched from Spain to Babylon (Rom 15:24; 1 Pet 5:13). It is that network, and the organization those people employed that is of chief interest. This study aims to present the network of leaders' positions/offices or roles in the public body of the First-Century Church, which comprised more than deacons, bishops, and elders, including how they functioned and also trained others in those functionalities.

## THE THESIS: THE STRATIFIED LEADERSHIP MODEL

This study argues for and will demonstrate from selected New Testament scriptures that God's design of leadership, promoted by the apostles of the First-Century Church, was a stratified model, different and superior to the hierarchical models of the temple cult and synagogue of the Second Temple era, which could adapt to suit any size congregation without sacrificing the personal attention needed by its followers.

This study focuses on three parts: the first is that most churches under the banner of Christianity are unaware of the leadership structure of the First-Century Church led by Jesus' apostles. Instead, they followed traditional formats adopted or inherited from the temple in Jerusalem or Jewish synagogues. The second is that in the First-Century Church, there were more than three leadership roles in operation—instead, possibly eight served the church's members. Sometimes, these positions were filled by apostles, prophets, evangelists, pastors, and teachers, and sometimes they were alongside those five spirit-energized ministries. Subordinate to those five ministries, eight positions of leaders served the early church, as signified in the Scriptures. As a standard, women were also capable and accepted in leadership roles throughout the church because, within the confines of the culture of the day, the church was egalitarian. The third part is the proposed theory that modern Christian churches could strengthen themselves via an increase in the quality of spiritual care extended to their members by reinstating the leadership structure of the First-Century Church. This study's purpose is to present the concept of the stratified model of those leadership roles of the First-Century Church from a new vantage with possibly overlooked details.

## METHODOLOGY

The method employed to explain the stratified leadership system of the first century is a hermeneutical one utilizing historical-cultural analysis, contextual analysis, and literary analysis.[16] The position of this study is that when God's holy men originally recorded the Scriptures of both the Old Testament and New Testament of the Holy Bible, before translations, redactions, and revisions were applied, those writings were perfect, absolutely truthful, without error or contradiction (2 Pet 1:20–21; 2 Tim 3:16–17). By that standard, each word chosen had a distinct purpose in its utilization. Unless a passage was figurative to illustrate some greater truth, each Scripture should be understood to state what it meant with proper respect given to its near and remote contexts. Finally, one must

---

16. Köstenberger and Patterson, *Invitation to Biblical Interpretation*, 57–68.

understand the text of the Scriptures within the framework of the cultures and ages in which its writers transcribed it.

## Historical–Cultural Analysis

A historical-cultural study explains why Christianity deserted the model of the First-Century Church in favor of adapting older formats. The historical–cultural analysis also permits the contrast and comparison of the neophyte church with Jewish leadership models and that of other cultures that surrounded and interacted with the first-century followers of Christ. The research for this dissertation will focus on the Bible's teachings, examples, and history. Still, noncanonical sources of that period will be employed, and other religions will be compared and contrasted, where applicable, for further cultural insights and information.

## Contextual and Literary Analyses

Contextual and literary analyses that concentrate upon the eight possible positions of service recognized in the NT and signified by the titles of θεράπων (*therápōn*), δοῦλος (*doulos*), διάκονος (*diakonos*), οἰκονόμος (*oikonomos*), ὑπηρέτης (*hypēretēs*), θυρωρός (*thyrōros*), πρεσβύτερος (*presbyteros*), and ἐπίσκοπος (*episkopos*) need be performed. These positions make up what this author calls the stratified model of leadership within the *ekklēsia* of the First-Century Church. This study will pursue a quantitative methodology to discover the depth of meaning of those eight titles, and the Greek language will be explored according to the usage within biblical texts and from other Greek texts of that period. While some may promote that a few of these titles are interchangeable and synonymous, the position of this study is that each title had a specific purpose in the church. The similarity observed between them is due to their functional servile nature, that those leadership roles were not yet fully codified, and adaptation and flexibility were the norms; therefore, leaders sometimes took on multiple roles and figuratively wore many hats. Finally, the interrelationships of those roles and positions will be examined for a qualitative methodology, as witnessed from the Scriptures, to produce a possible practical application.

## CHAPTER SYNOPSIS

Chapter one introduces a situation currently confronting all Christianity: the declining attendance and memberships within Christian churches of North America. This situation was the catalyst that started an investigation to answer the question: is modern Christianity a reflection of the ways and means by which the disciples of Jesus Christ communicated and evangelized the gospel of Christ in the first century? The desertion of followers from Christian churches in North America is evidence of the contrary. Therefore, this study proposes that Christian churches re-examine the means and methods by which they minister to their people. Furthermore, historical analysis shows that Christian churches' most common leadership structures today were inherited through traditions stemming from the Jewish temple or synagogue format. Those older formats, which have survived so long, have all the appearance of wearing out and wearing thin in the face of the modern age. But the followers of the First-Century Church, led by Jesus' apostles, separated from the temple and synagogue; they evolved and established new ways and means for disseminating the Gospel of Christ. The system they developed based on Jesus' example and teachings is the focus of this study. This study's thesis presents the prospect that embedded within the New Testament's Scriptures is an overlooked leadership model that is superior to the traditional formats to which Christianity has clung and, in so doing, introduces it as a possible solution to Christianity's declining membership.

Chapter two briefly overviews the historical progression and evolution of the Christian church's leadership structure from the NT through the early apostolic fathers. This chapter observes when the leaders' roles were first called "offices" and the implications this tradition drew. It also reviews the current state of modern research concerning the New Testament leadership roles.

Chapter three performs contextual, historical, literary, and comparative analyses from the Second Temple period pertaining to the leadership models of the temple at Jerusalem, Jewish synagogues, and Roman temple cult formats. Next, this study compares the similarities between the Jerusalem Temple of the Second Temple era with the Roman Catholic Church of modernity and the synagogue format from the same period corresponding to the Greek Orthodoxy and typical Protestant churches of today. The collected information on the religious environment of the first century forms a baseline for contrast and comparison with the neophyte church of the followers of Jesus Christ led by his apostles. Finally, in contrast, this work delves into Jesus' example and instructions to his followers and the difference those bore against established models and traditions. As the new church grew in numbers, the ways that the leadership guided the congregation were of the utmost importance to its advancement.

Chapter four examines the functions of apostles, prophets, evangelists, pastors, and teachers within the First-Century Church, including the difference between ordained leadership positions versus spirit-energized ministries. This chapter focuses on performing grammatical analyses scrutinizing the various Greek and Hebrew words within their contexts and conveyed meanings. The apostles were to emulate Jesus' example and treat others in that manner; their examples are a necessary component for understanding titles and the functions of those titles. Next, this study presents the proposed theory of the stratified leadership model. Each of the eight titles and their roles within the *ekklēsia* of the believers is detailed in this chapter. This chapter begins by establishing what the apostle Paul intended in 1 Cor 12:28, where he related the functions of "helps and governments" and what the people of the first century would have understood by his use of *kybernēsis*. One of the primary principles observed from the Scriptures was that these leaders' roles were not rigid or unchanging but, in contrast, were malleable according to the people's spiritual needs. The foundation for all the leadership roles was service, with Jesus' example of sacrificing all he had in the name of service to God and people as their primary frame of reference. Service first in spread of the message of the gospel of Christ, then secondarily in ministering to the lives of those won to the church. Due to their utilization across the NT, this author theorizes eight Greek titles: *therápōn, doulos, diakonos, oikonomos, hypēretēs, thyrōros, presbyteros,* and *episkopos*, were the titles of positions of leadership within the First-Century Church. This study examines the given definitions, the historical usages, and the scriptural uses to formulate a scripturally accurate description for each leadership role within the First-Century Church.

The fifth chapter scrutinizes the continuation of the church from one generation of leadership to another. The First-Century Church leaders never intended for the movement to end with the passing of their lives. This study explores the active roles performed by women in the First-Century Church and their valuable contributions. Paul's metaphor of the husbandman or farmer and Peter's analogy of the shepherd will also be reviewed. Peter's reference to "the Shepherd" in his epistle reflects the topic of "the great shepherd" (Heb 13:20–21), a reference to Jesus, and directly connects to Jesus' sermon from John chapter ten and Ps 23. Because it had been proven effective, the stratified model was to be replicated wherever there were followers of Christ. In his epistles, Peter stressed that the church would continue after his death, and his letters were intended to confirm that. Paul detailed instructions to Timothy and Titus, two of his closest trainees, on how to raise and install others as leaders in the church. Their instructions to a second generation of leaders were meant to ensure the church's perpetuation.

The sixth and concluding chapter of this dissertation recounts the subjects previously covered. First, the advantages of the stratified leadership model are illuminated and summarized. Next, this study reviews the scriptural evidence promoting the stratified model over the traditional leadership formats present in Christianity. Leadership is essential to the Great Commission, its promoters, pace-setters, instructors, mediators, pastors, and advocates for the members of the church body. Next, this study attests to the practicality of the stratified model. It also promotes that Christian churches re-examine the means and methods by which they minister to their people to ensure they are operating most effectually. Finally, this study argues for the superiority of the stratified model as a doctrinal and practical formula for modern Christianity.

# CHAPTER 2

# The State of the Research

THE CURRENT STATE OF the research related to the leadership offices of the First-Century Church is scant compared to the studies and writings that concern other biblical issues in the last twenty years. The goal of research should always be the continued exploration of different possibilities and new perspectives. While a few scholars have written on the topic of leadership in the early church, more scholarly efforts have been spent debating whether or not there were two or three administrative offices in the First-Century Church rather than the further development of the subject or possible reworking of the issue for any overlooked aspects, facts, or truths. None have explored the option of the existence of other leadership positions resident in the early church beyond that of deacons, elders, and bishops. This study proposes that there were more positions and that they had an organized network and a structure to be replicated from town to town.

## ISSUES IN CHURCH TRADITIONS

This research work aims to present the topic of the leadership positions of the First-Century Church with possibly overlooked details and new perspectives. For example, Mary MacDonald explored early church leadership's social and historical aspects regarding women's roles in the church, challenging church traditions and making her work an asset to this endeavor. Additionally, this dissertation focuses on the leadership positions and the titles of those who directed the movement of the First-Century

Church; any research already produced is valuable as a foundation for this study's efforts. An issue this chapter must contend with is, Were the leadership roles of the First-Century Church recognized as offices of authority, or were they entitled positions filled by individuals due to how they ministered to the church? Finally, this chapter will also account for what happened in Christianity's evolution that caused the functionaries of the *episkopos, presbyteros,* and *diakonos* to gain elevation in status, while since that time, *doulos, hypēretēs, oikonomos,* and *thyrōros* have somehow become forgotten. With these issues accounted for, this study may explore the various strata and roles of leadership within the First-Century Church.

## SCRIPTURAL TRUTHS VS. CHURCH TRADITIONS

In the First-Century Church, the offices of the bishops, deacons, and elders were not governing offices of authority comparable to politicians and priests of Hellenistic culture, as some might suppose. Instead, the followers and disciples of the Lord Jesus Christ operated in the fashion of sailors on a ship at sea, who, in an egalitarian and democratic manner, conferred the responsibilities of leadership upon the individual(s) deemed most capable. Nevertheless, the mother church's rule, order, and commanding dominance that she became known for would arise in the following centuries. This study stresses biblical accuracy within the cultural context of the day over traditions people established sometime later. As the Scriptures have been translated from language to language and from one era of civilization to another, meanings and understandings of words and phrases have morphed the original messages.[1] The words used within the context of the Scriptures must be understood in compliance with when they were written, to whom they were written, and with respect to the message communicated according to contexts.[2] Then, the intent of the message and theological principles may be applied to modern Christianity.

---

1. Duvall and Hays, *Grasping God's Word*, 23–38.
2. Duvall and Hays, *Grasping God's Word*, 42–47.

## The Usage Of "Office" And Its Implications

An issue that this study addresses is, Were the positions of *episkopos* (bishops), *presbyteros* (elders), and *diakonos* (deacons) recognized in the First-Century Church as offices of authority? Were they roles filled by individuals revered and entitled as such by others because of how they ministered to the church? If the NT Scriptures do not present the church's leaders as "officers," then when did people's perception change, and when did bishops, elders, and deacons appropriate such commanding authority?

### Usage of "Office" in the New Testament

It is in the apostle Paul's writings in the NT where the word "office" is utilized in the King James Version of the Bible. In Rom 11:13, he states, "For I speak to you Gentiles, inasmuch as I am the apostle of the Gentiles, I magnify mine office." In the epistle of 1 Timothy, he refers to "the office of a bishop" and "the office of a deacon," but this is an English translation and not the same Greek word used in Romans (1 Tim 3:1, 10, 13). In the reference from Romans, the corresponding Greek word for "office" is διάκονία (*diakonia*), which is more commonly translated as "ministry" or "ministration."[3] The phrase "desires the office of a bishop" from 1 Tim 3:1, in actuality, is only two words in the Greek text: ἐπισκοπῆς ὀρέγεται, which the NIV renders as "aspires to be an overseer."[4] Likewise, the references from verses ten and thirteen of the same chapter do not speak of an office but rather the actions of service rendered by a deacon.[5] The Gospels of Matthew and Luke provide the closest references to a person holding an "office" of authority in New Testament Scriptures, which speak of an officer who could haul people off to prison (Matt 5:25; Luke 12:58). There is no scriptural reference of this term specifically to an office of authority in the First-Century Church. For at least its first two generations of leadership, the early church depended upon charismatic individuals endowed with demonstrable spiritual gifts that served the body of believers.[6] In Acts 1:25, Peter states, concerning the candidates to take Judas Iscariot's place, "That he may take part of this ministry

3. Thayer, "διάκονία," *Thayer's Greek-English Lexicon*, 137.
4. Mounce and Mounce, *Interlinear New Testament*, 808.
5. Mounce and Mounce, *Interlinear New Testament*, 808–9.
6. Ehrman, *After the New Testament*, 429.

and apostleship." Comparing Rom 11:13 with Acts 1:25, Peter and Paul distinguished between their position as apostles and their ministerings and church responsibilities. They defined their roles by their actions of service but did not regard it as an office that commanded authority. According to Paul, one's role, function, and authority within the collective body of believers is determined by the gift imparted to him by God (Rom 12:3, 6). In the forthcoming chapters, this study will explore the difference between a supportive, service-oriented role and an authoritative-commanding office.

When considering the duty codes that Paul laid out for overseers of the early church (1 Tim 3:2–7; Titus 1:6–9), scholars have observed a solid resemblance to attributes, qualities, and qualifications of military leaders, dancers, and Roman senators.[7] The organization of the positions and requirements for bishops, deacons, and elders and the behaviors expected from those individuals have led scholars to refer to them as early church offices.[8] The doctrine laid out in the Pastoral Epistles for the arrangement of the leadership positions arrived late in the first century, while the events recorded in the book of the Acts of the Apostles occurred sometime between 30–60 CE (allowing for a variance of a few years). These facts do not discredit the Pastorals but show development and adaptation within the evolution of the early church. The titles for the leadership positions may not yet have existed in Acts, but by the time of the Pastoral Epistles, the roles were formalized and entitled.

## Usage of "Office" in the Apostolic Fathers' Writings

In comparison, the church in the first century was egalitarian. However, driven by its third generation of leaders, a hierarchy formed within the church as it transitioned to the second century. Clement, Ignatius, Polycarp, and their contemporaries are referred to as early apostolic fathers of the church, for they followed after the last of the NT elders and endeavored to imitate the practices of the apostles Peter and Paul. Considering when they wrote their letters for the church, these men were possibly third-generation leaders after Timothy, Titus, Silas, and others mentioned in the NT. Nevertheless, the ways in which they handled the

---

7. Goodrich, "Overseers as Stewards."
8. MacDonald, *Pauline Churches*, 210.

titles and authority of leaders' roles in the church formed the foundation of lasting traditions that are followed to this day.

The letter of 1 Clement, estimated to have been written in the late first into the early second century, contains the earliest reference to the leadership roles of the church outside of biblical texts. Traditionally, Clement, perceived to be of the line of bishops descending from the apostle Peter, is credited with authoring the letter in approximately 96 CE. First, in 1 Clement 40.5, the author refers to the "proper office" of the priests and the "proper ministrations" of the Levites.[9] Then, in 1 Clement 44.1, he refers to the "bishop's office," which, by the similitude of his phrasing, would place the bishop on the same level of authority as a priest from the OT.[10] In his introduction to 1 Clement, Michael W. Holmes wrote, "Tradition identifies him (the epistle's author) as the third bishop of Rome after Peter, but this is unlikely because the office of monarchical bishop, in the sense intended by this later tradition, does not appear to have existed in Rome at this time. Leadership seems to have been entrusted to a group of presbyters or bishops."[11] There is no lording over the church by its presbyters found in 1 Clement, but rather the body of believers are encouraged to "be at peace with its duly appointed presbyters" (54.2).[12] This statement is similar to Paul's exhortation to the Thessalonian Church: "And we beseech you, brethren, to know them which labour among you, and are over you in the Lord, and admonish you; And to esteem them very highly in love for their work's sake. And be at peace among yourselves" (1 Thess 5:12–13). The communal quality of fellowship read of in the book of Acts was still present in Clement's letters.

Lightfoot places Ignatius's letters in the early to middle of the second century; their author was en route to Rome to be martyred, and the church was into its third generation of leadership.[13] Ignatius claimed an apostle's position and authority for himself and organized a hierarchal structure across several passages.[14] In his letter to Polycarp, the bishop of the Smyrnaeans, Ignatius instructs him to "vindicate thine office" (1.2).[15] The rhetoric of his letters bears a stringency that may reflect his times but

9. Lightfoot and Andrews, *Apostolic Fathers*, 22–23.
10. Lightfoot and Andrews, *Apostolic Fathers*, 23.
11. Holmes, *Apostolic Fathers in English*, 26–27.
12. Lightfoot and Andrews, *Apostolic Fathers*, 27.
13. Lightfoot and Andrews, *Apostolic Fathers*, 42–44.
14. Lightfoot and Andrews, *Apostolic Fathers*, 60.
15. Lightfoot and Andrews, *Apostolic Fathers*, 73.

was not present in the writings of his predecessors. In Ignatius's letter *To the Trallians*, he directed them to "let all men respect the deacons as Jesus Christ, even as they should respect the bishop as being a type of Father and the presbyters as the council of God and as the college of Apostles" (3.1).[16] Another example reinforcing Ignatius's doctrine and furthering the confusion concerning the authority and positions of bishops, deacons, and elders in the church can be found in the *Didascalia Apostolorum*. The *Didascalia Apostolorum* is a text authored in the mid-third century AD, foundational to the practices of the organization that would become the Roman Catholic Church, which teaches that the bishop "is to be honored by you in the place of God . . . the deacon, however, is present as a type of Christ . . . the deaconess is to be honoured by you as a type of the Holy Spirit . . . the presbyters are also to be reckoned by you as a type of the apostles."[17] It also directs the followers to present gifts and offerings in an increasing amount for the office receiving it: a single portion unto the pastors, presbyters, and widows of the church, double that to the deacons, "and a quadruple portion to the one who is pre-eminent, to the glory of the Almighty."[18] The "one who is pre-eminent" is understood to be the bishop, as Jesus Christ is not mentioned, nor could he receive physical offerings. Such an overt hierarchy was not present prior to Ignatius, and seemingly placing Jesus Christ beneath the "college of Apostles" and likening the office of the bishop to the regnancy of God is not in agreement with the Scriptures.

The letters of Polycarp, *The Shepherd of Hermas*, and the *Fragments of Papias* refer to a leader's "office" once each, but they do not differ from Ignatius's example. Holmes puts forth that dating *The Shepherd* is difficult but estimates its text to have been written mid- to late second century, making it the last work of the apostolic fathers.[19] Citing the Muratorian Canon, Holmes presents the strong possibility that Hermas was a brother of Pius, who served as a bishop of Rome approximately 140–154 CE.[20] Near the conclusion of *The Shepherd of Hermas*, the text illuminates that those who operate an office of leadership receive the Lord's honor and esteem and are to exercise power and authority.[21] Compared with the examples

16. Lightfoot and Andrews, *Apostolic Fathers*, 60.
17. Stewart-Sykes, *Didascalia Apostolorum*, 150–51.
18. Stewart-Sykes, *Didascalia Apostolorum*, 152.
19. Holmes, *Apostolic Fathers in English*, 174.
20. Holmes, *Apostolic Fathers in English*, 174.
21. Holmes, *Apostolic Fathers in English*, 247.

from the book of Acts, the original apostles operated the power granted them by God because the situation warranted it to serve the betterment of the people. The congregation of believers revered them out of a mutually beneficial relationship, not because the apostles commanded power and authority over the people but because of how they ministered to them. *The Didache* also bears a passage highlighting the authority of bishops and deacons within the second century of the church's evolution. *The Didache* 15:1–2 instructed the Christian followers to elect honorable members from the congregation to serve as their bishops and deacons. However, charismatic spiritual gifts are not mentioned as a qualification for these electees.[22]

Paul referred to himself as the least of all the saints, and Peter exhorted all believers to submit to each other in an egalitarian manner (Eph 3:8; 1 Pet 5:5–7). Unfortunately, the letters of the early apostolic fathers do not discuss the positions or roles of the *doulos, hypēretēs, oikonomos,* and *thyrōros,* which only generates more unanswered questions. Likewise, the book of Acts also ignores them within the body of the church, yet they appear consistently in the apostle Paul's writings. Thus, the only logical conclusion is that the apostolic fathers followed and supported Ignatius, who was the first of the early church fathers to assign levels of charge to the positions of the *episkopos* (bishop), *presbyteros* (elders/presbyters), and *diakonos* (deacons). Ignatius can be credited with establishing the traditional perception of these levels of leadership and the distinctions between them.[23] In comparison, the church in the first century was egalitarian. Then, driven by its third generation of leaders, they formed a hierarchy as the church transitioned to the second century. Through their writings, one observes bishops taking charge of the Christian community, assisted by a board of elders (presbyters), with deacons serving under both in administrative roles.[24] The roles of the *doulos, hypēretēs, oikonomos,* and *thyrōros* were then dropped by the wayside and forgotten. Thus, the body of leaders was reduced to the *episkopos, presbyteros,* and *diakonos,* causing their exercise of authority and power in the church to expand. The evidence from letters of the apostolic fathers shows that it was in their generation when the tradition began to regard the positions of the bishop, elder, and deacon as offices commanding authority in the church.

*The Apostolic Tradition* is an essential document in Christian literature and tradition authored sometime in the late second to third centuries

22. Ehrman, *After the New Testament,* 437.
23. Elliott, "Elders as Leaders," 689.
24. Ehrman, *After the New Testament,* 430.

and attributed to the prominent presbyter in Rome, Hippolytus, who gained a reputation as an anti-pope and a martyr.[25] In its pages, this document provided the church with instructions for installing bishops, deacons, presbyters, subdeacons, and readers within the church.[26] First, only bishops could ordain another to the office of a bishop or a deacon (*The Apostolic Tradition* 2.1–3; 8.5). Next, the bishops and the presbytery installed a new presbyter (7.1; 8.6–7). *The Apostolic Tradition* cites Moses' example from Exodus as their criterion for appointing presbyters (7.3). The bishops also bore the responsibility of selecting readers of the liturgy (11.5). Finally, the subdeacons seemed of a lower class than the others mentioned because their appointment was not limited to the bishops alone, nor did they require a laying on of hands like the other positions (13.1). As with the apostolic fathers, *The Apostolic Tradition* does not mention the *doulos*, *hypēretēs*, *oikonomos*, or *thyrōros*, which may indicate that those positions were not in use or deemed significant. However, the formation of the hierarchy of that time is present in the text: the bishops were foremost, assisted by the presbytery second, then the deacons, followed by the readers and subdeacons. Later, in the third century, the hierarchy of offices within the church expanded to include exorcists, acolytes, and doorkeepers.[27] Upon its adoption and establishment under Emperor Constantine, the Roman Catholic Church would remain unchanged in its hierarchical leadership offices and exercise a draconian chokehold on Western European countries until the 1600s. Thus, *The Apostolic Tradition* and not the Scriptures became the manual for arranging and installing the religious hierarchy within the Christian church.

## RESEARCH IN MODERNITY

In modern times, the majority of those researching church leadership have not gone beyond the traditions established by the apostolic fathers. However, a few outliers have examined the issues of women's leadership roles in the church or the topics of the *oikonomos* and *thyrōros*. Scholars who have produced works that contribute to the subject and premise of

---

25. Baldovin, "Hippolytus and the Apostolic Tradition," 520–42. Baldovin raises objections against Hippolytus as the rightful author of *The Apostolic Tradition*, but that is not the concern of this study. The testimony the document provides of the morphing of the church to its teaching is of primary interest.

26. Ehrman, *After the New Testament*, 442.

27. Eusebius, *History of the Church*, 282.

this dissertation are assembled here. This overview is not exhaustive, but it will strive to include significant contributors on the topic of the early church's leadership from the last thirty-five years. These scholarly sources are arranged chronologically, beginning with the most distant.

In the spring of 1985, the *Presbyterion* published the article "Office of Deacon" by Richard Fraser, an ordained minister serving in the Presbyterian Church in America (*Presb*).[28] The significance of that article is the connections it presents between Jesus' teachings and the office of a deacon in the First-Century Church. "Office of Deacon" also draws a sharp distinction that a deaconship is lower than and, therefore, is a proving ground for the office of an elder.[29] Fraser focuses on the office of the deacon from its initiation to its maturity with light comparisons to other offices. He emphasizes the service rendered to other believers to the degree this office leads by serving.[30] This article addresses attributes that are lacking in some of the other writings referenced, which this study will illuminate.

The essay "The Uniqueness of New Testament Church Eldership" by David W. Miller investigates the office of the elder to discover whether early Christianity appropriated it from societal uses of the day or if it was something unique to the Christian movement.[31] Miller expresses that "the church today should consider the uniqueness of the NT eldership as motivation to study NT church polity. Our Lord's church should be organized the way he has designed it in his word."[32] He compares the position of authority with the two most significant influences on the early Christian, Hellenistic, and Jewish societies. Miller contrasts the leadership structure with that of the early church. Miller's writing also questions whether or not age indeed had a bearing on the office of the *presbyteros*. Miller challenges hypotheses offered by scholars such as Donald L. Norbie and Andre Lemaire, and he does so with Scripture rather than theory. David W. Miller received a PhD.in ethics and is the director of Princeton University's Faith & Work Initiative.

"Church Offices by the Time of the Pastoral Epistles" was written by Father Kevin Condon (1932–2021) in 1985, in which he performed an analysis of the offices of *episkopos, presbyteros,* and *diakonos* from the time

---

28. Fraser, "Office of Deacon," 13–19.
29. Fraser, "Office of Deacon," 19.
30. Fraser, "Office of Deacon," 15.
31. Miller, "Uniqueness of New Testament Church Eldership," 315–27.
32. Miller, "Uniqueness of New Testament Church Eldership," 327.

of the Pastoral Epistles, which would have been towards the end of the first century.[33] Condon compared the Scriptures with the writings of the church fathers, including *1 Clement*, *The Didache*, and the *Letter of Ignatius Martyr*, to set forth the early fathers' understanding of these offices. These early fathers are often credited with continuing the early church into the second and third centuries. Their proximity in history to the first-century believers affords them a unique perspective. According to his understanding of the Scriptures, the *episkopoi* are superior in spiritual stature to the *presbyteroi*.[34] Condon also presented how the Roman Catholic Church adapted these offices into its hierarchy of church leaders.

Robert S. Rayburn is one of two other authors referenced by this study who debated whether the NT promoted two or three offices of leadership, and his opponent was George W. Knight. Rayburn's position supports the triarchy of the early church offices: ministers, elders, and deacons. In his essay, "Three Offices: Minister, Elder, Deacon," Rayburn aimed squarely at the traditional teachings of the Presbyterian Churches in America as the staunchest promoters of the dual-office system of the minister and ruling elder.[35] One of the most beneficial aspects of this essay is Rayburn's connection of the dual-office doctrine within his survey of past scholars. Another is his debunking of the theory of the doctrine's origin in the Old Testament. Dr. Rayburn, the son of Robert G. Rayburn, is the senior minister of Faith Presbyterian Church in Tacoma, Washington, and he studied at Covenant College, Covenant Theological Seminary, and the University of Aberdeen.

Margaret Y. MacDonald authored the monograph *The Pauline Churches: A Socio-Historical Study of Institutionalization in the Pauline and Deutero-Pauline Writings* in 1988. The importance of this monograph is the factual manner in which MacDonald handled the social and historical information from the NT as she traced the process by which the early church became a religious institution from the first century into the second century. In her study, she presented the tactics of Paul's ministry that contributed to building, supporting, and protecting the church community. MacDonald presented that within the NT, one may observe the establishment of early church traditions from their initiation in Paul's early writings to their affirmation in the letters of Ephesians and Colossians and their legacy in the Pastoral Epistles to the next generation. In

33. Condon, "Church Offices," 74–94.
34. Condon, "Church Offices," 81.
35. Rayburn, "Three Offices," 105–14.

her observations, women were an essential asset to church leadership in the early development, but as institutionalization set in, they became prohibited from leadership roles.[36] Very few authors in the bibliography of this study pay attention to women's contributions to the early church; thus, MacDonald's study adds a critical perspective. MacDonald earned her doctorate in New Testament Studies from Oxford University and is a professor at Saint Mary's University in Halifax, Nova Scotia, Canada.

The essay "On ΕΠΙΣΚΟΠΟΣ AND ΠΠΕΣΒΥΤΕΠΟΣ," written by Frances M. Young OBE, FBA, appeared in the *Journal of Theological Studies* published in 1994. In it, she focused on the offices of the *episkopos* and *presbyteros*, illuminating their origins in the First-Century Church and the differences between them and the *diakonos*. Young elevated the offices of the *episkopos* and *presbyteros* above that of the *diakonos* due to the required ecclesiastical code found in the epistles of Timothy.[37] She also distinguished officers of the church who bear this title from members of the public community who are of advanced age.[38] Thus, in her analysis, she contrasted the common Hellenistic societal customs versus the applications found within the church. In addition, Young observed the placement of the *oikonomos* within the organization of the First-Century Church and provided facts other scholars mentioned herein did not, which aided her illustrations and is an essential resource for this study. Young is an emeritus professor at the University of Birmingham in Edgbaston, United Kingdom; she taught and served as dean of the faculty during her time there.

R. Alastair Campbell (1942–2021) was a New Testament scholar and a Baptist minister who earned his doctorate at the University of London. In his first published post-doctorate work, *The Elders: Seniority within Earliest Christianity*, he argued against the use of the term "elders" as designating an official position or office in the early church but instead that it was indicative of a respected senior individual who represented a family, extended family, or clan.[39] "Elder" in the English texts is derived from the Greek word πρεσβύτερος (*presbyteros*). In addition, Campbell presented a scope of early church leadership as having existed in binary patterns that sometimes opposed one another until it finally reverted into a hierarchical institution. In his essay *"The Elder and the Overseer: One*

---

36. MacDonald, *Pauline Churches*, 105.
37. Young, "On ΕΠΙΣΚΟΠΟΣ AND ΠΠΕΣΒΥΤΕΠΟΣ," 142.
38. Young, "On ΕΠΙΣΚΟΠΟΣ AND ΠΠΕΣΒΥΤΕΠΟΣ," 143.
39. Campbell, "Elders: Seniority in Earliest Christianity," 183–87.

*Office in the Early Church*, by Benjamin L. Merkle," Campbell contended with Merkle's position, and the ensuing debate would continue in the two men's published works and articles.[40] The two authors provide the opposing sides of the scholarly debate on whether "elders" were a recognized office of authority within the early church or something more socially conventional and traditional. For his part, Campbell maintains that "the only church offices known to the New Testament writers were those of overseer and deacon," and he refers to the title of elder as an honorific.[41] This study also will engage with Campbell's position on aspects of early church leaders he presented in "The Elders of the Jerusalem Church."[42]

In his article, "Elders as Leaders in 1 Peter and the Early Church," Dr. John H. Elliott (1935–2020) shines a spotlight on the doctrine contained in the epistle of 1 Peter, which parallels Paul's teachings in 1 Timothy and Titus.[43] Though Elliott attends to 1 Peter, chapters 2:4–10 and 4:7–11, his essay spends more effort expounding upon the section of Scriptures in chapter 5:1–4. He seizes a binary unit between the elders and younger persons as the leaders and dedicated subordinates.[44] Elliott compares the use of elders in the Scriptures with other areas of the Greco-Roman world to aid in drawing this title out beyond the familial environment and showing it to have been a titular office in the church.[45] He also compares the instructions of 1 Peter with those of the letters of Ignatius of Antioch, crediting those letters with the triarchy of *episkopos* (bishop), *presbyteroi* (elders)—subject to bishops, and *diakonoi* (deacons)—subject to both bishops and elders.[46] Elliott credits Ignatius with institutionalizing the distinct levels of leadership and drawing the distinctions between the three offices.[47] Elliott retired as an associate professor Emeritus of Theology and Religious Studies at the University of San Francisco.

The monograph "Overseers as Stewards and the Qualifications for Leadership in the Pastoral Epistles," by John K. Goodrich, has contributed to this study's recognition of other offices of service in the

40. Campbell, "*Elder and the Overseer*," 281–83.
41. Campbell, "*Elder and the Overseer*," 281.
42. Campbell, "Elders of the Jerusalem Church," 511–28.
43. Elliott, "Elders as Leaders," 681–95.
44. Elliott, "Elders as Leaders," 690–92.
45. Elliott, "Elders as Leaders," 686.
46. Elliott, "Elders as Leaders," 688.
47. Elliott, "Elders as Leaders," 689.

First-Century Church.[48] In "Overseers as Stewards," Goodrich presents social and cultural comparisons between the early church leaders and other occupations of Hellenistic culture. Goodrich states, "By portraying church leaders as officers entrusted with considerable structural authority they signal an important stage in the institutional development of the early church."[49] Another study by Goodrich dealing with the sociopolitical background of one the focal titles of this study is "Erastus of Corinth (Romans 16.23): Responding to Recent Proposals on his Rank, Status, and Faith."[50] In this work, Goodrich examines the socioeconomic rank and position of Erastus as an οἰκονόμος (*oikonomos*) as it related to Corinthian and Roman society (Rom 16:23). The societal utilization of this title had to have some bearing and influence upon Paul's use of it within his teachings for he employs it for five of its ten occurrences in the NT. Therefore, the knowledge of the Greco-Roman meaning and intent that underscored οἰκονόμος (*oikonomos*) forms its context and is profitable to doctrinal understanding. Goodrich also responds to Alexander Weiss's and Steven Friesen's assessment of the meaning of οἰκονόμος (*oikonomos*) as it pertained to Erastus. John K. Goodrich currently serves as a professor of the Bible at the Moody Bible Institute.

Robert N. Swanson's essay "Apostolic Successors: Priests and Priesthood, Bishops, and Episcopy in Medieval Western Europe" presents historical information concerning leadership roles in the church a millennia after the First-Century Church had passed into history. This information provides a basis for comparisons between the leadership structures of today's churches, those of the Middle Ages, the First-Century Church, and the temple cult of the Second Temple age. The information he provides has more to do with the application of the hierarchical structure of the Christian church in the Middle Ages than with scriptural doctrine. That structure owed more to the inherited traditions from the Old Testament (OT) priesthood than the structure established under the New Testament (NT) apostles of Jesus.[51] Robert N. Swanson is an Emeritus Professor of Medieval History, having retired in 2016 from his active position with the history department of the University of Birmingham in the United Kingdom.

---

48. Goodrich, "Overseers as Stewards," 77–97.
49. Goodrich, "Overseers as Stewards," 77.
50. Goodrich, "Erastus of Corinth," 583–93.
51. Swanson, "Apostolic Successors," 6.

Alexander Strauch is the author of *Paul's Vision for the Deacons: Assisting the Elders with the Care of God's Church*, in which he discusses the relationship between the offices of the elders and that of the deacons in the first century.[52] Strauch endeavored to present a critical explanation of what a deacon was and what it should be according to the Scriptures.[53] Strauch focuses on the office of the deacon, its responsibilities, and the role the office played in the early church. In his work, Strauch interprets the Greek word *episkopos* as "overseer," and he compares and contrasts the requirements of the two offices (deacons and overseers) to set forth their differences.[54] From his analysis, Strauch esteems overseers to be superior in authority to deacons and that one must be a deacon before attaining the office of an overseer.[55] Strauch is a prolific author and public speaker who has taught philosophy and New Testament at Colorado Christian University. He received his bachelor's degree from Colorado Christian University and his Master's in Divinity from Denver Seminary and has served as a church elder.

*Sacred Thresholds: The Door to the Sanctuary in Late Antiquity* is a collection of essays edited by Emilie M. van Opstall released in 2018, covering the subject of sacred thresholds, doorways, and those who kept them and their importance to religions of antiquity.[56] This volume is the only modern resource outside the Bible to offer a comparative understanding of the importance of the doorkeeper or porter (*thyrōros*) to ancient Near East religions. This text compares the cultural and religious importance of the long-overlooked role of the porter from other faiths to early Christianity to show the doorkeeper to have been a universally recognized role. In addition, this collection of works was the only resource, outside of a concordance or lexicon, to present information on the position of the *thyrōros*. Van Opstall is an assistant professor of Ancient Greek at the Vrije Universiteit in Amsterdam.

*God, Hierarchy, and Power: Orthodox Theologies of Authority from Byzantium*, published in 2018 by Ashley M. Purpura, focuses on the dynamics of hierarchy and the exercising of power in Christianity and Eastern Orthodoxy. Purpura received her doctorate of philosophy degree from Fordham University in 2014, specializing in the historical

---

52. Strauch, *Paul's Vision for the Deacons*.
53. Strauch, *Paul's Vision for the Deacons*, 12–14.
54. Strauch, *Paul's Vision for the Deacons*, 23–50.
55. Strauch, *Paul's Vision for the Deacons*, 25–26.
56. van Opstall, *Sacred Thresholds*.

research of Orthodox Christian theology from the traditional Byzantine perspective and the effects that historical religious practices and thought have had on modernity. Concerning Byzantine Christianity, Purpura promotes that within the Orthodox Church, the structure, the concept, and the exercise of hierarchy differed from the Roman Catholic Church or many Christian churches of modernity. She states, "In the Byzantine Christian theological tradition, hierarchy appears elusive and yet constant, affirmed and yet subverted, inequitable and yet the only means of true equality, and the source of ecclesiastical authority and the limit of it."[57] Such a description relates a flexible, almost liquid relationship between the church leadership and its followers, reflecting how the first-century leaders interacted with the believers. Her historical research and insights aid this study in understanding and describing the symbiotic relationship that existed in the First-Century Church, which is a focus of this discourse.

In the New Testament, discipleship is a critical concept that resurfaces time and again, beginning with the first dedicated followers of Jesus through to Paul's ministry to the gentile peoples. In his essay "Diakonos and Doulos as concepts of True Discipleship in Mark 10:43–44: A Social Scientific Reading," Mookgo Solomon Kgatle endeavors to expound the meaning and understanding behind the Greek words *diakonos* and *doulos* through a social scientific analysis of those verses of Scripture.[58] Because tradition holds that John Mark, the companion of Paul and Barnabas, was also the author of the Gospel bearing his name, the understanding of the words *diakonos,* and *doulos* as they relate to the concept of discipleship also frame the ideas of service and leadership across the NT. Kgatle currently serves as an Associate Professor of Missiology at the University of South Africa. In his essay, he advocates for a robust understanding of discipleship as Jesus taught it to the sons of Zebedee. This understanding was also foundational to Paul's teachings and lifestyle.

David M. May presented the apostle Paul's perspective on the positions of *doulos, diakonos, hypēretēs,* and *oikonomos* and how he applied them to himself in his epistles.[59] May teaches at Central Baptist Theological Seminary, where he serves as Professor of the New Testament and Director of the Master of Arts (Theological Studies) programs. A central focus of May's essay is the book of Colossians and Paul's view of himself

57. Purpura, *God, Hierarchy, and Power*, 6.
58. Kgatle, "Diakonos and Doulos as Concepts of True Discipleship," 71–83.
59. May, "Servant and Steward of the Mystery," 470.

as Jesus' servant-steward of the mystery, which May cites as "a rather unique self-designation."[60] Furthermore, he writes "that Paul is privy to this unique revelation invested him with even more authority for his vocation as a servant/steward."[61] As Paul was responsible for the outreach of the First-Century Church unto the gentiles and oversaw the appointment of many of the leaders in the gentile churches, his example to them and his perspective on the various leadership positions are necessary. Yet Paul's vision was never that only an elite few would rise to the level of service that he and the other apostles exhibited; instead, he desired that everyone who believed in Jesus' name would reach maturity in Christ. According to Paul, achieving such maturity required an apprenticeship in selfless service, as this study will demonstrate.

In his work, Benjamin L. Merkle labored to present an uncomplicated understanding of διάκονος (*diakonos*), as it occurred in Paul's writings with respect to the cultural landscape of the period, rather than today's modern understanding of the word. He contrasted his analysis against the works performed by Hermann W. Beyer and Eduard Schweizer, which had previously received wide acceptance.[62] Merkle is an author who specializes in the subject of eldership in the early church and currently serves as an Associate Professor of the New Testament and the Greek language at Southeastern Baptist Theological Seminary. He has authored or co-authored several books on New Testament Greek syntax. Merkle's research has dealt with the leadership roles within the early church in the New Testament, beginning with his doctoral dissertation, which he submitted in 2002 to Southern Seminary, which was revised and published in 2003 as *The Elder and Overseer: One Office in the Early Church*. This text focused upon the terms πρεσβύτερος (*presbyteros*), generally rendered as 'elder,' and ἐπίσκοπος (*episkopos*) as 'overseer' in the English NT.[63] This study will interact with the research in his dissertation and include other scholars who do as well. Merkle has also co-edited a text, *Shepherding God's Flock: Biblical Leadership in the New Testament and Beyond*, a collection of writings by eleven different authors, including Merkle, published in 2014.[64] This study interacts with the knowledge collected from *Shepherding God's Flock* while disagreeing with its Baptist

---

60. May, "Servant and Steward of the Mystery," 470.
61. May, "Servant and Steward of the Mystery," 472.
62. Merkle, "Authority of Deacons in Pauline Churches," 309–25.
63. Merkle, *Elder and Overseer*, 57.
64. Merkle and Schreiner, *Shepherding God's Flock*.

interpretations, as demonstrated in forthcoming chapters. The assessment provided by *Shepherding God's Flock* of the hierarchies resident in the Roman Catholic Church, the Anglican Church, the temple of the Second Temple era, and the Jewish synagogue was most valuable. This treatise disagrees with their assessment of leadership in the First-Century Church because the authors of *Shepherding God's Flock* only recognize three tiers—bishops, elders, and deacons—while declaring there to have been a plurality of leaders.[65]

This research aims to present the topic of the leadership positions of the First-Century Church with possibly overlooked details and new perspectives, such as that there were more than three positions, an organized network, and a design they replicated from town to town. The early church leaders defined their roles through service actions but did not regard them as offices that commanded authority. The evidence from letters of the apostolic fathers shows that it was in their generation when traditions emerged that regarded the positions of the bishop, elder, and deacon as offices commanding authority in the church. How the apostolic fathers handled the titles and authority of leaders' roles in the church formed the foundation of lasting traditions that are followed today. The objective of this study is to present the structure of First-Century Church leadership roles from a new perspective, in a new light. God's design for leadership, witnessed in the Scriptures and promoted by the apostles in the early church, was a stratified model, superior to the hierarchical models of the temple cult and synagogue of the Second Temple era, which could adapt to meet the personal attention needed by its followers. This study proposes that Christian churches of the modern age would benefit through the rediscovery and application of the leadership structure and methodology of the First-Century Church.

---

65. Merkle, *Shepherding God's Flock*, 225.

# CHAPTER 3

# The Emergence of the First-Century Church

THE FIRST-CENTURY CHURCH LED by Jesus' apostles appeared on the scene of the Second Temple period near its close between 30–40 CE, following the crucifixion of Jesus Christ. The temple at Jerusalem, the Jewish synagogues, and the Roman cultic pantheon dominated the religious climate. The First-Century Church drew its practical form by following or reacting against those influences surrounding it. In this chapter, this study will assess the temple's leadership structures, synagogue formats, and the arrangements of the Roman cults to form a baseline for understanding religious hierarchy. Next, it will provide evidence that the Roman Catholic Church and Greek Orthodoxy inherited their leadership hierarchies from Jewish and Roman traditions and arrangements. Finally, this study will examine Jesus' example and the teachings he imparted to his followers to establish the difference between his paradigm-altering doctrine and the dominant formats of the day. In addition, this study will assess how Jesus' followers practically implemented his teachings for the fledgling church.

## LEADERSHIP MODELS OF THE SECOND TEMPLE PERIOD

This section concerns an overview of the First-Century Church's historical and cultural context. In addition to cultural analysis, this study engages in a comparative analysis of the leadership models from the Jerusalem

Temple, Jewish synagogues, and temple cult formats of cultures of the late Second Temple era. Roman culture, with its acceptance and homogenization of other religions, is a significant source for comparison to the Jewish and early Christian leadership models. The assembled information forms the baseline for juxtaposing those models with church leadership formats of modernity and the structure of the First-Century Church.

## The Jewish Temple Hierarchy from the Second Temple Era

The Second Temple period ranges from the return of the diaspora Jews to the region of Palestine and the building of the Second Temple in Jerusalem in approximately 515 BCE until 70 CE, when Titus Vespasianus led the Roman army, laid siege to Jerusalem and razed the temple to the ground. Cyrus the Great had ended the exilic period of the Jewish people, which began in the sixth century BCE. With their return to their homeland, the Jews initiated the rebuilding of their temple. Three religious groups were present for it: the priests, the Levites, and the sons of Asaph (Ezra 3:10). Asaph was a Levite's son and had been one of King David's head musicians and singers; the "sons of Asaph" were his descendants or students who followed after and imitated his style of singing and playing in the temple.[1] The Levites were originally members of the tribe of Levi, which, by God's direction, had been appropriated for service in and of the sanctuary.[2] The priests consisted of the anointed priests and the high priest, and though they were initially of the tribe of Levi, Scriptures show they were not always of that bloodline; for example, some of the chief ministers in David's kingdom were priests but not Levites (1 Chron 18:16; 24:31).[3] One observes the addition of a subordinate fourth level to the tripartite hierarchy consisting of the high priest, the priesthood, and the Levites. Ezra 7:7 records, "And then went up some of the children of Israel, and of the priests, and the Levites, and the singers, and the porters, and the Nethinims, unto Jerusalem, in the seventh year of Artaxerxes the king." The singers and porters were subdivisions of the Levites, and the Nethinims were slaves dedicated to the priests and the Levites of the sanctuary.[4] Then, in 515 BCE, when the Second Temple was completed,

---

1. "אָסָף," BDBG, 63.
2. "לֵוִי," BDBG, 532–33.
3. "כֹּהֵן," BDBG, 463–64.
4. "נָתִין," BDBG, 682.

the staff of priests (*cohanim*), attendants (*leviim*), and other temple staff were reinstated; the temple once again became the central fixture for the Judean community's religious, financial, and social life.[5]

Chief in the order of the Israelite priesthood was the high priest, for he was the singular individual responsible once a year for entering the holy of holies, burning incense, and pouring some of the blood from the sacrifices onto the lavers as an offering of atonement for the people unto God (Heb 9:7; Lev 16). Under the rule of the Persian Empire, first, followed by the Hellenistic Empire, the Jewish people were permitted to conduct their traditional religious practices. Still, they were not allowed to re-establish their monarchy. The Greek historian, Hecataeus of Abdera (est. 300 BCE), testified that the high priest and subordinate priests assumed leadership roles over the people, becoming teachers, legislators, and judges, interpreting the Law, and dispensing justice, in addition to their cultic religious duties for the Jewish community (Hec. Ab.).[6]

The Jewish people gained substantial autonomy in the region during the Second Temple period after the Maccabean revolt. After a victorious uprising against their Seleucid overlords, Jonathan Maccabeus successfully negotiated for peace and independence for the Judean people, and he also assumed both the rulership of the region and the office of the high priest.[7] His consolidation of these powers in one individual established the temple's hierarchy as the ultimate authority over the Jewish people and transformed Judea into a theocracy versus a monarchy or an oligarchy separate from the temple. Another development within the temple hierarchy was a sub-sect to the priesthood called the Sanhedrin to assist the high priest in governing the people.[8] This court of elders acquired its name from the Greek word *synedrion*—a small council of elected citizens. The Sanhedrin's purpose was to aid the high priest as the highest court of Jewish law, responsible for interpreting the laws and instructing the people how they might conduct themselves accordingly.[9] Thus, the temple priesthood evolved into the dominating authority in the Jewish people's lives. A series of Hasmonean priest-kings followed in Jonathan's wake until, with the assistance of the Roman Empire, the Idumean, Herod the Great, wrestled power away from the Jewish people, placing them under

---

5. Goldhill, *Temple of Jerusalem*, 46–48.
6. Grabbe, *History of the Jews and Judaism in the Second Temple Period*, 231.
7. Green and McDonald, *World of the New Testament*, 43.
8. McLaren, *Power and Politics in Palestine*, 10–11.
9. Grabbe, *History of the Jews and Judaism in the Second Temple Period*, 188–90.

Roman authority with himself as regent.[10] Appointed as king over the Jewish people by Julius Caesar, Herod also exerted control over the office of the high priest, securing their submission and allegiance and reducing their power in the region.[11] Despite the hobbling of his power, the high priest, his subordinate priests, and the Sanhedrin maintained dominance over the Jewish people as valuable instruments of authority subject to the will of Herod the Great. Under the Hasmoneans, the temple priests collected taxes for their priest-king, a practice Herod continued that filled not only the high priest's pockets and Herod's coffers but also paid for Herod's renovation and expansion of the temple. Josephus documented that Ananias, the high priest during Jesus' time (a.k.a. Annas, Luke 3:2; John 18:13, 24; Acts 4:6), "was a great hoarder up of money" (Josephus, *A.J.* 20.9.2 §§ 205).[12]

Scholars have estimated that in the first century CE, the high priest had an estimated 20,000 priests who assisted with the affairs of the temple, including singers, collectors of tithes, and gatekeepers (*thyrōros*), subdivided into twenty-four companies that served via rotating shifts.[13] The Gospel of Luke provides an example: "And it came to pass, that while he (Zacharias) executed the priest's office before God in the order of his course, according to the custom of the priest's office, his lot was to burn incense when he went into the temple of the Lord" (1:8–9). Other priestly duties included liturgical worship, butchery, sacrificial performances, receiving confessions, prayer offerings, and other responsibilities.[14] In the Second Temple period, the Levites were a part of the priesthood, but not every priest was a Levite. Instead, the Levites, mostly temple attendants (*leviim*), tended to carry out more laborious functions such as collecting and distributing firewood, assisting worshippers with their sacrificial animals, coordinating the affairs of the women's court, and serving as the gatekeepers (doorkeeper—*thyrōros*) of not only the main entrances of the temple but also the doors of its inner courts.[15]

Two other religious groups contributing to the temple's spiritual environment during the Second Temple period were the Sadducees and the Pharisees. The Sadducees and the Pharisees were rivals over the

10. Green and McDonald, *World of the New Testament*, 47–48.
11. Goldhill, *Temple of Jerusalem*, 58–59.
12. Flavius Josephus, *Works of Flavius Josephus*, 538.
13. Sanders, *Judaism*, 130–32.
14. Sanders, *Judaism*, 134–35.
15. Sanders, *Judaism*, 136.

interpretation and implementation of the *Halakha* or the Holy Law.[16] A majority of scholars promote that the Sadducees followed after the division of the Levitical priesthood established by Zadok under King David (2 Sam 15:24–29).[17] The Sadducees strove to exercise political and religious authority over the region.[18] They exemplified the elite social class of the Palestine region and were strict interpreters of the Torah, keeping only to what was written in the scrolls.[19] John Hyrcanus (the Hasmonean) and the high priests Annas and Caiaphas (Luke 3:2; Acts 4:6) are examples of some Sadducees.[20] John Hyrcanus was previously a Pharisee but switched parties to join the Sadducees; he abolished the proclamations issued by the Pharisees not written in Moses' Law and nullified the Pharisees' power in the temple.[21] By the first century, Hellenization had corrupted the sect of the Sadducees, evidenced by their grasping for more power through politics and their lack of interest in the intent and meaning of the Mosaic Laws (*Halakhah*).[22] The contention between Jesus and Sadducees was partly due to their greed, corruption, and hypocrisy (Matt 16:1, 6, 11–12).

The Pharisees received education in the Torah and were considered "doctors of the law" capable of teaching and explaining its subject matter (Luke 5:17; Acts 5:34) but were of lower social strata than the Sadducees (Acts 5:34, 23:6). Though the Pharisees presented themselves as representing the common people of Palestine during the same period, in truth, they did not. Under the ten-year reign of Queen Shlomzion (76–67 BCE), the Pharisees regained their power and position within the Jewish hierarchy.[23] Traditionally, they advocated that an oral version of the Torah had been handed down in addition to the written one and deserved as much reverence.[24] This oral Torah, of which conveniently they were

16. Regev, "Sadducees, the Pharisees, and the Sacred," 126–40.

17. Newman and Ludlam, *Proximity to Power and Jewish Sectarian Groups of the Ancient Period*, 77.

18. Regev, "Sadducees, the Pharisees, and the Sacred," 126.

19. According to Philip Stern, the Torah began as a collection of individual divinely inspired laws (Heb. *tôrōt*) which became known as the Torah of Moses and later included the books of the Pentateuch. Use of the term *torah* could specifically refer to the five books of the Old Testament attributed to Moses or divine revelation in its entirety. "Torah" in Metzger and Coogan, *Oxford Companion to the Bible*, 747–48.

20. Regev, "Sadducees, the Pharisees, and the Sacred," 126.

21. Josephus, *A.J.* 13.10.6 §§ 295–98, 355.

22. Newman, *Proximity to Power and Jewish Sectarian Groups*, 78.

23. Newman, *Proximity to Power and Jewish Sectarian Groups*, 78.

24. Neusner, "'Pharisaic-Rabbinic' Judaism," 250–70.

the custodians, was the basis for many of their unwritten traditions and proclamations. The oral Torah was codified and edited for publication as the Mishna in roughly 200 CE.[25] However, they sacrificed accuracy for traditions and practices and adopted laws and customs incompatible with Moses' Laws.[26] While claiming to be pious, their lack of reverence for Moses' Laws earned them Jesus' reproof, correction, and disdain (Matt 15:1–9; 22:34; 23:13–27).

The Scriptures cite that the Sadducees and Pharisees only clashed over the subject of the resurrection (Matt 22:23; Acts 23:7 ff.). However, their political discord, which was undocumented in the Scriptures, was recorded by others, and this rivalry further expanded the temple hierarchy and neglected the needs of the people. The Sadducees moved to exclude lower-income people from temple activities, reserving openings only for those able to pay more. The Pharisees recommended reducing the tax offering for the lower-class citizens, posturing that it was for the populace's benefit, yet the suspicion was that they were conspiring with the Hasmoneans to rake in more wealth.[27] The Pharisees would ally themselves with the Herodians, presumably for increased political power and to catch Jesus contradicting the Scriptures (Mark 12:13). The Sadducees inflicted harsher punishments than those dispensed by the Pharisees—for example, their literal interpretation of "an eye for an eye."[28] The Pharisees and the Sadducees disagreed over several traditional holidays/festivals because they were absent from the Torah scrolls. Both groups wrestled for superiority to control the temple, with the Pharisees speaking for the masses and the Sadducees representing the upper class, resulting in the temple cult's Pharisaic coup.[29]

## The Hierarchical Format of the Synagogue

In the Second Temple period, though their forced exile was over, much of the Jewish population lived beyond the region of Palestine. Due to the immense distances many faced, Jews built the first synagogues as a substitute for visiting the temple so they might continue their religious

---

25. Britannica, Editors of Encyclopedia, "Mishna."
26. Newman, *Proximity to Power and Jewish Sectarian Groups*, 54–55.
27. Regev, "Sadducees, the Pharisees, and the Sacred," 131–32.
28. Regev, "Sadducees, the Pharisees, and the Sacred," 134.
29. Regev, "Sadducees, the Pharisees, and the Sacred," 131–32.

practices, except for the major annual festivals, which required a pilgrimage. Archeological evidence dates some synagogues in Egypt back to the third century BCE.[30] Their original function was as houses of prayer; however, upon becoming more commonplace across Jewish culture, the uses for synagogues diversified, such as for education or social functions.[31] Though synagogues have been found in Palestine and Judah, it is estimated they were not erected there until the first century BCE.[32]

Jewish traditions required an organization of a minimum of ten men to form a new synagogue, as any male was permitted to preach and read from the Scriptures or lead the prayer service.[33] Several traditions are drawn from the Mishna concerning the need for a minyan (ten Jewish adult males that have accomplished the *bar mitzvot*), and based upon *Berakhot* 6b, the formation of a synagogue is such a tradition.[34] As a result, towns could have multiple synagogues within their populations. A council of elders appointed officers to their synagogue, elected a leader, ordained priests (they wore the priestly garb of the temple, though most had no direct connection to it), and hired attendants to care for it.[35] It was not uncommon for the synagogue leader to have earned some notoriety, respect, and standing within his community. The leader was known in Greek sources as the *archisynagogos* or "ruler of the synagogue," while the attendants were the *hypēreton* (pl.), charged with fulfilling various roles from that of a janitor, to a porter, to a schoolteacher, to the charge of the scrolls, and the collector of offerings.[36] The *archisynagogos* may be viewed as the president of a synagogue because he is elected to that position, and his duties include conduct of worship services, management of finances, and delegation of responsibilities to subordinate individuals such as reading the Scriptures, leading prayers, and conducting singing.[37] In Mark 5:38, Jesus visited the home of a "ruler of the synagogue," and the Greek word employed is ἀρχισυνάγωγος (*archisynagogos*) and appears nine times across the NT.[38] In Luke 4:20, after Jesus finished reading, he

---

30. Ferguson, *Backgrounds of Early Christianity*, 573.
31. Ferguson, *Backgrounds of Early Christianity*, 575.
32. Grabbe, *History of the Jews and Judaism in the Second Temple Period*, 235–38.
33. Ferguson, *Backgrounds of Early Christianity*, 581.
34. Millgram, "Minyan."
35. Freeman, *Manners and Customs of the Bible*, 335.
36. Rajak and Noy, "Archisynagogoi," 75–93.
37. Miller, "Uniqueness of New Testament Church Eldership," 320.
38. Thayer, "ἀρχισυνάγωγος," 78.

closed the book and returned it to the minister. The word "minister" in the English text is derived from the Greek ὑπηρέτης (*hypēretēs*) and often translated as an officer, minister, or servant in the KJV but is also translated as an attendant.[39] Ὑπηρέτης (*hypēretēs*) is defined as "one who renders service; a helper, attendant in a varying official or assigned capacity."[40] Though a synagogue would only have one ruler, there were often several *hypēreton*, depending on the size and needs of that particular synagogue. For example, the *hazzan* was the attendant in charge of the scrolls, while other functionaries included the scribes, readers, singers of psalms, financial officers, and others.[41] Portraying themselves as representing ordinary people, the Pharisees extended their influence into local synagogues as much as the temple. They demanded special privileges, such as prearranged seating, and to be addressed as "Rabbi."[42] As the temple was the prototype for the synagogue, following its example, the lowest attendant employed by the synagogue would have also held the doorkeeper's duties. Thus, a hierarchical format of leadership, influenced by the temple and Jewish political traditions, operated in the Ancient Near East synagogues.

## Roman Religious Cultic Hierarchy

Unlike Jewish culture, Roman culture accepted many different styles and practices of religious rites and traditions. They inherited much of their pantheon of deities from the Greek and Egyptian civilizations, and they were not against adopting the gods from other cultures they encountered or conquered, as they feared offending any deity.[43] A biblical example occurs in Acts 17:23, where Paul states, "As I passed by, and beheld your devotions, I found an altar with this inscription, TO THE UNKNOWN GOD." Roman open polytheism, according to Beard, North, and Price, "reflected Rome's changing social, political, and military circumstances; they responded to new manifestations and new interpretations of divine power."[44] They also respected the Jews' religion because it had preceded

---

39. Strong, "ὑπηρέτης—*hypēretēs*," *Strong's Exhaustive Concordance*, 258.
40. Danker, "ὑπηρέτης," *Concise Greek-English Lexicon of the New Testament*, 364.
41. Merkle and Schreiner, *Shepherding God's Flock*, 19.
42. Newman and Ludlam, *Proximity to Power and Jewish Sectarian Groups*, 153–54.
43. Beard et al., *Religions of Rome*, 41.
44. Beard et al., *Religions of Rome*, 41.

their own and that of the Greeks; they even made equivalencies between Yahweh and Jupiter.[45]

Roman culture did not have a singular priesthood but many collectives of priests and priestesses, such as the *pontifices*, the *flamines*, the *curiones*, the *haruspices*, the vestal virgins, and the priests of the Imperial cult.[46] A *flamen* was a priest dedicated to one of the eighteen deities of the Roman pantheon of gods. However, the deities of chief importance to most Roman people were the triad on Capitoline Hill—Jupiter Optimus Maximus, Juno, and Minerva—the Roman Imperial cult, and the gods and ancestors of one's hearth (called *gens*).[47] The *pontifex maximus*, followed by the *flamens Dialis* (priests of Jupiter), were the most essential priests and commanded the most reverence.[48] Many public priests were also Roman politicians drawing on power and authority from both sides of the aisle, but while a political office was temporary, a priesthood was for life.[49] In serving the gods, a singular priest was charged with caring for a particular temple, such as a temple dedicated to Jupiter. In addition, that priest was assigned necessary underlings to aid in the sacrificial rites and maintain the temple's cleanliness. Beard reports that some priests were elected by popular vote; however, "the priest of Jupiter (*flamen Dialis*) was always chosen by the *pontifex maximus*—even sometimes against the will of the nominee himself."[50] As evidence that Roman religions were hierarchical, according to Cicero, Roman ancestors, under divine inspiration, entrusted both the worship of the gods and the matters of Roman governing to the men.[51] In addition, Augustus is one example of a Caesar nominating himself as the *pontifex maximus*, leaving him virtually unchallenged in authority. After him, the office passed to his successor, ensuring the priestly power, influence, and control remained with the emperor. Other Caesars followed his model, for the Romans understood the primary ways to direct and control a population were through military might, political power, and religious authority.

These three models, the Jewish Temple, synagogue, and the Roman pantheon of deities were significant contemporaries to the First-Century

45. Beard et al., *Religions of Rome*, 320.
46. Beard et al., *Religions of Rome*, 194–207.
47. Beard et al., *Religions of Rome*, 17, 24, 207.
48. Beard et al., *Religions of Rome*, 197.
49. Beard et al., *Religions of Rome*, 197.
50. Beard et al., *Religions of Rome*, 199.
51. Beard et al., *Religions of Rome*, 198.

Church as it formed and broke from their Jewish traditions. The brief overview of each presented is necessary for the analysis of the leadership model of the First-Century Church as they provide a baseline for comparison and contrast. These three sources—the Jewish Temple, synagogue, and the Roman temple cults—were the primary influences surrounding the early church in its embryonic stages. This overview forms a baseline for the study of the First-Century Church. The early church either adopted, adapted, or rejected the patterns of religious leadership they observed around them. This summary also provides essential evidence displaying the sources for the leadership formats of modern Christian churches.

## LEADERSHIP MODELS OF CONTEMPORARY CHRISTIAN CHURCHES

The leadership structures for the majority of churches across Christianity follow the forms of the Roman Catholic or Eastern Orthodox churches. The top-down format by which they lead their congregations removes the highest official from the public, comparable to the fashion that drew the high priest from the people (Heb 4:15). In contrast to such models, there are approximately thirty records of Jesus entering into people's homes, ministering and teaching from a domestic setting. Likewise, Paul, Peter, and others imitated his example, making themselves available to the lowliest members of the church.

The Roman Catholic or Eastern Orthodox churches have inherited and adopted their arrangements from the temple and the synagogue of Second Temple Judaism. The temple hierarchy derived its structure from the model instituted by Moses and Aaron for the tabernacle, which kings David and Solomon later modified. Within that hierarchy, the high priest (Lev 21:10; Num 35:25) and those who served directly under him (Num 11:16) were the only individuals anointed with the spirit of God. That anointing separated them from all others who served in the tabernacle and later the temple, thus establishing the Jewish hierarchy. After the passing of Moses and Aaron, the priesthood guided and directed the people; even Joshua and subsequent judges yielded to their authority. At that time, such a hierarchy was necessary because the spirit of God resided with a minority of the nation of Israel's population.

In variance to the model of the priesthood, at the outpouring of the gift of the holy spirit on the day of Pentecost, approximately three thousand plus souls were baptized and consecrated with that gift (Acts 2:41). The spirit from God was no longer for a select minority but unto all who believed, just as Peter had preached (Acts 2:17, ff.). That consecration separated those who believed in Jesus from all others and formed for the first time the *ekklēsia*, fulfilling Jesus' prophesy (Matt 16:18; Acts 2:42–47). Furthermore, the new church had no hierarchy, for the Scripture states, "all that believed were together, and had all things common" (Acts 2:42). The following verses display all the believers shared all things communally to care for each person's needs; at that time no individual was treated any better than any other (Acts 2:44–46). Likewise, the testimony of the Scriptures displays that the twelve apostles and the estimated 120 people who abode with them (Acts 1:15) were treated no better or with any superiority to the believers who joined the church. Such a witness displays two factors that indicate a departure from the tabernacle/temple format. First, all the people who believed were baptized of the spirit the same as the apostles—virtually equal standing. Under the tabernacle/temple formats, only a minority of the people obtained a spiritual anointing. Second, the members of the newly-formed church bore equal respect and treatment for one another (Acts 10:25–37), negating any hierarchy and thus forming an egalitarian movement.

The formation of the Roman Catholic Church hierarchy mirrored the top-down leadership style of the temple's priestly format.[52] During the Middle Ages, the Catholic priesthood exerted efforts to tie the model of its orders back to the leaders of the NT but instead copied the OT temple model and presented it under the guise of a consolidation that was the next evolution of the church structure.[53] The hierarchy of the Catholic Church places the pope at its apex, followed by the college of cardinals (senior bishops), archbishops, bishops, and priests. The standard of governance within the Catholic Church is rulership exercised by the priesthood.[54] Such an arrangement places power and control with the minority and sets them above the congregation, as in the OT temple format. The earliest source setting forth the pattern of exercised authority over the church's followers is *The First Letter of Clement*.[55] Clement

---

52. Swanson, "Apostolic Successors," 5–6.
53. Swanson, "Apostolic Successors," 10–11.
54. Walsh, *Roman Catholicism*, 38.
55. Walsh, *Roman Catholicism*, 36.

wrote concerning a dispute in the church and declared that authority was to be inherited in a traditional manner.[56] In *1 Clement* chapter 42, he begins with Jesus Christ, sent by God, who entrusted his gospel and authority to his apostles, and from the apostles, it was transferred to the bishops and deacons.[57] Regarding the transference of power from those in charge, *1 Clement* chapter 44, verse 2b reads: "They appointed those we have already mentioned; and afterward they added a codicil, to the effect that if these should die, other approved men should succeed them in their ministry."[58] The initial "they" refers to the apostles, and the latter "they" refers to the bishops and deacons who succeeded them. Next, the quote states the bishops and deacons who continued the church ministrations added a "codicil"—an additional supplementary council responsible for appointing other bishops and deacons.

Later, the mode of operations within the church would adapt and change, reflecting a hybrid of the temple format with a pseudo-military style due to adding other necessary positions. Cyprian (died c. 258), a bishop of Carthage, reportedly compared the church's priesthood with the Levitical priesthood of the OT.[59] In the middle of the third century, a bishop, Cornelius, giving an account of the hierarchy within the city of Rome to Eusebius, documented having "forty-six presbyters, seven deacons, seven sub-deacons, forty-two acolytes, fifty-two exorcists, readers, and doorkeepers."[60] Under the Roman Catholic Church, the presbyter ruled over the parish, collecting offerings from the parishioners, which he paid to his superior, the bishop; if need be, with the bishop's permission, the presbyter could ordain deacons, not for service in the priesthood, but as his personal assistants.[61] Such doctrines and practices formed the foundation of the leadership hierarchy within the Roman Catholic Church.

The Roman Catholic Church would like its followers and the rest of the world to believe that its leadership format is ideal, straightforward, and directly inherited from apostolic authority, but this is not factual. Emperor Constantine, via the Council of Nicaea in 325 CE and his following decrees, organized the Roman Church (not yet recognized as

56. Walsh, *Roman Catholicism*, 37.
57. Ehrman, *After the New Testament*, 433–34.
58. Ehrman, *After the New Testament*, 434.
59. Frend, *Rise of Christianity*, 405.
60. Eusebius, *History of the Church*, 282.
61. Frend, *Rise of Christianity*, 406.

"Catholic") to provide for the inclusion of all faiths in his empire, making room not only for diversity in the name of peace but also for compromise.[62] Previously, in 314 CE, Constantine wrote in a letter to Aelafius, vicar of Africa, that God had committed to his charge the managerial authority over all earthly affairs.[63] His intent was rulership and dominion over all in the same manner as Augustus Caesar and others before him. Like Augustus, Constantine and his successors took on the title of *pontifex maximus*.[64] Under his dominion, he established the hierarchy of what became the Roman Catholic Church by gathering the various bishops from across the empire under the ascendancy of the ruling episcopate centered in Rome, with himself as its head.[65] The church's history became a hybridization of fact and fiction with decrees, legal mandates, and documents designed to authenticate the organization it had transformed into.[66] Although verbally and through developed codifications, the Roman Catholic Church claimed connections to Christ, his apostles, and disciples; contrarily, their leadership arrangement took the form of the temple priesthood.[67] Constantine had been a successful military commander and established an empire unrivaled in its time through military order and control. He would employ a regimented religious hegemony within the realm to maintain control without appearing aggressive. Constantine had corrupted the church, supplanting patriarchs for martyrs and exchanging pacifists for militants; Stephenson argues the church became an instrument of the state and that the original message of Christianity was lost.[68] The hierarchical control and domination would continue through to the modern age through the arrangement and exercise of its leadership.

The Eastern Orthodox movement of Christianity was the first exceptional spinoff with any staying power from the church in Rome. They credit Dionysius the Areopagite (fifth-sixth c. CE) as the originator of the term "hierarchy" and its definition and justification, which are foundational to Byzantine religious traditions.[69] The structure of the Eastern

---

62. Stephenson, *Constantine Roman Emperor*, 270–71.
63. Optatus, *Work of St. Optatus*, 384–85.
64. van Haeperen, "Des pontifes païens aux pontifes chrétiens," 137–59.
65. Merkle, *Shepherding God's Flock*, 122–23.
66. Swanson, "Apostolic Successors," 8.
67. Swanson, "Apostolic Successors," 9–12.
68. Stephenson, *Constantine Roman Emperor*, 277–78.
69. Purpura, *God, Hierarchy, and Power*, 7.

Orthodox Church is decentralized and flexible, following Dionysius's teachings from *Ecclesiastical Hierarchy*, with a bishop appointed as the head of the particular church for a community, who acts as a stand-in for Jesus Christ.[70] This model is similar to the synagogue's design for serving a smaller community of people, with the synagogue's ruler as its head, the stand-in for the temple's high priest, and the congregation's mediator unto God. There may be a few Greek Orthodox churches in a town and many more for a city with a substantial population to maintain a lower number of members in a given congregation. This pattern contrasts the Roman Catholic Church's design that sets up a significant cathedral over a diocese of an extensive populous led by a bishop. Eastern Orthodox bishops operate independently of each other, furthering the decentralized model, but they form councils that maintain a loose association, referred to as a synod. While there is a sense of leadership and order in the Eastern Orthodox Churches, they do not operate under the same hierarchy and rigor as the Roman Catholic Church. Recently, the Ecumenical Patriarch Bartholomew was given the honorific title of *primus inter pares*, or "first among equals," to preside over the "Holy and Great Synod" in Crete.[71] Subordinate to that position, in order of declensions, are the offices of the archbishop, the archimandrite, the oeconomos, the archdeacon, and the office of the deacon.[72] Beneath the deacons are any further church ministers and attendants. Though the titles Greek Orthodoxy utilizes for their officials are similar to or after the fashion of those found in the Greek texts of the NT, their hierarchy bears a similitude to the Roman Catholic Church. Like the Greek Orthodoxy, Protestant, Presbyterian, Methodist, and Baptist churches maintain similar loose associations within their respective denominations but have dispensed with the position and titles of bishop and deacon. Instead, the leaders of these Christian churches are appointed by a church council like a synagogue's "council of elders." Some modern Protestant churches may combine to form a "megachurch" for specific events and functions. Such assemblies resemble an Eastern Orthodox synod, though a synod comprises only the leadership body.

The Lutheran Church, the Church of England, and the Church of Jesus Christ of Latter-Day Saints follow the Roman Catholic Church model derived from the Jerusalem Temple. The decentralized leadership

---

70. Purpura, *God, Hierarchy, and Power*, 30–35.
71. Leustean, "Eastern Orthodoxy, Geopolitics," 201–16.
72. Orthodox Times, "Archdiocese of Thyateira."

model of the Jewish synagogue influenced the Eastern Orthodox Church. Most Protestant churches in Europe and the Western hemisphere adopted Eastern Orthodoxy's pattern or a similar version. A commonality of all these models is that the person in charge leads a congregation of hundreds and, in some cases, thousands of people. Yet, as this study attested, people become marginalized, ignored, and left in the shadows in large congregations. How can the leader of such a large body of people attend to each member's individual needs? The teachings that Jesus left his followers were intended to replace and improve upon the temple cult format.

Roman Catholic and Greek Orthodoxy designs are entrenched in traditions—the temple and synagogue—that existed before the advent of Christ and were faltering or failing during the first century. Jesus and his followers of the First-Century Church broke away from the structures and traditions of their culture's history to form something new. The church established by Jesus and his apostles, committed to those who followed after, was meant to tend to the spiritual needs of God's people as a shepherd tends his sheep. Instead, they introduced a service-oriented paradigm shift that put people first before the leaders and set up an organizational structure that served their spiritual needs and practices. The transformation began with Jesus and his doctrine and examples.

## JESUS' EXAMPLE AND INSTRUCTIONS

Jesus Christ, in both word and deed, was a revolutionary for his day, who taught his disciples and later his apostles to take the Scriptures of God's word to the people and minister to them where they lived. Before this maverick appeared on the scene, men and women had to visit the temple to have a priest hear their confession, present offerings, and remit their sins. At least, they would have to visit their local synagogue. Documentable as early as the second century BCE, the Roman Empire taxed all foreign nations under her control to fund further expansion efforts and military conquest.[73] The synagogues and the temple paid taxes to their draconic overlords, and the staff of either location asked for an offering from their patrons for upkeep, food, and clothing (Matt 17:24–27; 22:15–22). Jesus broke with tradition many times across the records of the canonical Gospels, purposing to bring love, truth, healing, and deliverance

---

73. Grant and Kitzinger, *Civilization of the Ancient Mediterranean*, 809–27.

to the people where they resided. He repeatedly demonstrated that anyone who claimed to be an emissary for the almighty should operate a ministry of service to others.

## Jesus' Living Example for Leadership

At the initiation of his earthly ministry, Jesus began by meeting people in their synagogues (Mark 1:21). In the Gospel of Luke, it is written that after his baptism in the Jordan, and his temptations, it was his manner to visit synagogues on the Sabbath to read and preach to the people (Luke 4:15). Concerning his ministry, he quoted the book of Isaiah: "The Spirit of Lord is upon me because he hath anointed me to preach the gospel to the poor; he hath sent me to heal the brokenhearted, to preach deliverance to the captives, and recovering of sight to the blind, to set at liberty them that are bruised, to preach the acceptable year of the Lord" (Luke 4:18–19). He was sent to serve others rather than demand service and obeisance from those who came to see him. In Matt 20:28 Jesus declared, ". . . the Son of man came not to be ministered unto, but to minister. . ." Both "ministered unto" (διακονηθῆναι) and "to minister" (διακονῆσαι) have the verb διακονέω as their source, which means "serve, take care of, wait upon; be a deacon," and in the case of this Scripture it means "to render assistance or help by performing certain duties, often of a humble or menial nature."[74] The noun form of this word is διάκονος (*diakonos*), and it is translated most commonly across the King James Version (KJV) of the NT as "minister" or "servant" (e.g., Matt 22:13; Rom 13:4). However, in only three verses διάκονος is rendered as "deacon," and in each of those references, the context refers to people bearing an office of leadership (Phil 1:1; 1 Tim 3:8, 12). The true nature of a deaconship is in extending selfless service to others.

At the start of his earthly ministry, Jesus taught and spoke in the synagogues because that was the chief place, apart from the temple, where people gathered to hear the Scriptures (Matt 4:23; Mark 1:21; Luke 4:15). As he garnered a reputation for his miracles and healings, fame preceded him, and multitudes followed him (Matt 4:25). Jesus went to where there was a need for his service, and as people followed, he taught and ministered to them. For example, in Matt 8, he visited Peter's house and healed his mother-in-law, and many gathered, bringing others for

---

74. "διακονέω," L&N 1:460.

him to recover. Mark 2:15 records that he and his disciples ate with "the publicans and sinners." In addition, he accepted people suffering from leprosy, but in contrast to the temple's priests, Jesus embraced and ministered to those of society's lowest caste in their settings and homes.

Jesus refused to permit cultural traditions, prejudices, and mores of the day to interfere with delivering his gospel and ministering to people. An example of his behavior as a radical of his time is observed in Jesus' interactions with a Samaritan woman in the Gospel of John chapter four, verses one through twenty-six. As Jesus traveled, the most direct route from Judea to Galilee was through Samaria (John 4:3–4). In the Second Temple age, rivalry, hatred, and prejudice existed between Jews and Samaritans, motivating Jewish travelers to pass the long way around the region of Samaria by crossing the Jordan River and continuing through Perea.[75] Though they followed the Torah like the Jews, Samaritans were not permitted in the temple at Jerusalem due to established traditions and edicts; similarly, Jews were not expected to pass through Samaria but avoid the area. Traveling the route due North through Samaria, Jesus takes on the schism between the two cultures. Shechem, located near Mount Gerizim, has remained the Samaritan people's capital through the eons. There is a high probability that the town Sychar in this record is Shechem, but scholars have yet to conclude so unanimously. The Samaritan people long endured a reputation as foreigners or intermarried half-breeds at best and had to deal with the disdain of their Jewish neighbors.[76] The Gospel text acknowledges such prejudice when the woman matter-of-factly states that the Jews have nothing to do with her people (John 4:9). Some Jewish sources cite the Samaritans as "semi-pagans who rejected the Jerusalem Temple and regarded Mount Gerizim as the exclusive legitimate place of worship," a position reflected in John 4:20.[77] Following an exchange between Jesus and the woman at the well, she attains conversion and rouses her village to come to meet the Messiah. In verse nineteen, the KJV has "Sir" in the text; however, the corresponding word in Greek is κύριε (kurie).[78] Κύριε is a form of κυριος (kurios), which translates as "supreme authority, master" or, more commonly, the respectful and honorable title: "Lord."[79] In the Gospel of John, the first

75. Robertson, *Word Pictures in the New Testament*, 199.
76. Robertson, *Word Pictures in the New Testament*, 199–200.
77. Novakovic, "Jews and Samaritans," 208.
78. Mounce and Mounce, *Interlinear New Testament*, 360.
79. Thayer, "κυριος," *Thayer's Greek-English Lexicon*, 365.

person to revere Jesus as "Lord" before anyone else was someone society would have judged condescendingly as a half-gentile woman at a well.[80] Jesus was a radical who broke from traditions, cultural mores, and racial barriers in ministering and bringing his gospel to others.

When Jesus commissioned his twelve disciples (who would later become his apostles), he did so with specific instructions to seek homes where they might enter and teach people his gospel (Matt 10:1–14; Mark 3:14–19; Luke 9:1–6). In Matthew chapter nine, Jesus visited the homes of Matthew, the ruler of a synagogue, and two blind men (Matt 9:10, 23, 28). Each time he did so, he ministered to the people's needs, and when others found out and gathered at that home, he would teach them. Sometime later, in Luke chapter ten, Jesus commissioned seventy disciples in pairs to deliver the message of his gospel to others. Again, like the twelve before, he instructed them to enter people's homes to teach, minister, and heal (Luke 10:1–9). He referred to the seventy as his laborers who were sent to prepare cities and homes for Jesus, to find the areas that would receive his gospel upon his coming to them. The word laborer in the Greek text is ἐργάτης–*ergatas*, "a workman, a laborer: usually one who works for hire."[81] However, Jesus didn't pay any of them, yet they dedicated themselves to serving and working for Jesus as if he had. These ambassadors only received food, drink, or other necessities if their would-be hosts provided them. In essence, they were so committed to their master's work and ministry that it was as if they were his servants (δοῦλοι–*douloi* [pl.]).

A hospitality custom of the Ancient Near East is washing a guest's feet or permitting them to wash their feet when they enter their host's abode, which is as important as providing them with food.[82] For example, in Luke chapter seven, a Pharisee invited Jesus Christ into his home for a meal (Luke 7:36). During their exchange, a woman, whom the text stresses was a sinner, entered the scene and washed, kissed, and anointed his feet with ointment (vs. 37–38). The Pharisee had disparaging thoughts within himself of this woman because of her known sinful ways, and Jesus, perceiving this, reproved his host for not upholding the customs of their culture (vs. 39–46). Under everyday circumstances, washing a guest's feet would be the lowliest servant's responsibility—most likely the responsibility of the doorkeeper. Jesus later utilized this custom to teach his apostles the degree of service they were to render to others. In

---

80. Lawler, *Well of Living Water*, 32.
81. Thayer, "ἐργάτης," *Thayer's Greek-English Lexicon*, 248.
82. Freeman, *Manners and Customs of the Bible*, 17–18.

John chapter 13, at the event often referred to as "the Last Supper," when Jesus and the twelve apostles finished eating, Jesus commenced washing their feet (vs. 5). Then he taught them afterward that their behaviors and manners in treating others should mimic his. "For I have given you an example, that ye should do as I have done to you," and Jesus continued, "Verily, verily, I say unto you, the servant is not greater than his lord; neither he that is sent greater than he that sent him. If ye know these things, happy are ye if ye do them" (vs. 15–17). Jesus' purpose of debasing himself without any shame to perform one of the lowliest forms of service (for indeed he could have called any disciple to perform it) was to teach his apostles how to extend themselves in humble, loving service to others. Such service, with humility, was to be the hallmark of their leadership in his absence because that was how he, Jesus, had led them.

## Jesus' Doctrine for Leadership

In Matt 20:20, the mother of Jesus' disciples, James and John, had requested that her sons be granted the seats of honor on Jesus' right and left when he assumed authority over his kingdom. Her appeal to Jesus reflected the common knowledge that in a realm after the king, the seats which received the highest honor and wielded the most power over the people were directly on the right and left of the throne. Following her request, Jesus set the standards for all that followed after him when he stated, "Ye know that the princes of the Gentiles exercise dominion over them, and they that are great exercise authority upon them. But it shall not be so among you: but whosoever will be great among you, let him be your minister; and whosoever will be chief among you, let him be your servant" (Matt 20:25–27). Jesus' disciples were not to exercise power or dominion over others; instead, they were to serve others selflessly, just as he had. In this passage of Scripture, a particular figure of speech, antithetic parallelism, or "a parallel of opposites," is utilized to emphasize the lesson Jesus taught them. Antithetic parallelism is "when words are contrasted in the two or more lines being *opposed in sense* the one to the other."[83] For example, Jesus contrasted "great" versus "minister" and "chief" versus "servant" to form a dichotomy. Jesus employed this dichotomy, illustrating and calling attention to the principle that authentic, godly leadership comes from serving and lifting one's people rather than

---

83. Bullinger, *Figures of Speech Used in the Bible*, 351.

dragging them down or berating them. Searching the Greek language for a deeper understanding of the verses, one finds that "great" is *megas*, of relation to the Latin words *magnus* and *magister*, and means "great, predicated of rank, as belonging to persons, eminent for ability, virtue, authority, power."[84] "Minister" is διάκονος (*diakonos*), interpreted as "one who executes the commands of another, especially of a master; a servant attendant, minister; it is used universally of a servant of a king; figuratively of one who advances others' interests even at the sacrifice of their own."[85] The occurrence of the word διάκονος (*diakonos*) in verse 26 is its first usage in the NT, setting a precedent for understanding its meaning in future uses. This word/title gains importance later when one considers the apostle Paul's utilization of it in his writings. "Chief" is the noun πρῶτος (*protos*), bearing the meaning of "first in rank, influence, honor; chief; principle."[86] Next, in direct opposition to the chief, is the lowly position of the "servant," which is δοῦλος (*doulos*), meaning "a slave, bondman, man of servile condition; metaphorically one who gives himself up wholly to another's will."[87] Paul, speaking about Jesus, declared, "But made himself of no reputation, and took upon him the form of a servant, and was made in the likeness of men: And being found in fashion as a man, he humbled himself, and became obedient unto death, even the death of the cross" (Phil 2:7–8). "The form of a servant" is μορφὴν δούλου in Greek, which is to say his outward appearance embodied and reflected the very nature of a devoted servant—δοῦλος (*doulos*)—dedicated to accomplishing the will of his Father, God, even to the terminal degree of the death of the cross.[88] Jesus' dedication exemplifies that of a δοῦλος (*doulos*) and thus sets the example for any who might follow him. Previously, in Matt 16:24–25, Jesus had declared to his disciples that if any desired to follow him as their Lord, that person was required to "lose his life" or, in other words, give it up freely. In chapter 23, verses 8–12, he reiterates the sentiments of this teaching in his disciples' ears but adds, "Neither be ye called masters: for one is your Master, even Christ." The word "master" is not like the master-slave dynamic but instead designates an individual as one "to go before, lead, a guide, a teacher."[89] Jesus' disciples were to look

84. Thayer, "μέγας," *Thayer's Greek-English Lexicon*, 394–95.
85. Thayer, "διάκονος," *Thayer's Greek-English Lexicon*, 138.
86. Thayer, "προτος," *Thayer's Greek-English Lexicon*, 554–55.
87. Thayer, "δοῦλος," *Thayer's Greek-English Lexicon*, 157–58.
88. Thayer, "μορφὴν," *Thayer's Greek-English Lexicon*, 418.
89. Thayer, "καθηγητής," *Thayer's Greek-English Lexicon*, 313.

to him as their master teacher, leader, and guide, but they were to treat each other as brothers. If any of them wished to be "greatest," that person was to become a "servant"—διάκονος (*diakonos*) of all the others (vs. 11). Jesus' teachings concerning leadership and service overturned the typical administrative model for exerting governance, management, and control of people. Jesus promoted a people-first model that led through service, motivating others to imitate his example of ministering.

The other Gospels do not add different perspectives to Jesus' doctrine witnessed in Matthew but reinforce it. For example, the Gospel of Mark contrasts first—πρῶτος (*protos*), with servant—διάκονος (*diakonos*) (9:35), and 10:43 uncannily duplicates Matt 20:26. The Gospel of Luke does not utilize the word servant—διάκονος (*diakonos*) in its Scriptures. Chapter two of the Gospel of John relates the incident of Jesus turning water into wine at a wedding feast where he and his disciples were guests. The word διάκονος (*diakonos*) is employed for the individuals who were servants of "the ruler of the feast" (2:5, 9). These servants were the caterers, ministering to the needs of the people gathered; in society's eyes, they were nothing special. John 12:26 states, "Whoever serves (διακονῇ) me, must follow me; and where I am, my servant (διάκονος) also will be. My Father will honor the one who serves (διακονῇ) me."[90] In Eastern culture, the most trusted servant, the master's personal attendant, was the one permitted to accompany him as the master conducted his affairs. The verb form of "serves" (διακονῇ) is in the passive, third-person, singular, and the context portrays the meaning that underscores this mode of service as one who waits upon another in servitude as an attendant or assistant.[91] Thus, this Scripture promised that if a person were to dedicate himself to Jesus as his personal attendant, the Father, God, would honor him.

In John chapter ten, Jesus taught a most important lesson concerning the style of leader he was and implied that his disciples should follow his example. His parable spoke of the tender relationship between a good shepherd and his sheep. Jesus said, "But he that entereth in by the door is the shepherd of the sheep. To him the porter openeth; and the sheep hear his voice: and he calleth his own sheep by name, and leadeth them out. And when he putteth forth his own sheep, he goeth before them, and the sheep follow him: for they know his voice" (John 10:2–4). His lesson drew from Psalm twenty-three, in which David spoke of the LORD God as

---

90. Mounce and Mounce, *Interlinear New Testament*, 410.

91. Mounce and Mounce, "διακονέω," *Interlinear New Testament*, 1040.

his shepherd, the one above all who cared for, preserved, and blessed his life just as a shepherd would tenderly care for his sheep. Later in the tenth chapter, Jesus applied the analogies of the gate of the sheepfold and the good shepherd to himself. The flock could depend on him as the gate, for he provided safety and salvation (vs. 7–9). As the good shepherd, Jesus was willing to sacrifice himself for his flock and come between them and eminent danger (vs. 11–18).

Sheep are inherently timid creatures, and a shepherd must be firm and consistent because they require constant direction, goading, oversight, training, and tending. Still, the shepherd must also be gentle and mild because of their nature. Freeman informs that shepherds in the Palestinian-Middle Eastern region name each sheep in their flocks much like people in the Western hemisphere give names to their pets; the sheep recognize their name and respond to their shepherd's call.[92] The shepherd in the Middle East would sleep with his sheep in the field, and the sheep would know their shepherd's scent and the sound of his voice and respond accordingly. Likewise, Jesus endeared himself to his followers, and frequently, he referred to them as his sheep (Matt 9:36; 15:24; Mark 6:34). Many great men from the OT, whom the Jewish people revered, were herdsmen, such as Moses and Abraham, Isaac, Joseph, David, and Amos. The parable's lesson described Jesus' character and set the attributes necessary for his disciples, and later his apostles, to lead others in his stead. The example of a Middle Eastern shepherd was the prototype for a pastor's ministry within the public body of the church. This study discusses the comparison of the shepherd and the prophet in a later chapter. Towards the end of the first century, the author of the book of Hebrews and the apostle Peter, in his letters, would reference Jesus' parable of the good shepherd to remind the church of these principles. In some of his final instructions to Peter, in which Jesus put authority over the church in his hands, he said, "Feed my sheep" (John 21:15–19). His commands implied that Peter would need to lead the church, just as Jesus had. In his master's absence, Peter would have to become the good shepherd for the church and an example for those who joined its ranks later.

The culture of the Ancient Near East was deeply rooted in an agricultural way of life. Jesus, the master teacher, employed imagery in the society around him to impart truths and lessons to his followers. In the record where he visited Samaria, as the townspeople came en masse to

---

92. Freeman, *Manners and Customs of the Bible*, 428–29.

meet him, he said to his disciples, "Look on the fields; for they are white already to harvest" (John 4:35). The fields ready for picking were the people coming to hear his testimony. His parable of the sower and the good seed, his lesson about the trees and the fruit they produce, himself as the true vine, and many more all utilized agricultural symbolism to impart greater truths about the nature of people. In John 15 Jesus taught, "I am the true vine, and my Father is the husbandman. Every branch in me that beareth not fruit he taketh away: and every branch that beareth fruit, he purgeth it that it may bring forth more fruit" (John 15:1–2). Jesus doesn't leave the interpretation to chance, for, in later verses, he explains to his apostles that metaphorically, they were his branches bearing spiritual fruit to be harvested by God; the fruit they bore were people newly come to Jesus' gospel (John 15:5). The branches that bore no fruit were also followers of Jesus, but they were fake and needed to be pruned and discarded, cleansing the vine (John 15:2, 6). Jesus never placed the responsibility of the vine's maintenance on any of his followers. Their duty was to produce spiritual fruit, i.e., bring more people to Christ; in turn, these new people would grow and produce their own fruit. They would achieve this through keeping Christ's commandments and loving others as he loved them (John 15:8–10). This agricultural metaphor utilized the practices of how husbandmen of the East cultivated their vineyards and applied to people. In fostering and nurturing a vineyard, one must pay close attention to the weather it receives, remove weeds, and protect it from insects and animals. Likewise, for Jesus' apostles to produce a full church, the congregation would require comparable treatment to ensure they achieve spiritual maturity in Christ and win others to the Lord. The task would require the apostles to lead and love others the same way Jesus had served them. The apostles and disciples could no more scream, insult, abuse, or ignore would-be believers, lest those neophytes turn away from God's church. The husbandry metaphors and language also appear in Paul's letters to the churches in Asia Minor to help them understand how to nurture and raise others after Christ's example and doctrine.

The canonical Gospels contain many examples of Jesus opposing traditions, situations, or features found in the culture of that day. For instance, in the Gospel of Matthew, Jesus warned his disciples, "Beware of the leaven of the Pharisees and of the Sadducees," which was metaphorical for the doctrines of these two parties vying for control of the temple in Jerusalem (Matt 16:6–12). Leaven was fermented dough, which, when added to a new lump of dough, gave it the ability to rise like yeast, affected the flavor of the fresh dough, and metaphorically symbolized corruption.[93] Again, in Matthew, Jesus confronted the Pharisees concerning their hypocrisy, for they appeared pleasing to the eye on the outside when their souls were as filthy as sepulchers (Matt 23:23–28). The Pharisees and Sadducees were not the only groups adversely aligned against Jesus but so also were the chief priests, the scribes, the elders of the temple, and the Herodians (Mark 3:6; 12:13; Luke 20:1). The Herodians were a political group often at odds with the Pharisees concerning legislative control and power in the region and that supported Herod as a Roman vassal king and his family.[94] Herod, being an Idumean and not Jewish, was viewed as a friend of the Romans and a betrayer of the people because he punished members of the Pharisees and executed some of the Sadducees to advance his control over the temple and the Jewish people.[95] Herod's four sons, Archelaus, Antipas, Aristobulus, and Philip, inherited their father's dominion, cared nothing for Jewish religious society, and endeavored to keep the region peaceful and in good standing with their Roman overlords. Agrippa II, the great-nephew of Herod, ruled the area when the Jewish people revolted against Roman control, and due to his failure, their family's dominion ended with the Roman siege of Jerusalem in 66–70 CE.[96]

In 2 Chronicles, at the dedication of Solomon's Temple, the LORD made a solemn promise that if Solomon and the people did not remain faithful to his statutes and commandments, the edifice would become a desolate ruin (2 Chron 7:19–22). God would only be present in a particular dwelling as long as the people there were faithful to him and his Word. The prophet, Isaiah, inspired by God, declared, "Thus saith the LORD, the heaven is my throne, and the earth is my footstool: where is the house that ye build unto me? And where is the place of my rest?" (Isa 55:1). People are not capable of building an edifice that could house almighty God. Instead, he dwells with those who love him and keep his Word in their hearts (Ps 119:1–11).

When Jesus entered Jerusalem on a colt, duplicating Solomon's coronation ride, the people gathered and honored Jesus as a king for the first time (1 Kgs 1:39–40; Luke 19:30–38). As he approached the city, he paused and prophesied Jerusalem's destruction, which would come to

93. Manning and Coogan, *Oxford Companion to the Bible*, 428.
94. Freeman, *Manners and Customs of the Bible*, 365.
95. Manning and Coogan, *Oxford Companion to the Bible*, 280–84.
96. Manning and Coogan, *Oxford Companion to the Bible*, 284.

pass in 70 CE (Luke 19:41–44). What Jesus discovered in the temple revealed why God would permit such consequences. The traditions people participated in involving the commerce of animals in the temple courtyard for their sacrificial rites had corrupted and polluted the temple with sin. In Luke 19:46, Jesus quotes the prophet Jeremiah (Jer 7:11), stating, "It is written, my house is the house of prayer: but ye have made it a den of thieves." He routed their businesses and cleaned the temple of their traditions, which the chief priests and other authorities had permitted and no doubt profited from (Luke 19:45–47). Jesus' actions and teachings set him at odds with the religious leaders of the day.

Herod's renovation of the Second Temple at Jerusalem made it wonderful and majestic to view, rivaling other notable structures and architecture of the ancient world, and was meant to curry favor with the people as much as promote his stature.[97] The Gospel of Mark records, "And as he (Jesus) went out of the temple, one of his disciples saith unto him, Master, see what manner of stones and what buildings are here!" (Mark 13:1). Josephus's account of the temple states that it was constructed of white marble, its front was covered in gold, its nine gates were covered in silver and gold, the vestibule inside had been ornately decorated with gold grapevines and grape clusters, and the veil of the temple was "a Babylonian curtain, embroidered with blue, and fine linen, and scarlet, and purple . . . a kind of image of the universe."[98] The presence of a Babylonian curtain inside the house of God was indicative of the corruption that had infiltrated from gentile and pagan sources. Jesus' response to his disciple's awe prophesied the temple's destruction, which arrived in 70 CE at the hands of Titus Vespasian. "And Jesus answering said unto him, 'Seest thou these great buildings? There shall not be left one stone upon another, that shall not be thrown down'" (Mark 13:2). Yet the gaping maw of hell would not overcome his church, once established. How would his church prove superior to anything that humanity had erected?

Jesus prophesied in Matt 16:18, "And I say also unto thee, that thou art Peter, and upon this rock I will build my church; and the gates of hell shall not prevail against it." He was speaking about the church, ἐκκλησία (*ekklēsia*), that would be formed from his followers after the outpouring of God's gift of the holy spirit in Acts chapter two. Though the Scriptures never referred to Jesus as an οἰκονόμος (*oikonomos*) or manager over God's

---

97. Richardson and Fisher, *Herod King of the Jews and Friend of the Romans*, 276.
98. Josephus, *W.J.* 5.5.2–4 §§ 190–212, 706–7.

household or his family, this utterance provides a connection. The phrase "build my church" οἰκοδομήσω μου τὴν ἐκκλησίαν speaks of erecting his church from his called-out body of followers drawn together because they all chose to believe on Jesus as their savior.[99] This statement was not a literal reference to a physical building but a metaphorical one, such as Paul utilized in 1 Tim 3:15. The word οἰκοδομήσω is derived from the same root word as οἰκονόμος: οἶκος–*oikos*, meaning "an inhabited house; any building whatever: the palace, the house of God, the tabernacle; any dwelling place."[100] This word, *oikos*, while most commonly utilized for a house/home that someone or something dwells in, is also used in reference to the human body and the family and household of God (Matt 9:7; John 7:53; Luke 11:24; 1 Tim 3:15; 1 Pet 4:17). Jesus Christ is the head of the church of the living God, and his ministers serve as its household managers (*oikonomoi*, pl.). Jesus' twelve apostles would have been his first οἰκονόμοι (*oikonomoi*). They would form a spiritual edifice that replaced the physical temple, with Jesus as the cornerstone, never to be demolished (Acts 4:11; 1 Pet 2:6–7). Paul declared that through Jesus, those who believed through the spirit "are of the household of God and are built upon the foundation of the apostles and prophets, Jesus Christ himself being the chief corner stone in whom all the building fitly framed together growth unto an holy temple in the LORD" (Eph 2:19–21). In his holy temple for the Father-God, Jesus is first at its base, the chief cornerstone. The apostles form the foundation, serving, supporting, lifting, and raising all other believers from beneath. Not a hierarchy of authority leading from the top-down, ruling and commanding the congregation, but instead forming a stratification of layers of strength and faithfulness in love growing from the bottom-up, bearing the lowliest and weakest member figuratively upon their shoulders, bringing them into the presence of God as their heavenly Father.

## THE APOSTLES' IMPLEMENTATION OF JESUS' INSTRUCTIONS

The Acts of the Apostles (Acts) is the testimonial account of the rise and the expansion of the First-Century Church of Jesus' followers, as led by his apostles. Beginning with Jesus' ascension into heaven, he left the

---

99. Mounce and Mounce, *Interlinear New Testament*, 66.
100. Thayer, "οἶκος," *Thayer's Greek-English Lexicon*, 365.

twelve apostles with instructions to await the outpouring of the gift of the holy spirit (Acts 1:5, 8), which later transpired in Acts chapter two on the day of Pentecost. Obeying his directions, the eleven Apostles (Judas Iscariot had hung himself by that point) returned to Jerusalem. They stayed in an upper room, continuing in fellowship with some women and a host of Jesus' disciples so that their total number was approximately one hundred and twenty (Acts 1:12–15).

The next noteworthy occurrence in Acts is that they had an election to fill Judas's vacancy in the twelve apostles. An apostle's exact functions and responsibilities differ from any other office or position of leadership and are handled in a later chapter. Peter has assumed the lead role of the group, presumably due to Jesus' instructions (Matt 16:18–19). He declares, "For it is written in the book of the Psalms, 'Let his habitation be desolate, and let no man dwell therein: and his bishoprick let another take'" (Acts 1:20). They agree together to appoint their thirteenth apostle of Jesus Christ to fill Judas's position, and they might number as twelve on Pentecost as Jesus intended. In Greek, the phrase reads, Τὴν ἐπισκοπὴν λαβέτω ἕτερος, "the responsibilities his let-take-over another."[101] For ἐπισκοπὴν (*episkopēn*), some versions render it "bishoprick" (KJV), while others have "office" (ESV) and "place of responsibility" (NIV). Mounce and Mounce detail ἐπισκοπὴν (*episkopēn*) as from "ἐπισκοπὴ *episkopē* 4x inspection, oversight, visitation; of God, visitation, interposition, whether in mercy or judgment; the office of an ecclesiastical overseer; from the Hebrew, charge, function."[102] A later chapter handles further depth and details concerning ἐπισκοπὴ—*episkopē*. Therefore, the apostles were also the first generation of "overseers" of the newly forming church.

Peter and the other ten held two authoritative roles—they bore two levels of responsibility in the early church: apostle and overseer. Many times in the book of Acts or Paul's letters, one observes that a leader may perform the functions of more than one office. Such is always a display of humility and meekness in attending to the people's needs. It is essential to note the humility the apostles displayed in the election of Matthias to their number. A vote was cast not only of the eleven remaining apostles but also of the entire group Peter addressed (Acts 1:23–26). The text does not separate them from the congregation of about one hundred and twenty, so it should not be assumed so. From the very beginning,

---

101. Mounce and Mounce, *Interlinear New Testament*, 455.
102. Mounce and Mounce, "ἐπισκοπὴ," *Interlinear New Testament*, 1068.

the heads of the church are "in the trenches, shoulder to shoulder," with the ones they guide. Thus, the group chose two well-known individuals: Barsabas and Matthias. These candidates had to be eyewitnesses of Jesus' ministry, from his baptism to his ascension, displaying their faithfulness. Though not of the original twelve, they most likely participated in Jesus' commissioning of the seventy. They added Matthias to their number in an egalitarian manner, their ranks numbering twelve again.

One of the early Christian fathers of the second generation, Ignatius of Antioch (died c. 107), wrote in his letters to Polycarp that "I am devoted to those who are subject to the bishop, the presbyters, the deacons," and a little later added, "a Christian hath no authority over himself, but giveth his time to God."[103] His statements express admiration for the freewill subjection, rather than subjugation, that believers rendered to the bishops, presbyters, and deacons because of their devotion to God first and foremost. This study of leadership offices in the first century bleeds into the second century because the second generation inherited their modus operandi from the Apostles and leaders recorded in Acts. Where did the offices of the deacon or the elder (presbyter) originate in the Scriptures?

In Acts chapter six, the neophyte church had grown to include so many people that they were becoming cumbersome for the apostles to manage. The Scriptures state, "And in those days, when the number of the disciples was multiplied, there arose a murmuring of the Grecians against the Hebrews, because their widows were neglected in the daily ministration" (Acts 6:1).

The number of disciplined, devoted followers had increased, to say nothing of the casual attendees, and this generated a problem: certain people, Grecian widows, became marginalized.

"Ministration" is διαχονία (*diakonia*), understood as "a procedure for taking care of the needs of the people; provision for taking care of, arrangement for support; money given to help someone in need–contribution, help, support."[104] Including this understanding behind the word διαχονία–*diakonia*, one discerns that the communal support witnessed in Acts chapter two faltered in chapter six because the congregation grew too large for the apostles to minister appropriately, in addition to their other responsibilities before the Lord. The apostles had been serving and ministering to their people from the initiation of the new movement, for

---

103. Lightfoot, "Ignatius, Letter to Polycarp" 6.1, 7.3., *Apostolic Fathers*, 23.
104. "διαχονία," L&N 1:462, 571.

when Peter referred to the duties they carried out in Christ's name, he referred to them as "this ministry," and the word ministry is διάκονία—*diakonia* (Acts 1:17). The solution they chose was adding a new level of assistants to the apostles and delegating authority to these new attendants to minister to the disciples.

The ministration of daily affairs conducted by the apostles was comparable to that of Moses in Exodus before he heeded his father-in-law's wisdom by adding individuals to assist him (Exod 18:13–20).[105] Peter and the apostles called the congregation and, out of their humility, requested the people to recommend "seven men of honest report, full of the Holy Ghost and wisdom, whom we may appoint over this business, But we will give ourselves continually to prayer, and to the ministry (διάκονία–*diakonia*) of the word" (Acts 6:3–4). This passage records the formation of the office of the deacon as a needed adaptation for the First-Century Church. The Scripture of the Word of God was their rule of faith and practice. The apostles delegated spiritual authority to the seven individuals the congregation had chosen from among their numbers. These men already served the church, had an outstanding reputation in the public's eye, and proved capable of ministering to their needs.

The first record of elders in the church in Acts was in Acts 11:30 when the disciples in Antioch sent relief for the Judean believers "to the elders by the hands of Barnabas and Saul." All previous uses of "elders" in Acts referred to elders of the temple in Jerusalem. Acts 14:23 declares that Paul and Barnabas ordained "elders" in every church they established along their evangelical journey. These churches were held in believers' homes or possibly in buildings they had access to, but the focus was never an actual physical structure but the gathering of those faithful called-out believers in Christ. A debate exists amongst scholars on whether these "elders" were mature believers (without an age qualification), individuals who held prominent positions in their family/community, or members with possibly both of those statistics in addition to being aged. This study's examination and findings concerning this debate are handled in the later section dedicated to πρεσβύτερος (*presbyteros*). In both of these verses, the Greek word for "elder" is indeed πρεσβύτερος (*presbyteros*), and it has several possible meanings determined by both its usage in the verse and the context about it. *Thayer's Lexicon* defines it as "among

---

105. Thayer, "διάκονία," *Thayer's Greek-English Lexicon*, 137–38.

Christians, those who presided over the assemblies (or churches)."[106] What is evident by the context is that Paul and Barnabas had the authority from the apostles and elders in Jerusalem to ordain elders in each of the assemblies they established. These offices were for serving and maintaining the churches after Paul and Barnabas departed.

In summation, when the First-Century Church, formed by Jesus Christ's followers and led by his apostles, erupted onto the scene, the religious landscape was already dominated by the Jewish temple, the synagogues, and the Roman pantheon of deities. As the early church evolved, they either adapted or rejected the patterns of leadership observed in the cultures around them. Jesus and his followers broke from religious traditions about them to form something new. His apostles and those they commissioned were committed to tending to the spiritual needs of God's people, like shepherds tending their sheep. They introduced a service-oriented organizational structure that put people's spiritual needs first before the leaders.

The Jewish temple, the synagogues, and the Roman pantheon were hierarchical and led from the top-down, ordering and commanding the lives of their followers. The Roman Catholic Church's organization mirrored the leadership style of the temple's priesthood, and the Lutheran Church, the Church of England, and the Church of Jesus Christ of Latter-Day Saints have followed their example. The structure of the Eastern Orthodox Church, like the synagogues, is decentralized, and the Protestant churches in Europe and the Western hemisphere have followed their style. An attribute shared among all these examples is that the person in charge leads a congregation of hundreds and, in some cases, thousands of people, which leads to some people feeling neglected, lost to the shadows, and treated as outliers.

The First-Century Church did not base the initial generation of leadership offices upon traditions but on the congregation's and its leaders' necessities. The apostles served as the first overseers and handled the duties of ministering to the congregation's needs in addition to their responsibilities of studying and attending to the Scriptures. When the community grew to numerous, the whole church adapted to the situation's needs, generating the deacon's office. The apostles heeded their people, and the people worked with and obeyed the counsel of the apostles in a symbiotic fashion, in accordance with the Scriptures' examples. Such humility, meekness, and

---

106. Thayer, "πρεσβύτερος," *Thayer's Greek-English Lexicon*, 535–36.

practicality exemplified the development of the leadership positions within the First-Century Church. The model they developed for their leadership was adaptable to congregations of any size and could be replicated from town to town. The following two chapters of this study investigate this leadership structure further to reintroduce it to the modern age.

# CHAPTER 4

# The Stratification of Leadership

IN THE NEW TESTAMENT, the majority of passages that address the topic of the early church's leadership address the triumvirate of bishops (*episkopoi*), elders (*presbyteroi*), and deacons (*diakonoi*) but never all three within the same verses of Scripture. For example, Phil 1:1 and 1 Tim 3 speak about bishops and deacons but leave out elders. Meanwhile, 1 Tim 5 focuses on the church elders separately from the bishops and deacons. Therefore, a study of the interrelationship of these three leadership roles and the other subordinates resembles the assemblage of a jigsaw puzzle wherein one must exercise care and precision to avoid contradictions. Though some may present bishops and elders as interchangeable terms describing the same leadership position within the early church, this study will demonstrate they were distinct from one another and performed differing responsibilities.

By the end of the first century, the church had developed definite positions of authority: bishops (*episkopoi*), elders (*presbyteroi*), and deacons (*diakonoi*).[1] Unfortunately, confusion crept into the doctrine and practice of the greater body of the church sometime between the close of the first century and the beginning of the second century.[2] Due

---

1. van Zyl, "Evolution of Church Leadership in the New Testament," 585.

2. In chapter two of this study, the section "Usage of 'Office' in the Apostolic Fathers' Writings" presents detailed examples of the confusion mentioned. References from *1 Clement*, Ignatius' letters, *The Shepherd of Hermas*, and *Fragments of Papias* bear evidence of the integration of the tradition for calling a bishop or other leaders' positions offices. Ignatius' writing bears witness to the establishment of a hierarchical model of authority. References from *The Shepherd of Hermas* and *The Didache* display assumptions of rule and reign by church leaders. Further misrepresentation and evidence for

to that muddying of the waters, some scholars have argued that elders and bishops were two names for the office.³ Others have made the case that the church only had two leadership roles: bishops and deacons.⁴ The majority of scholarship has remained satisfied in the tradition that there were and are only three leadership roles within the body of the Christian church: bishops, elders, and deacons.⁵ Interestingly, Dr. Robert Rayburn observed that Presbyterian Churches were deeply confused concerning the principles and practices of the First-Century Church, for he stated, "Church government has been largely neglected as a field of study by Presbyterians in the present century. The major works on the subject to which appeal is presently made are old and must be admitted to have left the debate in a seriously imperfect state."⁶ This research work will display several leadership roles that developed within the early church, as was necessary to meet the needs of the people.

Nevertheless, roles within the early church did not always maintain a rigid separation of the duties and responsibilities performed by each. While assignments and responsibilities defined a leader's position in the church, they did not restrict or inhibit that leader from going beyond and doing more to serve the church. For example, a single individual might serve the church as both an apostle and an overseer, or an overseer might also manage an in-home church.⁷ In the early years of the newly developing movement, apostles went where required and performed according to the people's needs. In addition, it was not outside the norm for an apostle, prophet, or another held in high esteem to take on menial tasks because others needed help. Not until late in the first century does one

---

possible confusion are presented in an analysis of Ignatius' comparison between deacons, bishops, and the presbytery to Jesus, God, and the College of Apostles.

3. Merkle, *Elder and Overseer*; Knight, "Two Offices," 1–12.

4. Knight, "Number and Functions of the Permanent Offices in the New Testament Church," 111–16.

5. Rayburn, "Three Offices," 105–14.

6. Rayburn, "Three Offices," 105.

7. In the New Testament, Paul is a primary example of an early church leader who "wore many hats." As an example, in Eph 3:7, he is a "minister"—*diakonos*; in Titus 1:1, he is a "servant"—*doulos* and an apostle; in 1 Cor 4:1, he is a "minister"— *hypēretēs* and a "steward"—*oikonomos*. Peter is another example, for in addition to being Jesus' disciple, then his apostle, he also served the church as an overseer (Acts 1:20 and 8:14). He refers to himself in 1 Pet 1:1 as "a servant," *doulos* and an apostle; in 1 Pet 4:10, he includes himself when he describes how every man who received the gift should minister (the verb form of *diakonos*) as "good stewards" *oikonomos*. In 1 Pet 5:1, he calls himself an "elder" *presbyteros*.

find an apostle receiving an assignment, such as Paul sending Titus to Crete or Paul assigning Timothy to the territory of Ephesus (Titus 1:5; 1 Tim 1:3). The apostle Paul often referred to himself as a *doulos* for Christ serving the church, meaning he was ready to take on any task to serve others in Christ's name (Rom 1:1; 2 Cor 4:5; Gal 1:10; Titus 1:1). Codification of leaders' roles and responsibilities with their titles arrived in the latter years of the First-Century Church with the epistles of Timothy, Titus, and Peter.

One must allow some latitude with the application of the various positions of authority as seen in the Scriptures because of the evolution the early church endured. Misinterpretation and scholarly private interpretation that favors a Scripture or passage of Scriptures over another is oft to blame for confusion in understanding; therefore, this study must evaluate usages in light of the weight of the evidence of available research. This study strives to exert scriptural and linguistic accuracy in the face of tradition and, in so doing, will define positions in the First-Century Church according to the inherent meaning of the word or words used within their given context. Where a clear delineation exists between leadership roles, further defining them one from another in the Scriptures, this study will endeavor to bring those characteristics to the forefront. Nevertheless, the First-Century Church leaders exerted efforts to follow Jesus' example; regardless of a title, they were willing to take on any task required to benefit the church and serve God's will.

Though the majority of the New Testament texts were written and addressed to gentile converts under the dominion of the Roman Empire and even beyond it, one must understand the New Testament Scriptures were penned by first-century Jewish men, who had inherited their knowledge from and owed their theological thinking and preaching to the Hebrew Scriptures of the Old Testament. The books of the Bible, collected together as the New Testament today, were not available until sometime in the middle to later years of the first century. The Hebrew Scriptures they quoted, preached from, and the apostles searched through concerning Christ are now called the Old Testament. In Phil 3:5, Paul presented his credentials and upbringing, and as a Pharisee, owing to his Jewish heritage, he had at one time adhered strictly to their code of conduct (Acts 23:6; 26:4–12). Paul declared that salvation through the gospel of Christ was made available first to the Jews and afterward the gentiles (Rom 1:16). The book of Acts records numerous occasions where Paul initiated his acts of evangelism in new cities from their local synagogues (Acts 13:14; 14:1; 17:1). To the gentile Corinthian Church, he preached that they should not be ignorant of the history of the Jewish people (1 Cor 10:1–14). Therefore, the theology that founded, undergirded, and molded the First-Century Church was born from those Old Testament Scriptures.

However, one cannot deny the Hellenistic influence or the Roman imperialism that shaped the culture of that era. Greek Hellenistic culture and philosophy, introduced by Alexander the Great some three hundred years before the advent of Jesus, left its marks on the early church. The most available form of the Scriptures to people outside of Jerusalem was the Greek Septuagint, produced by Hellenistic Jewish scholars who translated, revised, and redacted the Jewish scrolls (now known as the Old Testament) in Alexandria, Egypt, early in the third century BCE, into a single volume in Greek.[8] As this study will unfold, the cultures that abounded in the Second Temple period influenced the development of the First-Century Church. This work stresses that the First-Century Church, its doctrines, and its practices must be understood in light of its Jewish/Hebrew heritage, even as it evolved, comingled, and co-opted with the surrounding Greco-Roman societies.

The following subsections of this chapter will explore the significance of the word κυβερνήσεις (*kubernēseis*), translated as "governments," in 1 Cor 12:28, and how it encompasses all of the leadership roles and their order within the collective body of the church. A hierarchical polity did not control the First-Century Church but instead developed two aspects to its leadership body, similar to how a coin has two faces: the gift ministries and the organized ordained ministers. In its beginnings, the congregation recognized and followed charismatic individuals endowed with spiritual gifts, displaying the power of the Holy Spirit. This study will scrutinize the qualities of and determine the differences that separate these gift ministries from other church functions, which will aid in defining the leaders whom the church appointed and ordained. Lastly, this study will delve deeply into the leadership roles that the church ordained, elected, and selected into their positions of responsibility and service. This study is most concerned with this arrangement of leaders and has organized them herein as the stratified leadership model of the First-Century Church.

---

8. Arcari, *Beyond Conflicts*, 247.

## THOSE WHO STEERED THE SHIP

One passage in the apostle Paul's first letter to the Corinthians established a stratification of the various levels of authority within the church. He stated, "Now you are Christ's body, and individually members of it. And God has appointed in the church, first apostles, second prophets, third teachers, then miracles, then gifts of healings, helps, administrations, and various kinds of tongues" (1 Cor 12:27–28).[9] The word from the Greek text translated as "governments" in the King James Version and this reference as "administrations," is κυβερνήσεις (*kubernēseis*). Κυβερνήσεις (*kubernēseis*) can be defined as the ability to guide others and applies, per the context, to various leadership capacities within the church.[10] The difficulty encountered in understanding κυβερνήσεις (*kubernēseis*) exists because the Greek text of the NT utilizes it in this verse alone. According to *Thayer's Lexicon*, our understanding of κυβερνήσεις (*kubernēseis*) is based upon its Latin equivalent *gubernare*, meaning to govern, and from which the English language obtains its words "govern," "government," and "governing."[11] As the church became the Roman Catholic Church, Latin became the *lingua franca* of the church, and the Latin Vulgate superseded the Greek text; changes occurred within the doctrine, and leadership positions became governing offices within the church. The utilization of a younger language to understand its predecessor only results in an error; instead, one must utilize context, prior usage(s), and, when possible, the source origins to understand a word or words of the analyzed language.

The first occurrence of any specific word within the Hebrew Scriptures has always drawn particular attention from Jewish commentators and scholars.[12] The same standard has also applied to the study of the Greek texts of the New Testament writings. The first usage bears the significance of setting the standard for understanding a word's meaning and use. After an initial application, further usages permit expansions and comparisons of meaning, broadening understanding of that particular word. In Hebrew and Greek literature, when a word appears only once in a text and no other time, it stands apart meant to attract the reader's attention as a linguistic idiom or figure of speech, called a *hapax*

---

9. Mounce and Mounce, *Interlinear New Testament*, 677.
10. Danker, "κυβερνήσεις, εως, ἡ," *Concise Greek-English Lexicon*, 209.
11. Thayer, "κυβερνήσεις" *Thayer's Greek-English Lexicon*, 364.
12. Bullinger, *Number in Scripture*, 60.

*legomenon*, meaning a term utilized only once in a corpus.¹³ Κυβερνήσεις (*kubernēseis*) is a hapax legomenon. What makes these words special is their rarity; they need to be studied carefully to understand what they mean within a context and why the author utilized them.¹⁴ However, to properly understand a hapax legomenon, one must compare the word in question with its nearest textual relations because there is no other usage or context for analysis; one must consult external texts conducting comparisons with their application and utility of that specific word.¹⁵

According to Johannes P. Louw and Eugene A. Nida, κυβερνήσεις is "a derivative of κυβερνάω: to steer a ship, to guide; not occurring in the NT; the ability to lead—guidance, leadership . . .may be expressed in some languages as being able to lead others or being able to get others to follow."¹⁶ Indeed, the closest relative of the noun κυβερνήσεις (*kubernēseis*) is the noun κυβερνήτης (*kubernētēs*) meaning a steersman, helmsman, or sailing master and rendered in English as "shipmaster" (Acts 27:11; Rev 18:17).¹⁷ The Septuagint preceded the First-Century Church by nearly three hundred years becoming commonplace in Jewish synagogues before the first century AD, and influencing the authors of the NT with its jargon and phrasing, to which Paul was no stranger.¹⁸ In the Septuagint, the word κυβερνήσεις (*kubernēseis*), or a form of it, appears four times in the book of Proverbs. In Prov 1:5, 11:14, 12:5, and 24:6, the Septuagint utilizes κυβερνήσεις (*kubernēseis*) as the transliteration of the Hebrew word תַּחְבֻּלָה (*tachbulah*).¹⁹ תַּחְבֻּלָה (*tachbulah*) is understood in both Greek and English to mean "direction, counsel and guidance" and "steering, directing a ship."²⁰ For example, Prov 1:5 reads, "Let the wise listen and add to their learning, and let the discerning get guidance" (NIV). Thus, the understanding of κυβερνήσεις (*kubernēseis*) is counsel, direction, and guidance, like a helmsperson or sailing master guiding their ship across the waters. In conclusion, Paul's use of κυβερνήσεις (*kubernēseis*) in 1 Cor 12:27–8 bears witness that the leaders of the church had the proven ability to get others to follow them because of their discerning

---

13. Stevenson, "Hapax Legomenon," *Oxford Dictionary of English*, 798.
14. Cateclesia, "Death by a Thousand Cuts."
15. Bullinger, *Number in Scripture*, 70–86.
16. "κυβερνήσις," L&N 1:466.
17. Thayer, "κυβερνήτης," *Thayer's Greek-English Lexicon*, 364.
18. Cook, "Septuagint as a Holy Text," 4.
19. Brenton, *Septuagint with Apocrypha*, 788, 798, 810.
20. "תַּחְבֻּלָה," BDBG, 287.

judgment, wisdom, and guidance; they steered those in-home churches as proficient helmspersons.

Returning to the strata of leadership listed in 1 Cor 12:28, it reads, "And God has appointed in the church first apostles, second prophets, third teachers, then miracles, then gifts of healing, those able to help others, those who can provide guidance, and various kinds of tongues."[21] The Scripture assigns priority to the gift ministries of apostles, prophets, and teachers within the church, and "those able to help others, those who can provide guidance," are subordinate to them, and it is within the space generated by those later categories that positions of the *episkopos, presbyteros, diakonos, oikonomos, hypēretēs, doulos, and thyrōros* find their placement within the body of Christ. There is a distinction and a separation between the gift ministries of apostles, prophets, teachers, evangelists, pastors, and preachers and the other ordained and appointed leadership positions, which this study must attend to before proceeding further.

This study will first present a brief analysis of the charismatic gift ministries to set a baseline for contrast and comparison and to aid in understanding the appointed leadership roles of the First-Century Church. Then, this study will delve into biblical, cultural, and social-scientific investigations of those elected and appointed leadership positions: *episkopos, presbyteros, diakonos, oikonomos, hypēretēs, doulos, and thyrōros*. Lastly, the unique role of the *therápōn* will be examined. This study shall display how, in an organized fashion, the First-Century Church leaders followed Jesus' example of "the greatest leader is the greatest servant," demonstrating a willingness to do whatever was necessary for the good of the church body in service to the Lord and the will of God.

## THE GIFT MINISTRIES

Paul lists apostles, prophets, and teachers as first in the order of strata within the church's leaders, but he does not say how these people arrived at their situation. Paul's Epistle to the Ephesians sheds more light and details upon these ministries. Writing to the church in Ephesus, he stated, "Now therefore ye are no more strangers and foreigners, but fellow citizens with the saints, and of the household of God; and are built upon the foundation of the apostles and prophets, Jesus Christ himself being the chief corner stone" (Eph 2:19–20). In this figure of speech, Christ is

---

21. Mounce and Mounce, *Interlinear New Testament*, 677.

compared to *the cornerstone* of a building, which sets the orientation and geometry of the edifice, joins two of the outer walls, and supports the structure; he directs the church towards God, joins together in unity Jews and gentiles, and sustains its members through his selfless sacrifice.[22]

Together with and following after Christ are the apostles and prophets, but they are not alone in forming the church's foundation, for the passage lists five energized gift ministries. Paul states, "And he (Jesus Christ) gave some apostles; and some prophets; and some evangelists; and some pastors and teachers; for the perfecting of the saints, for the work of the ministry, for the edifying of the body of Christ: till we all come in the unity of the faith, and the knowledge of the Son of God" (Eph 4:11–13b). This verse explains why they are called "gift ministries," they are gifts of God's grace through Christ manifested in people's lives for the benefit of the body of Christ. The revelation of the Scripture declares that all five are necessary to the church to stimulate, guide, promote, and encourage the church members' maturation. Their manifestation in a person's life is God's prerogative, not because they will it or give themselves a title; therefore, the energizing of these specific ministries does not come by men's wills, elections, or confirmations.

In Rom 12, Paul states that all people who have received salvation have also been given the duly fit measure of faith and grace from God (v.3). He discloses that while we all are of body (the body of Christ), we do not fulfill the same roles within that collective (v.4). "Having then gifts differing according to the grace that is given to us, whether prophecy, let us prophesy according to the proportion of faith," proclaims Paul, and he continues, "or ministry, let us wait on ministering: or he that teacheth on teaching" (vv. 6–7). Within the church, those God chose as his teachers, prophets, and ministering agents, he endowed through the gifts of his grace. Verse eight continues Paul's statement, including "he that ruleth, with diligence." In Greek, "that ruleth" is προϊστάμενος (*proistamenos*), better rendered in English as "leading, or managing, as a superintendent."[23] Indicating that those whose responsibility was the leadership and management of the church and setting in order all other subordinate stations of authority, i.e., the apostles, did so because of the gift of God's grace.

---

22. Thayer, "ἀκρογωνιαῖος," *Thayer's Greek-English Lexicon*, 24.

23. Προϊστάμενος (*proistamenos*) is the nominative masculine singular present participle middle-voice form of the verb προϊστημι (*proistēmi*): "to set or place before, to set over, to superintend, preside over"; see also, 1 Tim 3:4, 5, 12; 1 Tim 5:17; Thayer, "προϊστημι," *Thayer's Greek-English Lexicon*, 539.

According to the Scriptures, God's divine grace and providence called out and energized the holy orders of apostles, prophets, evangelists, pastors, and teachers from within the church; hence, this work addresses them as "the gift ministries" of the church (Eph 4:11–13b).

In 1 Cor 12:28, apostles are first, prophets second, and teachers are placed third to set an order within the church. In Eph 4:11, through the figure of speech *polysyndeton*, apostles, prophets, evangelists, pastors, and teachers equally form the church's foundational leadership stratum with Jesus as the head.[24] These ministries are God's gift by way of Christ unto the church, and their purpose is to equip and bring to maturity members of the church. In Luke 11:49, it is written, "Therefore also said the wisdom of God, I will send them prophets and apostles, and some of them they shall slay and persecute." They are not elected or selected by the body of the church, but in following the examples of the Scriptures and Paul's teachings (1 Cor 12:4–6), one or more of these ministries may be energized in an individual according to God's design to meet the need(s) of his people. The intent behind the gift ministries is to guide believers so they might mature in Christ.

## Apostles

An apostle is someone who is an authorized delegate dispatched on a mission with instructions, commands, a message to be delivered, or duties to be completed for another individual or collective: "In a broader sense, the name is transferred to other eminent Christian teachers," e.g., Barnabas, Timothy, and Silvanus.[25] The noun "apostle" is ἀπόστολος (*apostolos*) in Greek and is related to the verb ἀποστέλλω (*apostéllō*), "to cause someone to depart for a particular purpose," or "to send a message presumably by someone" (Acts 15:22, 19:31).[26] A simple understanding of an apostle could be "a sent one, or someone sent to deliver a message." According to Danker, the central meaning of the verb ἀποστέλλω (*apostéllō*) is "cause to move from one position to another, send, send away; of a person with focus on an assignment; send out word . . . messengers are sent out to inform the inhabitants of an order transmitted."[27]

---

24. Bullinger, *Figures of Speech Used in the Bible*, 208–37.
25. Thayer, "ἀπόστολος," *Thayer's Greek-English Lexicon*, 68.
26. "ἀποστέλλω," L&N 1:191.
27. Danker, "ἀποστέλλω," *Concise Greek-English Lexicon*, 49.

In Matt 10:40, Jesus stated, "He that receiveth you receiveth me, and he that receiveth me receiveth him that sent [ἀποστέλλω] me." The explanation presented by Danker of the commissioned, sent-out messenger on a specific mission, in the word ἀποστέλλω (*apostéllō*), is foundational to ἀπόστολος (*apostolos*) and ἀποστολή (*apostlē*).[28] Therefore, before the disciples received their commissioning from God by way of Jesus Christ, he sent Jesus (Mark 9:37; Luke 10:16; John 5:36). Peter referred to the "ministry and apostleship" Judas left vacant when he committed suicide; the word "apostleship" is ἀποστολή (Acts 1:25).[29] Hebrews 3:1 is the only Scripture to refer to Jesus as an apostle, appointed so by God. He sent Jesus as his chief emissary and ambassador with a particular mission, namely humanity's redemption. Jesus is the first example to all believers of a successful apostle (John 19:28–30).

The first twelve disciples of Jesus Christ became his first apostles, as recorded in Matt 10:2–4 and Luke 6:13–16. Matthew 10:5–6 relates, "These twelve Jesus sent forth, and commanded them, saying, 'Go not into the way of the Gentiles, and into any city of the Samaritans enter ye not: But go rather to the lost sheep of the house of Israel.'" The following verses of the chapter include Jesus' additional commands to preach a specific message, heal, raise the dead back to life, and perform other miraculous deeds. They were to enter people's homes, and from those who welcomed the apostles, they operated their ministry within that particular town, thus spreading Jesus' message and expanding his ministry.

An apostle's origin and nature are rooted in Hebrew jurisprudence in the Talmudical law of agency, wherein one individual is delegated and authorized to represent another.[30] An example of this custom and tradition occurs in Jer 49:14, "I heard a rumour from the LORD, and an ambassador is sent unto the heathen, saying Gather ye together, and come against her, and rise up to battle." In that verse, "is sent" is שָׁלוּחַ (*shālūah*), the verb form for the Hebrew word שָׁלִיחַ (*shāliah*), and שָׁלִיחַ (*shāliah*) is equivalent in meaning to the Greek word for apostle—ἀπόστολος (*apostolos*).[31] Just as an ambassador or an envoy was sent by God, in lieu

---

28. Danker, "ἀποστολή, ἀπόστολος, ἀποστέλλω, ἀποστολή," *Concise Greek-English Lexicon*, 50.

29. Danker states, "In NT specifically of the special role of an elite emissary in the service of the gospel, ambassadorship, apostleship Acts 1:25." Danker, "ἀποστολή," *Concise Greek-English Lexicon*, 50.

30. Simmons, "Talmudical Law of Agency," 614–31.

31. Thayer, "ἀπόστολος," *Thayer's Greek-English Lexicon*, 68.

of his divine presence but bearing a message in his holy name, such is the duty of an apostle for their master. L. M. Simmons writes, "Talmudical Law agrees exactly with other systems, in its definition of שָׁלִיחַ, and in allowing the appointment of a שָׁלִיחַ it is actuated by the same need as allows such appointments in all systems of Law."[32] Furthermore, he adds that "representation then, is the conclusion of a juristic act by one person acting for another."[33] Such is the very principle that Jesus claimed in Matt 10:40 when he commissioned his apostles to go in his stead and conferred upon them the authority God had given him. Similarly, one may consider individuals such as Timothy and Titus as apostles (with the possibility of others) because Paul commissioned them as his envoys to other areas and people, thus extending his apostolic office.

Two factors separated the ministry of God's holy apostles from any other שָׁלִיחַ or emissary that a person of authority might send in their stead. First, God's presence, either through his Son Jesus Christ or by spiritual manifestation, granted individuals that authority. Secondarily, the message they were to deliver was new, having never been heard before by the recipients. In Luke 6:13, Jesus gathered his disciples, selected twelve of them, and called those men his apostles. In Matt 10:7, the text records that Jesus gave them a specific message, which had never been uttered before because God's Messiah had never been present on earth before, and that message was, "The kingdom of heaven is at hand." As another example, in the books of Ephesians and Colossians, in his role as Jesus' apostle, Paul made known unto the churches that the fight, the struggle all believers endured, was truly with the spiritual realm, a subject which previously had been in the shadows of biblical knowledge. As Jesus had done, Paul, in his apostleship, made revelations, knowledge, and new light available for public consumption concerning the unseen happenings in the cosmos so believers could understand who their enemy was.[34]

The Canonical Gospels utilize the word "apostles" exclusively in reference to the twelve disciples whom Jesus elevated to become his personal emissaries and proclaimers of his gospel message.[35] In the Gospel of John, when Jesus washed the feet of his twelve apostles, he declared that as their master, they should follow his example (John 13:4–16). In verse 16, he said to them, "Verily, verily, I say unto you, The servant is

---

32. Simmons, "Talmudical Law of Agency," 614.

33. Simmons, "Talmudical Law of Agency," 615.

34. May, "Servant and Steward of the Mystery," 474.

35. See Matt 10:2; Mark 6:30; Luke 6:13, 9:10, 11:49, 17:5, 22:14, 24:10; John 13:16.

not greater than his lord; neither he that is sent greater than he that sent him." Jesus directed the reference of "the servant" to the twelve, and he was their lord. Interestingly, "servant" is δοῦλος (*doulos*), the abject, servile person devoted to another's will. In that verse, the phrase, "he that is sent," is ἀπόστολος (*apostolos*). Though the twelve were apostles, they were still Jesus' dedicated servants, committed to carrying out any task he required.

In the book of Acts, from chapters one through twenty-six, every usage of "apostle" or "apostles" refers to the heads of the early church. In the NT, 68 of the 79 occurrences of ἀπόστολος (*apostolos*) are found in the Gospel of Luke and Paul's letters without any variance in the meaning of the word.[36] The pattern continues in the book of Acts 13:2, which states, "As they ministered to the LORD, and fasted, the Holy Ghost said, Separate me Barnabas and Saul for the work whereunto I have called them." Thus, the Holy Spirit commissioned Barnabas and Saul (a.k.a. Paul) to take the message of the Gospel of Jesus abroad, first to Jewish synagogues and later to the gentiles (Acts 13:5, 14:21–27).[37] An apostle, therefore, is an elite emissary in the service of the gospel, an ambassadorship commissioned by the Holy Spirit in lieu of the Lord Jesus Christ. Their spiritual authority and message of salvation through Jesus, which was the brand-new message, and the miracles they wrought are why the author of Acts was justified in calling Barnabas and Saul apostles (Acts 14:14).

Some have argued that no more people were ordained as apostles after the twelve that Jesus selected and Paul. Still, such an argument is false because Acts records both Matthias and Barnabas as apostles (Acts 1:25–26; 14:14; 1 Cor 9:5–6). Some promote that there were no further apostles past the first century, and the basis for the disqualification of other individuals is because the requirements witnessed in the selection of Matthias in Acts chapter one cannot be met. That principle would disqualify others in the NT, which the Scriptures label as apostles. Moreover, evidence in the scriptures shows that, following the same pattern witnessed in the gospels and Acts, other men and women served as apostles in the church. For example, in 2 Cor 8:23, Paul includes Titus in a group of individuals as "messengers of the churches and the glory of Christ" (KJV,

---

36. Thayer, "ἀπόστολος," *Thayer's Greek-English Lexicon*, 68.

37. The King James Version of the Holy Bible interchanges the words "ghost" and "spirit" for the Greek word πνεῦμα (*pneuma*)—refer to Thayer, "πνεῦμα," *Thayer's Greek-English Lexicon*, 520–23. Other than when quoting the KJV text or another version of the Bible that may utilize the word "ghost," this study elects to use "spirit" for πνεῦμα (*pneuma*) in the text.

NASB). The Greek word employed for messengers is ἀπόστολοι (*apostoloi*), the nominative masculine plural form of ἀπόστολος (*apostolos*).[38] Titus, therefore, according to Paul, was an apostle.

Similarly, in Phil 2:25, Paul refers to Epaphroditus as a messenger (unto the church at Philippi), which is ἀπόστολον (*apostolon*), the accusative masculine singular form.[39] Both usages are interchangeable for "apostle" because these individuals are credited with "extraordinary status in the work of the gospel," comparable to Jesus' twelve disciples.[40] Likewise, in Gal 1:19, Jesus' brother, James, is included in the group of apostles at Jerusalem. In addition, Paul counts Silvanus (a.k.a. Silus) and Timothy as apostles in 1 Thess 2:6–7. Finally, in Rom 16:7, Paul states, "Salute Andronicus and Junia, my kinsmen, and my fellow prisoners, who are of note among the apostles, who also were in Christ before me." Andronicus and Junia were presumably each other's spouses, similar to Aquila and Priscilla (Acts 18; 1 Cor 16:19) and, according to the context, renowned leaders of the churches that Paul respected as his predecessors in Christ.

Andronicus and Junia were responsible, in part together with the others named, for bringing the gospel of Christ to Rome. The Scripture states that Andronicus and Junia were illustrious, "of note among the apostles," which is to say that in the church, they were marked and stamped as counted among the echelon of the apostles.[41] This passage of Romans displays evidence of at least one female apostle within the ranks of the First-Century Church leaders.[42] Concerning Junia, John Chrysostom (347–407 CE) stated, "To be an apostle is something great. But to be outstanding among the apostles—just think what a wonderful song of praise that is! Indeed, how great the wisdom of this woman must have been that she was even deemed worthy of the title of apostle."[43] This interpretation of the Scripture and the understanding of Junia as a woman's name would not be shared.

---

38. Mounce and Mounce, *Interlinear New Testament*, 713.

39. Mounce and Mounce, *Interlinear New Testament*, 768.

40. Danker, "ἀπόστολος, ον, ὁ," *Concise Greek-English Lexicon*, 50.

41. This conclusion is based upon Thayer's definition for "note," correlated with Danker's. Thayer, "ἐπίσημος," *Thayer's Greek-English Lexicon*, 242; Danker, "ἀπόστολος," *Concise Greek-English Lexicon*, 50.

42. "Junia," proper feminine noun, "a convert from Judaism, Paul's kinsman and fellow-prisoner; a woman's name." Thayer, "Ἰουνίας," *Thayer's Greek-English Lexicon*, 306.

43. Chrysostom, *Homilies on Galatians*, 441.

In his review of all of the apostles appearing the pages of the NT, Herbert Lockyer first reported concerning Andronicus that Paul lauded him as "my kinsman," presumably of the same Jewish nation or tribe; "my fellow-prisoner," they had been imprisoned together for spreading the gospel; "of note among the apostles," Andronicus was distinguished and highly esteemed by the other apostles; "in Christ before me," his conversion preceded Paul's.[44] Next, he states, "As Junias is paired with Andronicus, all we have written about him is applicable to Junias, seeing Paul's greeting at the close of his epistle to the Romans was addressed to them both."[45] Lockyer does not recognize Junia as a woman, referring to the person with male pronouns, but both Andronicus and Junia deserve to be acknowledged as apostles.

A study published by Cambridge University puts forth that the views on the subject have flipped back and forth through the years, beginning with the early church fathers sharing John Chrysostom's understanding, but later changed, favoring Junia as a man around the time of the reformation and continuing through the twentieth century, only to find them reverting in favor of Junia as a female since technology has made viewership of the Greek texts and papyri widely available.[46] Andrea Hartmann of the London School of Theology acknowledges that the grammatical gender of a person's name appearing in Rom 16:7 could be male or female and that Calvin's and Luther's interpretations promoted it as male.[47] After Luther and the other reformers, scholarship professed that a female apostle in the first century was unthinkable and that Junia was a contraction of the name Junianus, but that is not a name found in the NT.[48] Linda Belleville performed an exhaustive study of the Greek language, which produced more evidence in favor of Junia as female than male.[49] Beyond theological traditions established between the 1500s through the 1900s, there is a dearth of evidence to support reading Junia as a man.[50] As a result, lexicons and newer versions of the Bible now acknowledge Junia as a woman. Still, scholars engage in debates over Junia's persona, male or female, as an apostle.

44. Lockyer, *All the Apostles of the Bible*, 183–84.
45. Lockyer, *All the Apostles of the Bible*, 200.
46. Belleville, "Ιουνιαν," 231–49.
47. Hartmann, "Junia," 646–60.
48. Hartmann, "Junia," 653.
49. Belleville, "Ιουνιαν," 240–49.
50. Hartmann, "Junia," 657–59.

In summation, the word "apostle" may take on different meanings in accordance with the context of its usage. One must understand the historical and cultural settings surrounding a particular occurrence within a text for the word "apostle." In the framework of the NT, an apostle is an exceptional leadership role within the church, which was to act as an envoy in lieu of Jesus Christ in God's service to his people. An apostle was granted special authority and commissioned with a message, e.g., the gospel of Christ, that would be new in the ears of their audience.[51] God selected and energized the gift ministry of apostles within the church, where and when the people needed their unique service and leadership.

## Prophets

Prophets have a long and storied history in the Bible and extra-biblical Jewish texts as messengers of the will of the most high God unto his people. Abraham was the first recorded prophet of the Scriptures, yet there is no record of Abraham delivering a message containing portents of future events. Yet, in Gen 20:7, God tells Abimelech about Abraham: "Now, therefore restore the man his wife; for he is a prophet, and he shall pray for thee and thou shalt live." The word "prophet" is נָבִיא (*nabiy'*) in Hebrew and is understood to mean "spokesman, speaker, prophet."[52] E. W. Bullinger, concerning Abraham as the LORD's first prophet, stated, "We learn from this that the word *Prophet* does not mean merely one who *foretells*, but one who witnesses for God as His spokesman."[53] In addition to having a relationship with God as his prophet and spokesman, Abraham was called to be an intercessor for others unto God. God called both Moses and Aaron to function as spokesmen—Moses for God and Aaron for Moses—and therefore, both were prophets. The prophet's first job was forth-telling, speaking messages from Yahweh to his people, messages of guidance and instruction or reproof and correction to preserve, strengthen, or restore the people's relationship with their God. Later prophets, such as Isaiah, Jeremiah, Ezekiel, and others, delivered prophecies of future events and people. The style God chose for the message was ultimately his business; the prophet had the job of conveying it. As

---

51. Paul's epistles also contain examples of new messages which one does not find elsewhere in the Bible, such as the gifts and manifestations of the spirit in 1 Cor 12, or the hope of Christ's return in 1 Thess 4.

52. "נָבִיא," BDBG, 611.

53. Bullinger, *Number in Scripture*, 61.

an example, when God selected Jeremiah to be his spokesman, his command was, "Go to all that I shall send thee, and whatsoever I command thee thou shalt speak. Be not afraid of their faces: for I am with thee to deliver thee, saith the LORD" (Jer 1:7–8). The prophet of the LORD was his spokesman, whether foretelling or forth-telling, and he was to aid the people as their intercessor with God.

The apostle Paul, writing to Timothy, stated that Jesus Christ is the one mediator between God and humanity (1 Tim 2:5). Jesus' ministry, while he was present on earth, was built solidly upon Moses' example as God's prophet and mediator for the children of Israel. Deuteronomy records Moses' prophecy to the people, stating, "The LORD thy God will raise up unto thee a Prophet from the midst of thee, of thy brethren, like unto me; unto him ye shall hearken" (Deut 18:25). This verse is referenced two more times in Acts 3:22 and Acts 7:37 in confirmation that Jesus was a prophet on par with Moses. However, Jesus Christ expanded the role of a prophet from the framework with which Moses had operated as God's prophet. Luke 7:16 records the people's response after Jesus raised a man from the dead: "And there came a fear on all: and they glorified God, saying, that a great prophet is risen up among us; and that God hath visited his people." Jesus foretold a prophecy of the decimation of the temple (Matt 24:1–2; Mark 13:1–2; Luke 21:5–6). In AD 70, Titus Flavius fulfilled that prophecy when he laid siege to Jerusalem, culminating with leveling the temple to its foundation.

As a prophet following Moses' form, Jesus spent his entire earthly ministry making God's will known to the people. Both men died in service to God, faithfully proclaiming God's word until their last moments of life. Stephen Edmonson writes, "Calvin calls Christ, God's 'ambassador and interpreter,' for he would make God's ways plain to God's chosen, illuminating both God's gracious initiative in himself toward God's Church and God's requirements of the Church in response."[54] Jesus testified concerning his cousin John the Baptist, that as the forerunner to the Messiah, he was God's messenger, more significant than any prophet—"among them that are born of women there hath not risen a greater than John the Baptist" (Matt 11:10–11). Such a statement meant that John surpassed Elijah, Enoch, and Moses, and by fulfilling the role of the promised Messiah, Jesus Christ exceeded John.[55] Differing from Moses and all

---

54. Edmondson, *Calvin's Christology*, 154.
55. Thayer, "προφήτης," *Thayer's Greek-English Lexicon*, 553.

other prophets who preceded Jesus, death could not hold him, and after his resurrection, he resumed proclaiming God's will. Fulfilling the roles of God's spokesman and humanity's intercessor, Jesus became the prime example of a prophet in Scripture.

The first recorded prophetess in Scripture was Miriam, the sister of Aaron and Moses, and she set an example for women in Hebrew history. She led the women in a singing and dancing performance, praising God for the deliverance he brought the people (Exod 15:20–21). In Mic 6:4, by God's will, the prophet states, "I brought thee up out of the land of Egypt, and redeemed thee out of the house of servants; and I sent before thee Moses, Aaron, and Miriam." Next, in Judges, God raised Deborah, also his prophetess, to the authoritative level of a judge presiding over the nation (Judg 4:4). Her leadership gave the Israelites a decisive victory over their Canaanite oppressors. In Luke, chapter two, when, after his circumcision, Jesus was presented in the temple by his parents, one of the two people who recognized Jesus for who he would become was the prophetess Anna (Luke 2:36–38). The evidence abounds, showing that God was willing to work with women as well as men for the position of his spokesperson.

In the NT, the Greek word for נָבִיא (nabiy') is προφήτης (prophētēs) from which the English word "prophet" is derived, and it bears the meaning of "one who speaks forth; to divulge, make known, announce; an interpreter or spokesman for God; one through whom God speaks."[56] The author of the book of Acts states, "God hath spoken by the mouth of all his holy prophets since the world began" (Acts 3:21). God has never been silent but commissioned men and women as his spokespeople, proclaiming that the Messiah, the Christ was coming. Through Peter on the day of Pentecost, God's message changed, for speaking via the Spirit, he declared a new message: Christ had come, salvation was available, people needed to repent, be baptized in the name of Jesus Christ and receive the gift of the Holy Spirit (Acts 2:38). Peter was not only an apostle, but he had become God's first spokesman of the new church, it's first prophet.

In Peter's sermon in Acts chapter two, he cited King David and Joel and declared them God's spokesmen, his prophets (Acts 2:16, 25–30). His focus for quoting David and Joel is their recognized authority that God authorized the transpiring events the people have witnessed, which were not of any person's plans. Then he unfolded for his audience the

---

56. Thayer, "προφήτης," *Thayer's Greek-English Lexicon*, 553.

purpose of God's plans that his prophets from ages before had declared: salvation accomplished through the sacrifice and resurrection of his son Jesus Christ was now available to anyone who believed. This message was the new Gospel of Christ (Mark 1:1; Rom 1:16).

In the book of Acts, the first individual called a prophet by the author was Agabus. Acts 11:27–28 records, "And in these days came prophets from Jerusalem unto Antioch. And there stood up one of them named Agabus, and signified (*made known*) by the Spirit that there should be great dearth throughout the world: which came to pass in the days of Claudius Caesar." Multiple prophets journeyed from Jerusalem to Antioch, and Agabus was among their company. This occasion was not the only time he foretold an event that came to pass. In Acts 21, as Paul is making his return trip to Jerusalem, Agabus intercepts him and prophesies his capture and betrayal if Paul doesn't change his course (vs. 10–11). Unfortunately, Paul didn't heed God's prophet, and subsequently, he was captured and turned over to the Romans, who hauled him off to stand trial.

Other individuals served the church as God's prophets throughout the book of Acts, displaying that the gift ministry was alive in the first century. The city of Antioch became a locus for the church's operations and a jump-off point for outreach to Asia Minor. Acts 13:1 informs thusly, "Now there were in the church that was at Antioch certain prophets and teachers; as Barnabas, and Simeon that was called Niger, and Lucius of Cyrene, and Manaen, which had been brought up with Herod the tetrarch, and Saul." Six individuals were so noteworthy in their service to the church that the Scriptures had their names recorded. Prior to attaining apostleship, Barnabas and Saul (later Paul) were prophets, which shows, like Peter, that leaders often took on multiple roles throughout their tenure. Judas Barsabas and Silas are called prophets (Acts 15:32). In Acts 21:8–9, though they are not named, Philip the evangelist's four daughters prophesied in Paul's presence, presumably to keep him from going to Jerusalem. Therefore, the possibility existed/exists for women to serve as prophets for God. God energized the ministry of a prophet in a person's life where and when it pleased him to suit the needs and situations of the people.

## Evangelists

There are only three verses of Scripture in English where the noun "evangelist" appears. The Greek word from which the English language derives "evangelist" is εὐαγγελιστής (*euangelistēs*), defined as "a bringer of good tidings," and Thayer's Lexicon continues, "this name is given in the N.T. to those heralds of salvation through Christ who are not apostles."[57] Ephesians 4:11 lists evangelists third after apostles and prophets. Acts 21:8 states, "We entered into the house of Philip the evangelist, which was one of the one of the seven," and is referencing the first seven deacons who were promoted by the congregation of the early church in Acts 6:5. The third reference was written from Paul to Timothy. He states, "But watch thou in all things, endure afflictions, do the work of an evangelist, make full proof of thy ministry" (2 Tim 4:5). Εὐαγγελιστής (*euangelistēs*) comes from the verb εὐαγγελίζω (*euangelizō*): "Pass on information that spells good tidings to the recipient; spread good tidings of God's beneficial concern."[58] Louw and Nida translate εὐαγγελίζω (*euangelizō*) as "to communicate good news concerning something; in the NT, a particular reference to the gospel message about Jesus."[59] An evangelist's ministry differs from the ministry of an apostle in that the evangelist is not an official emissary, and the evangelist is not necessarily spreading a new message to their audience. In Romans, Paul states, "As it is written, How beautiful are the feet of them that preach the gospel of peace, and bring glad tidings of good things!" (Rom 10:15). In that passage, "preach the gospel," and "bring glad tidings" are the same Greek word: εὐαγγελιζομένων (*euangelizomenōn*).[60] Εὐαγγελιζομένων (*euangelizomenōn*) is the present participle of the genitive masculine plural verb form of εὐαγγελίζω (*euangelizō*), which is to say, those who deliver the message of the gospel of Christ at God's direction and energizing are carrying out the gift ministry of an evangelist. Similarly, 1 Pet 1:12 says, "Them that have preached the gospel unto you with the Holy Ghost sent down from heaven." In that verse, "them that have preached the gospel" is εὐαγγελισαμένων (*euangelisamenōn*), which is the aorist participle of the same verb as before, and the context declares the Holy Spirit inspired their preaching.[61]

57. Thayer, "εὐαγγελιστής," *Thayer's Greek-English Lexicon*, 257.
58. Danker, "εὐαγγελίζω, ον, τό.," *Concise Greek-English Lexicon*, 152.
59. "εὐαγγελίζω," L&N 1:412.
60. Green, *Interlinear Bible*, 879.
61. Green, *Interlinear Bible*, 940.

Like apostles and prophets, God energizes and activates the gift ministry of an evangelist within his chosen person.

The singular individual labeled an evangelist in the Scriptures was Philip of the first seven ordained deacons (Acts 6:5). The Scripture speaks, "Then Philip went down to the city of Samaria, and preached Christ unto them. And the people gave heed unto those things which Philip spake, hearing and seeing the miracles which he did" (Acts 8:5–6). Jesus had visited Samaria previously (Luke 17:11; John 4:5), so the message that Philip delivered was not wholly unknown to them. However, the evidence of the gift ministry of an evangelist in Philip was due to the presence of God's Holy Spirit manifested in the miracles he wrought, and the people responded positively to his preaching. After accomplishing the task in Samaria, in Acts 8:26, an angel directed Philip where to go next. He intercepted a devout and influential man and preached Christ to him. Later, verse 40 states that Philip preached the gospel of Christ in all the cities between Azotus and Caesarea. As an evangelist, Philip went where the Spirit of God inspired and energized him to preach the gospel of Christ.

In his letters to the church, Paul encouraged believers to follow his example and preach the gospel of Christ everywhere (1 Cor 11:1; 2 Cor 11:7; Gal 1:8). Paul excelled in many duties for the church and set an example of every gift ministry, which makes him a prime authority to teach them to others. In 1 Cor 1:17, he declared, "For Christ sent me not to baptize, but to preach the gospel." Christ had commissioned Paul not only as his apostle but also as his evangelist because "to preach the gospel" is εὐαγγελίζεσθαι (*euangelizesthai*), another form, but this is the present infinitive tense.[62] As the infinitive, Paul's commission to preach the gospel did not have a set ending, and with the action set in the present tense, the activity takes place *now*. Thus, following his example, an evangelist should always preach the good news of the gospel of Christ right now.

## Pastors and Teachers

In Eph 4:11, pastors and teachers, though they are unique roles within the church, each bearing a specific purpose, are coupled together almost like Castor and Pollux in the constellation Gemini. There are arguments for presenting this category as "pastor-teachers" or that teachers should

---

62. Green, *Interlinear Bible*, 884.

be considered a subset of pastors.⁶³ However, the two terms are not identical, synonymous, or interchangeable, or the Scripture would have stated *pastors and pastors* or *teachers and teachers*, but the text reads "pastor and teachers." Therefore, a significant difference exists between pastors and teachers, though they are coupled together in the phrasing of this verse. Other studies have promoted that the phrasing of "pastors and teachers" should be understood as a singular unit comprising a combination of the two words and their inherent and contextual meanings as "pastor-teachers." There is also a position proposing that teachers should be a group within but lower than the category of pastors. This study presents a more flexible third possibility: that one may excel in the church in the role of a pastor while still required to teach the congregation, but this is not their strength: a pastor-teacher. Conversely, an individual may be a model teacher, able to expound the details of the Scriptures, but is short-suited in pastoring: a teacher-pastor. The previous statements are not to say that the individual is deficient or lacking in any way but simply excels in one side over the other: *pastor*-teacher and *teacher*-pastor. The church's needs must come first and be the deciding factor, and God has the prerogative concerning what role is energized for the maturation and equipping of the saints.

Ephesians 4:12 contains the figure of speech *hendiadys*, which occurs when two words that are the same part of speech and the same case are joined by the conjunction "and" to intensify the meaning of what the statement expresses.⁶⁴ In the Greek text, this verse reads: Καὶ αὐτὸς ἔδωκεν οὺς ἀποστόλους τοὺς δὲ προφήτας τοὺς δὲ εὐαγγελιστάς τοὺς δὲ ποιμένας καὶ διδασκάλους. The verse bears five distinct nouns in four sections, with each section separated by τοὺς δὲ. The final section, τοὺς δὲ ποιμένας καὶ διδασκάλους, employs the figure *hendiadys*, evidenced by the different joining conjunction, καὶ. All five nouns in this sentence are in the accusative masculine plural. However, of these, ποιμένας (pastors/shepherds) and διδασκάλους (teachers) are linked together, presenting the implication that "a shepherd who did not feed would fail in his duty; and so would a teacher who failed to be a pastor."⁶⁵ Therefore, a person

---

63. Christopher Green presents the argument for combining pastors and teachers into "pastor-teachers." Green, *Message of the Church*, 254–56. Sydney H. T. Page presents each, pastors and teachers, as its own category while acknowledging the possibility of the subset. Page, "Whose Ministry?," 26–46.

64. Bullinger, *Figures of Speech Used in the Bible*, 657.

65. Bullinger, *Figures of Speech Used in the Bible*, 666.

called by God to be a shepherd will still be required to be adept at teaching, and likewise, one chosen to serve his people as their teacher will still need to manifest the care of a pastor.

*Pastors*

Interestingly, the KJV of the Holy Bible renders the Greek word ποιμένας (*poimenas*) as "pastors" in this reference alone; fifteen times it is "shepherd," and twice it is "Shepherd" about Jesus Christ.[66] The use of the word "pastor" instead of "shepherd" displays evidence of the influence of the Latin language in translations. "Pastor" is the Latin word for shepherd, from the root *past*, meaning "fed, grazed, from the verb *pascere*."[67] The illustration that the title would paint in the mind of a person from Asia Minor and the Mediterranean region would have likely been someone with a mild, patient, and caring temperament, which is necessary for handling sheep. Moreover, the illustration would have born a much more profound implication for the Hebrew people because some of their most illustrious leaders from history were herdsmen. People from the Old Testament, whom Yahweh had shown favor, like Abel, Abraham, Jacob, and Joseph, kept and tended flocks and herds of animals. As a young man, David maintained his father's flock of sheep and recounted to King Saul how he saved them from a lion and a bear (1 Sam 17:34–36). One of David's most famous psalms, Ps 23, attributed a shepherd's manner and practices to God to describe the care he bestowed upon David. The Scriptures refer to Jesus as "the Great Shepherd" (Heb 13:20) and "the chief Shepherd" (1 Pet 5:4). Concerning Jesus, Peter wrote, "For ye were as sheep going astray; but are now returned unto the Shepherd and Bishop of your souls" (1 Pet 2:25). Therefore, anyone aspiring to attain a pastor/shepherd's role should heed their lessons and examples, but especially those of Jesus.

A continuity exists between the OT and NT concerning the shepherd, as ποιμέν is the Greek equivalent utilized in the Septuagint for the Hebrew word רָעָה, meaning a herdsman, a shepherd, and in reference to Jesus' parables, ποιμέν is one to whom others have committed their care (Matt 9:36–7; Mark 6:34; John 10:2–12).[68] The parable of the good

---

66. Strong, "ποιμήν, -ένας," *Strong's Exhaustive Concordance*, 206.
67. Stevenson, "Pastor," *Oxford Dictionary of English*, 1299.
68. Thayer, "ποιμέν," *Thayer's Greek-English Lexicon*, 527.

shepherd from the Gospel of John chapter ten displays the prototypical relationship between the shepherd and the flock. Utilizing himself as their example, this was Jesus' instruction to his disciples for them to emulate, especially after his ascension. The leader of the flock enters boldly before the congregation because the flock has no fear of him because they know him; he is open, honest, and transparent unto them, engendering their trust, contrary to another who would steal and harm them (John 10:1–5). For one to be a shepherd, one must dedicate their life to the tending, care, and preservation of their flock of sheep, but someone who is doing the job simply for an income won't last but will desert the flock in the face of adversity and calamity (vs. 11–13). The sheep and the shepherd form a symbiotic relationship: they support and sustain him and provide him with food and clothing. The shepherd leads them away from dangers, tends to their wounds, and pastures them so they are nourished, healthy, and reproductive. Jesus intended the early church leaders to manage and care for their congregation like the shepherds of the Orient tended and cared for their flocks.

*Teachers*

The gift ministry of the teacher referenced in Eph 4:11 was not just anyone who might teach the Scriptures or a teacher of the Hebrew Law but was a master teacher adept in the Scriptures and able to fill an audience's spiritual needs via the inspiration provided by the Spirit of God. The Greek word for teachers is διδασκάλος (*didaskalos*), and in the KJV, when referencing Jesus, it is translated as "Master" forty times; separate from him, it is translated as "teacher" ten times, "master" seven times, and "doctor" once.[69] Several definitions are available for this word, depending on its context. This study focuses on "those who in the religious assemblies of Christians undertook the work of teaching, with the special assistance of the Holy Spirit."[70] It is these elite teachers that 1 Cor 12:28 speaks of in context with apostles and prophets.

Jesus earned the title of "Master" or master teacher from his opponents due to the deftness with which he handled the Scriptures and confounded them at every opportunity (Luke 20:19–40). Paul had served the church as a prophet and a teacher in Antioch, and with good reason,

---

69. Strong, "διδασκάλος," *Strong's Exhaustive Concordance*, 68.
70. Thayer, "διδασκάλος," *Thayer's Greek-English Lexicon*, 144.

because he had received training in the Hebrew Law at the feet of the renowned Pharisee Gamaliel (Acts 13:1, 22:3). His pharisaical training served him well because shortly after his conversion to following Christ, Acts records Saul (Paul) was preaching Christ in the local synagogues of Damascus and out-excelling those who debated with him (Acts 9:19–22). Paul told his successor Timothy that Christ had set him in place in the church as a preacher, an apostle, and a teacher (1 Tim 2:5–7). As his successor, Paul directed Timothy, "And the things that thou hast heard of me among many witnesses, the same commit thou to faithful men, who shall be able to teach others also" (2 Tim 2:2). Timothy could not have carried out this directive so that other men who had not known Paul were equipped to teach like the apostle if he were not a proven adept teacher himself. Thus, by implication of the greater context, one who manifests the gift ministry of a teacher will follow Jesus Christ's example as the master teacher.

The First-Century Church was not a hierarchically controlled organization but instead developed two aspects to its leadership body, similar to how a coin has two faces: the gift ministries and the organized ordained ministers. The leaders with gift ministries were charismatic individuals whom the body of believers recognized as operating spiritual gifts, thus proving the presence of the power of the Holy Spirit in their midst.[71] These five gift ministries– apostles, prophets, evangelists, pastors, and teachers– form the foundational level of the church, always looking to Jesus Christ as their primus, head, and chief cornerstone.[72] The Holy Spirit of God energized them into action based on the church's needs and not through an election or committee (Acts 13:1–13). They aimed to stimulate, guide, promote, and encourage the church members' maturation (1 Tim 2:7; 2 Tim 1:11). According to God's purposes, an individual may manifest one or more of these gift ministries to meet his people's needs, though they are not prerequisite for serving other believers.[73] These gift ministries set the

---

71. Ehrman, *After the New Testament*, 429.

72. "Gift," from the Greek, "χάρισμα,"—*charisma*: "The gift of divine grace . . . denotes extraordinary powers, distinguishing certain Christians and enabling them to serve the church of Christ superlatively, the reception of which is due to the power of divine grace operating in their souls by the Holy Spirit." According to 1 Cor 12:28, these ministries are a spiritual gift to the church; in Eph 4:8–13, after Jesus' ascension, God gave gifts unto men, which included apostles, prophets, evangelists, pastors, and teachers, hence why this study refers to them as "gift ministries" of the church. Thayer, "χάρισμα," *Thayer's Greek-English Lexicon*, 667.

73. The presence of a gift ministry within an individual and manifested in their life

pace for the church, and they led, guided, trained, and ordained the different subordinate leadership roles that stood on their shoulders.

Some promote the belief that the gift ministry of an apostle no longer functions in modernity. As the modern age and the First-Century Church are part of the same administration, the grace administration (seeing as Christ has yet not returned), the same rules, guidelines, doctrines, standards, and privileges must be available and applicable to both (Eph 3:2). Thus, if apostles, prophets, evangelists, pastors, and teachers were available to the church then, they must also be available in modernity. Some scholars have argued that there were no more apostles after the first century, after the completion of all the accepted books of the Bible or other boundaries they desired to insert into Scripture from their private interpretations.[74] The five are all grouped together in Eph 4:11, on equal standing with each other, and to say that one of the five is finished, over, and unavailable is to say they all are. However, no verse of Scripture plainly and pointedly states there would be no more apostles after the first century. To include necessary context for the review of this issue, Eph 4: 6–13 states:

> (There is) One God and Father of all, who is above all, and through all, and in you all. But unto every one of us is given grace according to the measure of the gift of Christ. Wherefore He [God] saith, "When he [Christ] ascended up on high, He [God through the completed works of the Messiah] led captivity captive, and gave gifts unto men. (Now that he ascended, what is it but that he also descended first into the lower parts of the earth? He that descended is the same also that ascended up far above the heavens, that he might fill all things.) And He [God] gave some, apostles; and some prophets; and some evangelists; and some pastors and teachers; For the perfecting of the saints, for the work of the ministry, for the edifying of the body of Christ: Till we all come in the unity of the faith, and of

---

and ministering to others is not a prerequisite for leadership within the church as shall be displayed in the coming second half of this chapter. However, the Scriptures do present the fact that the heads of God's church, as seen in the examples of the charismatic leaders in the NT, manifested one or more of the gift ministries.

74. George W. Knight's essay "The Number and Functions of the Permanent Offices in the New Testament Church" is one such example. In his article he states, "Christ does not continually give to the church those special and extraordinary offices of apostles and prophets." However, he does not provide scriptural support for when, where, or why these offices were terminated. Knight, "Number and Functions of the Permanent Offices in the New Testament Church," 111–16.

the knowledge of the Son of God, unto a perfect man, unto the measure of the stature of the fulness of Christ.

Beginning with the word "wherefore," at the start of verse eight, initiates an intermediate section that quotes Ps 68:18, discusses Jesus' death ascension and descension, and ends in verse ten with "he might fill all things." Because verses eight, nine, and ten form a parenthetical break, one may read from verse seven and skip to verse eleven without disrupting the message.

The essential word to understand clearly within the context of Eph 4:11 is "gave," in the phrase "And He (God) gave some apostles." The verb "gave" is ἔδωκεν (edōken), the third-person, aorist, indicative, active tense of δίδωμι (didomi).[75] Δίδωμι (didomi) is defined as "to give" and is translated in the NT as "add, allow, bestow, produce, grant" and many other possibilities of usage.[76] For comparison, verse seven reads, "Unto every one of us is given grace according to the measure of the gift of Christ." When a person believes in the Lord Jesus Christ, he receives, of God's grace, the gift of Christ, which is the gift of the holy spirit.[77] The words "is given" in Greek are one word, ἐδόθη (edothē), which is the aorist indicative passive tense of δίδωμι (didomi). The aorist tense in Greek, for the majority of uses in the NT, occurs in the past and shows completed action, but the time of the verb's action is undefined or indefinite in its parameters; it states "only the fact of the action without specifying its duration."[78] With Jesus Christ's ascension, God initiated the outpouring of his gift of holy spirit to humanity on Pentecost. The twelve apostles were the first to accept—receive passively—this gift, and then the thousands present who believed also received it. People of the twentieth and twenty-first centuries were not present for that initiation, yet they continue to receive that gift of God's grace and salvation unto this day. The aorist passive indicative tense of δίδωμι—ἐδόθη (edothē) is utilized because the

---

75. Mounce and Mounce, *Interlinear New Testament*, 753.

76. Thayer, "δίδωμι," *Thayer's Greek-English Lexicon*, 145–47.

77. As capital letters were not originally part of the first Greek texts but added much later by translators and redactors and to avoid confusion, this study chooses to address God, the giver, as the Holy Spirit with a capital "H" and "S," and his gift of holy spirit, with a lower case "h" and "s," that is given to the believer (Acts 2:38; 10:45; Heb 6:4), a.k.a. "inner man" (Eph 3:16), "inward man" (Rom 7:22 and 2 Cor 4:16), and gift of Christ: "Christ in you the hope of glory," (Col 1:27).

78. Mounce, *Basics of Biblical Greek*, 189–96.

gift was initiated in the past, but regarding any certain expanse of time is undefined and is therefore available to people today.

By saying in verse eleven, "He [God] gave,"—ἔδωκεν (*edōken*)—the aorist tense presents an inceptive action that is active because the subject "He [God]" performed the doing of the verb.[79] There is no clearly defined ending to the verb's action, so it is considered ongoing, just like the gift of Christ. These gifts were and are complete units, not lacking anything, but exist without regard to the finite definitions of time as we understand it. The indicative mood augments the aorist tense of both verbs to show their absolute certainty.[80] In conclusion, a more accurate English rendering of Eph 4:11–12 could state:

> And He, God, initiated and consecrated with Jesus Christ's ascension (ref. 4.8) until an undetermined future time, the gift of apostles, prophets, evangelists, and pastor-teachers (certainly all are gifts of God's grace, as Christ's understudies) for the maturation and equipping of the saints, for the work of service, to the building up of the collective body of Christ.

The gift ministries do not have a specified expiration date for their commissioning. They are a part of the package of salvation, which is the gift of God's grace through Christ unto all who believe. Ephesians 4:13 says they are available until all believers attain the unity of the faith and the knowledge of Jesus Christ. First Corinthians 13:10–12 states, "When that which is perfect is come," i.e., Jesus Christ, the perfect one's return, all the charismatic things bestowed upon the Christian believers, which are partial—awaiting their completion at his return—such as the manifestations of the gift of the holy spirit and the gift ministries of the holy spirit, then would be done away.[81] At that time, when every Christian believer is made complete and transformed (1 Cor 15:51–2; 2 Cor 3:18; Phil 3:21) at the return of Christ, then those gifts will no longer be necessary.

However, until that event occurs, the energizing of apostles, prophets, evangelists, pastors, and teachers to the church for the improvement,

---

79. Mounce states, "When the aorist describes an action as a unit event it may accentuate one of three possibilities, as, imagine, a ball that has been thrown: 1) *let fly* (inceptive or ingressive); 2) *flew* (constantive or durative); 3) *hit* (culminative or telic)." *Basics of Biblical Greek*, 189.

80. Wallace, *Greek Grammar Beyond the Basics*, 448–49.

81. First Corinthians 13:10–12 states, "when that which is perfect is come," usually understood as a reference to the expected return of Jesus Christ due to Paul's anticipatory statement in verse twelve of seeing the perfect one "face to face."

establishment, and maturation of God's people is his business and according to his prerogatives. The purpose for observing their roles in the First-Century Church is that the gift ministries were an indispensable part of the leadership and contributed to its success. Still, they should not be confused with the structure and stratification of the ordained leadership roles and their subordinates, which developed over time. This discourse concludes that the gift ministries were available to the church then; they were consecrated as Christ's substitutes here on earth for an undetermined length of time, and they should be equally available today because the church of modernity is of the same body of Christ.[82]

## ORDAINED AND APPOINTED LEADERS

As recorded in the book of Acts and the epistles, the positions observed in the early church earned respect and authority from their service and examples of humility; never once were they witnessed commanding the believers or their congregations like officers empowered to dole out punishments for disobedience. The early church did not regard their leaders as officers and, therefore, did not refer to their positions of authority as "offices." Applying such terminology was a construct of the apostolic fathers and later was adopted by the Roman Catholic Church. One might think this issue to be a simple matter of semantics, but this study aims to present the information as biblically accurately as possible. Therefore, these roles in the early church should not be seen as officers commanding authority and dominion over others but as leadership positions within the church, functions of service that needed to be filled to maintain order and unity through loving, caring guidance. The individuals that filled these positions were elected to the roles either by promotion from the congregation or appointment received from other leaders (Acts 1:23–26; 6:3–6; 13:1–2; Titus 1:5). A few of these roles received an ordination, while others that were subordinate or perhaps resembled in form and practice an apprenticeship did not. Frequently, individuals who served in these positions also exercised the charismatic gifts of the Holy Spirit; this way, they fit the church in a dual capacity. The apostle Paul expressed on several occasions, often utilizing himself or Jesus as the prime example,

---

82. For reference, see also 1 Cor 12:12–27; Eph 1:10, 3:2; Col 1:25.

that the function of leaders in the Christian community was the service of the public body.[83]

The primary assignment posts of *episkopos* (bishop), *presbyteros* (elder), and *diakonos* (deacon) have, throughout history, received the lion's share of scholarly attention. However, they did not operate without help, for as this study shall display, there were other subordinate positions within the church's leadership structure: the *oikonomos*, *hypēretēs*, *doulos*, and *thyrōros*. These functionaries shared the burdens of the *episkopos*, *presbyteros*, and *diakonos* and received the respect of the believers because of the assistance they rendered. These subordinate positions were recognized for how they served, and therefore, they also set an example within the church. In addition, they submitted themselves for training so that, like Timothy and Titus, those in the lesser roles would replace their masters, ensuring the continuation of the church. Scholars attribute the development of the other subordinate positions within the church to the influence of organizational models from traditional governmental structures, religious hierarchies, known social groups, and the *paterfamilias's* household influence.[84] Lastly, this study will bring to light the most obscure leadership role in the early church, that of the *therápōn*. All of these positions operated with an almost liquid, malleable flexibility. On many occasions, a church leader assumed the responsibilities of more than one role without question or resistance because the situation necessitated them to do so. Time and again, leaders showed the willingness to do whatever was necessary for the good of the church body in service to their Lord Jesus Christ and the will of God.

There are two perspectives with which one may observe these strata of leadership positions: how they functioned in service to each other and the church body, or how someone might rise through their ranks as they increased in maturity and responsibility within the church. As with anyone who receives training, counsel, and instruction from a more experienced person, the trainee is lower in rank and looks up to their trainer. So, was that principle also true with the early church. The beginning position then was the *thyrōros*, followed by the *doulos*, *hypēretēs*, *oikonomos*, *diakonos*, *presbyteros*, *episkopos*, and then those with the gift ministries. Finally, the level of the highest spiritual maturity and superior degree of selfless dedication possible was the *therápōn*. Each one trained, taught,

---

83. Pascoe, "Living as God's Stewards," 24.
84. Ehrman, *After the New Testament*, 430.

counseled, and aided those with lesser experience and proficiency, and they all helped each other out of godly humility.

In the second perspective, based upon Eph 2:20, Jesus and his ministers (apostles, prophets, evangelists, etc.) are at the foundational level, supporting all the other strata of leaders and believers from beneath. Such a perspective inverts the hierarchical pyramid wherein the most revered individual stands atop all those working for him; instead, within the church, the least experienced member is placed at the top as the recipient of the greatest quantity of care and ministering. Jesus, during his ministry, had taught, "For whomsoever much is given, of him shall much be required" (Luke 12:48). The lives of Peter, Paul, Stephen, and others are a testimony of this principle, for they followed Jesus into laying their lives down for the church. After the gift ministries, then come the bishops, elders, and deacons, with the caveat that God often energized the gift ministries in the lives of those who served in ordained positions. Upon their shoulders were those who managed the individual household churches—the *oikonomos*. On top of them were the three roles that assisted and served all who attended the churches: the *doulos*, *hypēretēs*, and topmost would have been the *thyrōros*. The members of the early church were expected to present their lives as open examples (2 Cor 3:2–3; James 1:22). As one increased in the knowledge, wisdom, and abilities within the church, so also their responsibilities of service increased proportionately.

## Misunderstandings and Misinterpretations

Disagreements and debates exist among scholars surrounding the roles of the bishop, deacon, and elder, which this study must address before proceeding. These disagreements have arisen partly due to interpretations promoting sameness between *episkopos* and *presbyteros* or *episkopos* and *diakonos*. Disputes may also be partly due to some early church members being styled as more than one of these roles within the church. Every language has synonyms: "a word or phrase that means exactly or nearly the same as another word or phrase in the same language."[85] The Greek language of the Bible is no different. Θεραπόν (*therapon*), δοῦλος (*doulos*), διάκονος (*diakonos*), οἰκέτης (*oiketēs*), ὑπηρέτης (*hypēretēs*) are styled as synonyms of one another because for each their simplest definition is

---

85. Stevenson, "Synonym," *Oxford Dictionary of English*, 1804.

"a servant."[86] However, this study promotes that while these words bear similarity because the Greek language is more precise than English, one must pay attention to the differences between these words to determine why the text does not simply repeat the same word in each instance. The biblical usage of a particular word chosen within a passage must be understood within the verse and context of that passage and relative to its previous uses, in addition to the meanings assigned by lexicons, dictionaries, and other reference materials.[87] This study promotes the following rule for understanding the Scriptures: there must be divine intent, purpose, and precision behind each word chosen to convey the will of the creator, God, and one must handle the words of the word of God with reverence, reflecting that purpose and precision (2 Tim 2:15). Based upon these tenets this study presents each one: *episkopos, presbyteros, diakonos, therápōn, doulos, oiketes, hypēretēs,* and *thyrōros,* as servants of God unto the church, but each possessing unique and defining characteristics which positions them as individual functionaries within the church. Each position has a specific role and responsibility(s) for furthering the gospel of Christ and ministering to the believers.

## Bishops and Elders

In the late 1800s, renowned scholar J. B. Lightfoot stated, "It is a fact now generally recognized by theologians of all shades of opinion, that in the language of the New Testament the same officer in the church is called indifferently 'bishop' (ἐπίσκοπος) and 'elder' or 'presbyter' (πρεσβύτερος).[88] Lightfoot based his statement upon his observation that in the introduction of Paul's Epistle to the Philippians where he addressed "bishops and deacons" and reasoned that because "elders" or "the second order" were left out, then they must be identical to bishops.[89] Lightfoot's conclusions seem to be heavily influenced by the weight of church traditions. But, of course, theories, interpretations, and conclusions, such as Lightfoot's, are subject to change and amendment at any time upon introducing new information or increased clarity. For if Lightfoot's conclusion was biblically accurate, why then does Paul, in 1 Timothy, direct Timothy concerning

---

86. Trench, *Synonyms of the New Testament*, 30–34.
87. Bullinger, *How to Enjoy the Bible*, 227–29.
88. Lightfoot, *St. Paul's Epistle to the Philippians*, 93.
89. Lightfoot, *St. Paul's Epistle to the Philippians*, 95.

the qualifications of bishops—ἐπίσκοπος in chapter three, and separately the elders—πρεσβύτερος (both men and women) in chapter five? Why not utilize the same word in all the references unless there exists a distinct difference between the roles and responsibilities that ἐπίσκοπος and πρεσβύτερος each bear to the church? Benjamin J. Merkle, in agreement with Lightfoot, promotes they both are the same except that "teaching is the responsibility of all overseers (1 Tim 3:2; Titus 1:9), but only some of the elders have this responsibility (1 Tim 5:17)."[90] That one role bore the responsibility of teaching others while another did not is a distinct difference; therefore the two are *not* the same. Merkle firmly rooted his position in Lightfoot, who, on one page, muddles the delineation between elders and overseers and claims "the two are only different designations of one and the same office."[91] Yet, later on, he states, "It is clear then at the close of the apostolic age, the two lower orders [elders and deacons] of the threefold ministry were firmly and widely established; but traces of the third and highest order, the episcopate properly so called, are few and indistinct."[92] Therefore, according to Lightfoot's statement, during the age of the First-Century Church, there existed *three distinct orders of leaders* (bishops, elders, and deacons), but much later, they were reduced, so only two of them dominated Christianity.

In the government of the United States of America, presidents, senators, and members of Congress have served as leaders of this country. They are all politicians and, on occasion, may have come from the same states in the union, *but* no matter their similarities, to say they are the same and minimize their roles is insulting. Again, this research work is concerned with the details, standards, and characteristics that defined the varied positions of responsibility and leadership in the First-Century Church and contributed to their success. That these positions bear similarities is noteworthy, but the fact that there are discernable differences is remarkable. Modern-day Christianity stands to profit from investing and paying attention to such details rather than allowing traditions to minimize their potential value. "Beware lest any man spoil you (takes you captive)," wrote Paul to the church in Colossae, "through (hollow and deceptive) philosophy and vain deceit, after (which depends on) human traditions, after the rudiments of this world, and not after Christ."[93]

90. Merkle, *Elder and Overseer*, 2.
91. Lightfoot, *St. Paul's Epistle to the Philippians*, 191.
92. Lightfoot, *St. Paul's Epistle to the Philippians*, 193.
93. This rendering of Col 2:8 is an interweaving of the KJV and NIV versions by this

Merkle also referenced and quoted Leonhard Goppelt to support his interpretation and theology. However, from the same pages from which Merkle so dexterously extracted quotations, he ignored the greater context where Goppelt stated:

> The next step in the development becomes when 1 Tim. v.17 says in the same context that those of the elders who then 'ruled well' (in contrast to those who had no ruling function) were to be especially honoured, in particular those 'who labor in preaching and teaching'. The role of ruling and teaching, however, according to 1 Tim. iii.2, 4 f. and Tit. i.9, is the task of the bishop, Apparently, therefore, only some of the elders were active as bishops, and the bishops now emerge into prominence from the circle of elders.[94]

In this quotation, Goppelt indicated a distinction that admits bishops could attain the honorific of elder, such as the apostle Peter (1 Pet 5:1), but not all elders previously served as bishops, nor was it a requirement to become an elder. Goppelt further stated there existed a distinction between the elders and the bishops: the bishops oversaw the management of the church as its "leader and representative, with a presbytery [council of elders] and a body of deacons subordinate to him." Furthermore, Goppelt acknowledged that bishops and presbyters became interchangeable sometime after the close of the Pauline era of leadership.[95] Richard Fraser is another author who, in his essay "Office of a Deacon," recognizes only two levels of authority in the early church, that of elders and deacons; either he completely ignores the bishops or, in his understanding, has combined the elders and bishops into a singular role (which is the belief of this author), for he argues that the office of a deacon was the proving ground for elders of the early church.[96] The adaptation and evolution of the early church in the second and third centuries, preceding Constantine the Great, wherein the blending and melding of these two roles occurred, is a worthwhile study for future endeavors, but this did not transpire during the time of the First-Century Church detailed in the Scriptures, which is this study's concern and focus.

---

author, the goal of which is the presentation of the stress and emphasis within in the verse of Scripture decrying traditions. The majority was copied from the KJV, while the words in parentheses are from the NIV to provide clarity.

94. Leonhard Goppelt, *Apostolic and Post-Apostolic Times* (London: Black, 1970), 190.

95. Goppelt, *Apostolic and Post-Apostolic Times*, 189.

96. Fraser, "Office of Deacon," 19.

During the Hellenistic age, the position of the ἐπίσκοπος developed in Jewish society due to Greek influences that combined with Hebrew heritage because ἐπίσκεπτ, the root for ἐπίσκοπος is analogous with פָּקַד—*paqad* (Gen 39:4).[97] Merkle calls for a generic interpretation of ἐπίσκοπος in 1 Tim 3:2 and Titus 1:7, since there is more than one overseer per church, and interprets the Scriptures to say that "the presiding presbyters (προεστωτες πρεοβύτεροι) mentioned in 1 Timothy 5:17 are then to be understood as overseeing elders (πρεσβύτεροι ἐπίσκοπουντες)."[98] However, that is not what the Scripture states, as R. Alastair Campbell reports that the passage from 1 Timothy does not merge the two distinct leadership roles. "Instead, the way in which they speak of elders in the plural, but of the overseer in the singular makes sense," writes Campbell, because, per the cultural use of the words ἐπίσκοπος and πρεσβύτερος in that day: there would have already existed multiple in-home churches, multiple elders were appointed within each city, but a single overseer appointed for the city.[99] Elders in Greek society emerged as an honorific position and title for respected members of families and within the social environments in Greek towns and cities. The function of the bishop, more properly ἐπίσκοπος (*episkopos*)—possibly overseer—has its origin in Hellenistic government almost five hundred years before Christ. The Athenian Empire utilized the office of the *episkopos*, adopted from the Achaemenid position for a royal executive, as an overseer of other areas of government as "Episkopoi periodically toured their respective territories to ensure that all allied governments were functioning in the interest of Athens, their imperial center."[100] In setting a similar standard for the church, Paul often visited and revisited his established churches (Acts 15:36; Rom 1:10–13; 1 Cor 16:5; Col 4:16).

When one observes the usages of the words ἐπίσκοπος and πρεσβύτερος, both in Scripture and in the Hellenistic culture of the day, ἐπίσκοπος (*episkopos*) may occur in plural or singular forms, and referred to overseers both in both spheres of influence.[101] Separately, πρεσβύτερος (*presbyteros*) implies an older, wiser, and dignified individual, and when referring to public servants, generally appears in its plural form, denoting

---

97. Goppelt, *Apostolic and Post-Apostolic Times*, 188.
98. Merkle, *Elder and Overseer*, 10.
99. Campbell, "Elders: Seniority in Earliest Christianity," 185–86.
100. Jack Martin Balcer, "Athenian Episkopos and the Achaemenid 'King's Eye,'" 252.
101. Condon, "Church Offices," 74.

a council of elders.¹⁰² The overseers of the church were present from its inception on the day of Pentecost, while elders were not introduced until some years later in Acts chapter eleven. In addition, "elder"—πρεσβύτερος (*presbyteros*)—does not appear in the Pauline epistles of Romans, Corinthians, Galatians, Ephesians, Philippians, Colossians, Thessalonians, or Philemon. The temple hierarchy of "priests and elders" opposed the apostles in Acts 4:23 and 6:12. The temple elders provided wisdom and sage advice to the priests who were esteemed as masters of the Scriptures. However, in Acts 11: 29–30, the elders in Jerusalem received a relief offering from the believers in Antioch delivered by Paul and Barnabas. Later, when Paul and Barnabas attend the Jerusalem Council in Acts 15, they are received by "the apostles and elders," which infers that the apostles maintained their position as the overseers of the church, but in a similar fashion to the Jewish temple and synagogues, they had added their own council of elders.¹⁰³ Campbell promotes that adding a council of elders was another leadership level that further assisted the apostles who seemingly never left Jerusalem.¹⁰⁴ Another cultural difference between elders and the other leadership positions was that "men were not appointed as elders so much as recognized as elders in virtue of being heads of their families."¹⁰⁵ The title of πρεσβύτερος (*presbyteros*) in the Greek world at that time was an honorific bestowed upon endeared members of the family and community revered for their wisdom, counsel, leadership as well as their advanced years.

Two particular passages of the Scriptures present evidence for the interchangeableness of the positions of the "bishop" or "overseer" (ἐπίσκοπος) and the "elder" or "presbyter" (πρεσβύτερος), Acts 20:17 and 28, and Titus 1:5–7. These Scriptures are in the minority for most of the usages of these two terms, but their differences are maintained. Both terms will be studied later in this chapter, and their differences will be illuminated. Within these two passages, the terms almost seem interchangeable. In Acts 20:17, Paul called the "elders of the church," and the word utilized is πρεσβύτερος. However, later in verse 28, he states, "Take heed therefore unto yourselves and to all the flock, over which the Holy Ghost hath made you overseers," and the word for overseers is ἐπίσκοπος. The position of the ἐπίσκοπος—overseer carries a different

---

102. Condon, "Church Offices," 74.
103. Roger, *Contextualisation of Leadership in Paul*, 38–39.
104. Campbell, "Elders of the Jerusalem Church," 512–14.
105. Campbell, "Elders of the Jerusalem Church," 514.

set of responsibilities and duties within the church than an elder, and the overseer is viewed as superior to the elder due to the longer list of requirements of their position.[106] For example, an overseer must be skillful in teaching the Scriptures (1 Tim 3:2; Titus 1:9). However, teaching is not a requirement for an elder, which is a distinct difference between the two positions. The potential is present for leaders such as overseers, deacons, and others within the church to become elders and continue serving the church as they grow older as will be seen in a future section, but not all elders were deemed worthy of the honor and reverence of an overseer. By this understanding, the overseers addressed in verse addressed in Acts 20:28 were a select subset of the elders Paul called together in verse 17.

In Paul's address to Titus, he presents his acolyte with instructions to "ordain elders [πρεσβύτερος] in every city" in verse five and follows this in verse seven with "for a bishop [ἐπίσκοπος] must be blameless." Again, this is a passage in which the two terms appear to be exchangeable, one for the other. These verses need to be compared with the passages in Timothy concerning overseers and elders (1 Tim 3:1–7; 5:1–17), which present a clear distinction between the duty codes of each position. In 1 Tim 5:17, Paul addresses certain elders of the church who were worthy of "double honour" because they "ruled well" and "labored in the word and doctrine." This verse is understood to mean these elders were exceptional because they served the church not only as counselors (a college of elders, Acts 15:23, 16:4) but also as active leaders and teachers of the word of God. Condon understands that the elders/bishops of Titus could be of this same kind of exceptional leader in the church, embracing dual roles and therefore worthy of double honor like Timothy.[107]

The Scriptures defined bishops/overseers and deacons/ministers by their ways and means of service to the believers and the church. Because the meetings were held in homes, undoubtedly, some elders served the church as fellowship leaders. It also would have been prudent for the apostles, overseers, and deacons to consult with elders of prominent local families to negotiate the regional political and religious environments. In the epistles of Timothy and Titus, bishops and deacons have qualifications and a code of conduct that must be manifested and evident to the church before they may be appointed as a bishop or deacon, but there is no such code presented for qualifying a person for the role of an elder.

106. Condon, "Church Offices," 77.
107. Condon, "Church Offices," 84.

One observes from the Scriptures that through the progress of time, as the church evolved, the position of the elders grew more expansive, and it might include the aging apostles and, most likely, others who had served in the various levels of leadership.[108] Peter's testimony in 1 Pet 5:1 shows an apostle taking up the position of an elder due to his longevity in service to the church.

The evidence presented thus far testifies that during the First-Century Church, the overseers and the elders differed in their roles and responsibilities within the church's organization. The primary function of an elder was that of sage advice, counsel, wisdom, and support, in contrast to the active ministrations of the overseers and the deacons. The roles of bishop/overseer and deacon/minister were primarily for the service of the people that attained reverence based upon their performance, while an elder was a title of honor and dignity brought on due to age and social position.[109] Instead of reviewing the roles of bishops, elders, and deacons from a hindsight perspective, and to avoid possible confusion, this study promotes their examination step-wise as they developed within the evolving church. The epistles of Timothy, Titus and Peter, which contain the codification of these leadership roles, were written near the end of the first century. Therefore, those letters will be investigated in the next chapter. In conclusion, overseers could become elders of the church, such as in the case of the apostle Peter, but not the other way around. Eldership developed much later in the church's evolution as a role that assisted the established governing bodies of bishops and deacons.

*Bishops and Deacons*

The utilization of these titles by the first two generations of believers within the early era of the church is of primary concern to this chapter. Beyond the period of Timothy, Titus, and their peers, into the second century, the third generation of leadership, known as the apostolic fathers, consisting of Clement I, Ignatius, Polycarp, and others, did not maintain the established standards, and confusion slowly crept in. As an example, Ignatius equated the bishop—ἐπίσκοπος to God, the presbyters—πρεσβύτερος to the college of the apostles, and the deacons—διάκονος to Jesus Christ in

---

108. Rayburn, "Three Offices," 110–11.
109. Campbell, "*Elder and the Overseer*," 282.

his letters to *Magnesians* and *Trallians*.¹¹⁰ His presentation in his letter to the Trallians is most confusing, for he states, "For when ye are as obedient to the bishop as to Jesus Christ . . ." and follows a sentence later with "do nothing without the bishop; but be ye obedient also to the presbytery, as to the Apostles of Jesus Christ our hope." Still, in the next paragraph, Ignatius presents to his audience, "In like manner let all men respect the deacons as Jesus Christ, even as they should respect the bishop as being a type of The Father and the presbyters as the council of God and as the college of Apostles."¹¹¹ Two factors become evident in this passage: the position of the bishop is singular, and the hierarchy Ignatius presents ranks the bishop as first, presbytery second, and Jesus Christ as third. In contrast, the Scriptures declare Jesus as the mediator of the new covenant through his blood (Heb 8:6; 9:15; 12:24), and Jesus proclaimed that he is the way unto God (John 3:16). Furthermore, 1 Tim 2:5 states, "For there is one God, and one mediator between God and men, the man Christ Jesus." Regarding any church leader as greater than Jesus Christ contradicts Scripture. The other apostolic fathers do not correct Ignatius but rather agree with and build upon his writings. Ignatius's letters, together with the writings of the other apostolic fathers, were the foundation for the arrangement of the clerical order in the Roman Catholic Church and influenced all of Christianity, spreading the confusion.¹¹² In analyzing Ignatius's letters, Frances M. Young finds them to be the primary source for the development of the monepiscopate, known today as the office of the Pope.¹¹³

The Pauline Epistles do not provide any information concerning elders or their role within the early church. First Timothy 3, often referenced as an ecclesiastical code of conduct for leaders, handles διάκονος (*diakonos*) and ἐπίσκοπος (*episkopos*), which links together with Phil 1:1 and the verses following, but the context of Philippians does not discuss any other positions of authority.¹¹⁴ Therefore, Young concludes that the overseers—ἐπίσκοπος were the first stratum, the ministers—διάκονος

---

110. Lightfoot, *Apostolic Fathers*, 57, 60. This author has compared Lightfoot's text with that of Michael W. Holmes, *Apostolic Fathers in English*, and Bart D. Ehrman's *After the New Testament*, for source references regarding the apostolic fathers. The dominant use of Lightfoot's text is due to it being the oldest of the three, but if there are any disagreements between these three authors, they will be examined and brought to light.

111. Lightfoot, *Apostolic Fathers*, 60.

112. Young, "On ΕΠΙΣΚΟΠΟΣ AND ΠΠΕΣΒΥΤΕΠΟΣ," 142.

113. Young, "On ΕΠΙΣΚΟΠΟΣ AND ΠΠΕΣΒΥΤΕΠΟΣ," 142.

114. Young, "On ΕΠΙΣΚΟΠΟΣ AND ΠΠΕΣΒΥΤΕΠΟΣ," 143.

were secondary unto the overseers, and the revered elders—πρεσβύτερος served as councilors to both.[115] The position of a διάκονος was distinctly separate from the πρεσβύτεροι and not directly subordinate to them, signified by their ministerial duties to the church body.[116] As the ἐπίσκοπος ordained the διάκονοι and appointed πρεσβύτεροι, they bore a weightier level of service than the other two. Because the direct function of the διάκονοι was subordinate to the overseers, sharing the responsibility of ministering to the congregation, they bear more responsibility than the πρεσβύτεροι.[117] A college of elders could have functioned as leaders, but most commonly, they were appointed advisors to overseers and ministers. However, overseers and ministers who served well could age into becoming esteemed elders of the church. In addition, because they developed later after the διάκονοι, they rank third within the First-Century Church.

## The Overseer

Before any other roles of responsibility and service developed in the early church, the first title encountered in Scripture is "Bishop/bishoprick" in Acts 1:20. Within the verse and its context, the word "bishoprick" references the duties, responsibilities, and oversight of an apostle, and thereby all apostles at that time were bishops (Acts 1:25). About the position Matthias took on in verse twenty-six, not only does verse twenty utilize ἐπισκοπήν (*episcopēn*) to describe the responsibilities the apostles administered, but also verse twenty-five employs ministry—διακονίας (*diakonias*) and apostleship—ἀποστολῆς (*apostolēs*) to describe the position. The use of all three signifies that at the beginning of the First-Century Church, the twelve apostles shouldered the duties later distributed between three differing leadership roles within the church body. Not until sometime later in the church's evolution and expansion across the Roman empire were there overseers/bishops who were not also apostles, indicating the possibility of a separation between the two positions in the church. The same applies to the development and separation between overseers/bishops and ministers/deacons. This distinction between apostles and overseers is evident in Paul's statement, "This is a true saying, if a man

---

115. Young, "On ΕΠΙΣΚΟΠΟΣ AND ΠΠΕΣΒΥΤΕΠΟΣ," 145.
116. Fraser, "Office of Deacon," 18.
117. Campbell, "Elders of the Jerusalem Church," 514.

desire the office of a bishop, he desireth a good work" (1 Tim 3:1). One could not desire or pursue the role of an apostle, for such is energized by God. The record of Simon in Acts 18 is an example of one who desired the gift ministry and attempted to buy it, to which Peter responded adversely, "Thy money perish with thee, because though hast thought that the gift of God [referring to the power, authority, and abilities Peter and John manifested, not witnessed in Philip] may be purchased with money" (Acts 18:20). Still, one could achieve the role of an overseer through dedicated, selfless service in the church. In the first half of the book of Acts, all the apostles, who were also the church's bishops/overseers, were located in either Jerusalem or Antioch, which were the two major centers of the early church's operations—first Jerusalem, and then they expanded further to Antioch. However, in the latter half of the first century, after the gospel of Christ spread across Asia Minor, then bishops became associated with specific locals such as Philippi, Ephesus, Rome, Crete, and others. In addition, later in the church's history, the oversight that began with the apostles evolved and became divided into the elected, ordained, or appointed roles of the overseers/bishops and ministers/deacons, apart from the gift ministries. These activities testify to the church body's escalating needs as the overall congregation increased, the flexibility and development of leaders' roles, and the evolution of the church.

The King James English word "bishop" originates from the Old English word *biscop*, derived from the Greek noun, *episkopos*, meaning "overseer."[118] The Hellenistic culture utilized *episkopos* similarly, indicating that the First-Century Church authors' use was a spiritual reflection of the culture around them. Concerning the culture of the day, J. Andrew Overman reports, "In pre-Christian and extra-Christian usage the Greek word rendered "bishop," *episkopos*, and its cognates, refers primarily to caring for something or someone."[119] The KJV New Testament utilizes *episkopos* only five times, of which once it is rendered "overseer" (Acts 20:28) and four times as "bishop" (Phil 1:1; 1 Tim 3:2; Titus 1:7; 1 Pet 2:25). Such limited use does not provide an extensive amount of information; therefore, to broaden the scope of understanding, this study includes three Greek words which are cognates of ἐπίσκοπος (*episkopos*): ἐπισκοπή (*episcopē*), ἐπισκοπήν (*episcopēn*), and ἐπισκοπέω (*episkopeō*). The investigation results show that within biblical context and presentation, all three

---

118. Stevenson, "Bishop," *Oxford Dictionary of English*, 170.
119. Overman, "Bishop," *Oxford Companion to the Bible*, 91.

cognates paint a picture of a role responsible for the spiritual oversight of all other positions and people of the household of God.

In Acts 1:20, the word for "bishoprick" is ἐπισκοπήν (*episcopēn*), the accusative singular feminine form of ἐπισκοπή (*episcopē*), and refers to the position of oversight and responsibility of caring for others in the First-Century Church.[120] In the OT, the Hebrew word פְּקֻדָּה (*pequddah*) is congruous with ἐπισκοπή (*episcopē*), for פְּקֻדָּה (*pequddah*) means "oversight, a charge, mustering, visitation, gracious visitation, and providence."[121] In Acts 1:20, Peter quoted Psalms 108:8 (109:8 in the English Bibles), and the Hebrew text utilizes the word פְּקֻדָּתוֹ (*pequddatow*), the third-person masculine form of פְּקֻדָּה (*pequddah*), which translates to "his office," in English.[122] The Septuagint, for the same verse, employs ἐπισκοπήν (*episcopēn*) for פְּקֻדָּתוֹ (*pequddatow*) and translates ἐπισκοπήν (*episcopēn*) to "office of overseer," in English.[123] In 1 Chron 26:30, the Scripture states, "Seven hundred were officers among them in Israel." The word "officers" in the English text is תִּפְקֻדַת (*pequddat*), the feminine singular noun form of the Hebrew word הַפְּקֻדָּה (*pequddah*), and in the Septuagint appears as ἐπισκέψεως (*episkepseōs*), which is the genitive singular feminine noun form of *episkopos*.[124] An example of God's gracious oversight is in Job 10:12: "Thou hast granted me life and favour, and thy visitation [פְּקֻדָּה] hath preserved my spirit." In Num 4:16, the priest Eleazar, Aaron's son, held the responsibility for "the oversight [פְּקֻדַּת] of all the Tabernacle. And of all that therein is, in the sanctuary, and the vessels thereof." The usage ἐπισκοπή found in 1 Tim 3:1, "If a man desire the office of a bishop," like as in Acts 1:20, references a role of service and leadership within the collective of the First-Century Church.[125] In addition, these overseers were to function as guardians of the collective church body just as shepherds kept watch over and guarded their flocks.[126] Thus, the leadership role within the church inferred that it brought God's power and providence and came to be defined by the service rendered unto the whole church.

120. "ἐπισκοπή, ης," L&N 1:463.

121. Thayer, "ἐπισκοπή," *Thayer's Greek-English Lexicon*, 242–43, in correlation with "מְקֻדָּה," BDBG, 824.

122. Green, *Interlinear Bible*, 500.

123. Brenton, *Septuagint with Apocrypha*, 766.

124. Brenton, *Septuagint with Apocrypha*, 562. Compared with *Interlinear Bible*, 376.

125. "ἐπισκοπή, ης," L&N 1:541–42.

126. Condon, "Church Offices," 77.

Ἐπισκοπή (*episcopē*) appears in 1 Tim 3:1 as "the office of a bishop" and in Luke 19:44 and 1 Pet 2:12 as "visitation." Regarding the passages of Luke and 1 Peter, the text describes the onset and arrival of divine power, bringing oversight and judgment of one's life.[127] One may infer from this explanation that when the ἐπίσκοπος (*episkopos*) visited the various home churches under their direction as the head of a metropolis, they brought God's divine power, doctrine, reproof, and correction depending on what was needed. Chapter eight of Acts presents an example of the church's overseers in action. Philip, a deacon/minister exercising the gift ministry of an evangelist, preached Christ in Samaria, and through his preaching and miracles, he won the whole town (Acts 8:5–6). The apostles in Jerusalem hear of Philip's success, and they dispatch Peter and John to deliver necessary oversight and spiritual visitation to Samaria (8:14). In Acts 15:36, the text states, "And some days after Paul said unto Barnabas, Let us go again and visit [ἐπισκεψώμεθα: "let us look after"] our brethren in every city where we have preached the word of the LORD, and see how they do." The Greek word for "visit"—ἐπισκεψώμεθα is the aorist subjunctive first-person plural middle voice verb form of ἐπισκέπτομαι, which is a cognate of ἐπισκοπή.[128] In excising a visitation unto the in-home churches and groups of believers they had established, Paul and Barnabas carried out the responsibilities of overseers—*episkopoi* within the First-Century Church, for the benefit of the people.

The Greek verb ἐπισκοπέω (*episkopeō*) has three possible meanings within the New Testament. The first is "to care for or to look after with the implication of continuous responsibility."[129] For example, Heb 12:15 states, "Looking diligently [ἐπισκοπέω] lest any man fall of the grace of God." The immediate context deals with individuals receiving correction from God via their overseers (contextually implied), similar to fathers training and educating their children (Heb 12:5–11). Therefore, the individual, an overseer, was charged with delivering instruction, reproof, and correction to preserve the believers and prevent them from falling from the grace of God. Another meaning of ἐπισκοπέω (*episkopeō*) is "to oversee," watch over, or to accept the oversight of another, such as in 1 Pet 5:2,

---

127. "ἐπισκοπή, ης," L&N 1:453.

128. Ἐπισκέπτομαι is utilized in the Septuagint often for פָּקַד: "To look upon or after, to inspect, examine with the eyes," ref. Acts 7:23; Judg 15:1; "Hebraistically, to look upon in order to help or benefit." Thayer, "ἐπισκέπτομαι," *Thayer's Greek-English Lexicon*, 242.

129. "ἐπισκοπέω," L&N 1:463.

which states, "Feed the flock which is among you, taking up the oversight [ἐπισκοποῦντες]."[130] The third meaning of ἐπισκοπέω (*episkopeō*) is "to visit, to take care of," as occurs in Matt 25:43: "(I was) sick and in prison and ye visited [ἐπεσκέψασθέ] me not." Ἐπισκοπέω is the root word for ἐπεσκέψασθέ in this verse reference.[131] Therefore, these examples of the verb ἐπισκοπέω present an understanding that an ἐπίσκοπος (*episkopos*) assumes the oversight of others and exercises continuous diligent care, visiting and looking after the wellbeing of those people in their charge.

Though the word ἐπίσκοπος (*episkopos*) is Greek, the position of the overseer did not originate with the Greeks, or more specifically, the Athenians. Instead, the Athenians copied the role from the Achaemenid empire's office of authority for their imperial overseer, "The King's Eye."[132] The king of the Achaemenid Empire, Cyrus the Great, anointed by God, ended the Babylonian captivity for the exiled Israelites, permitted them to return to Jerusalem and rebuild their temple, heralding the Second Temple era (2 Chr 36:23; Ezra 1:1–8; Isa 44:28, 45:1). Considering the honor—the OT Scriptures lauded Cyrus for his treatment and favor towards the Jewish people recorded in the books of Ezra and Isaiah—one should not underestimate the influence his reign and empire would have over the Israelites. Following Cyrus, the Hellenistic empire under Alexander the Great also granted the Jewish people the freedom to worship and conduct their lives again under the laws of the OT, for which they were grateful. One can see how, after enduring the Babylonian captivity and being freed from it, the Jewish people absorbed some of the influences of the two successive empires, which dealt more favorably with them, such as the role of the *episkopos*. In the Achaemenid empire, the "King's Eye" duties included oversite of the founding of new cities and legal advisement of foreign and domestic governing officials.[133] As a comparison, under the Athenian government, the *episkopos* were appointed civilians who did not have a specific physical station but toured the empire's major cities, like the King's Eye, and similarly, they too, were explicitly charged with tax and tribute collection and fraud prevention.[134] Their authority

---

130. In this usage, ἐπισκοπέω is in the nominative masculine plural active present participle form. Mounce and Mounce, "ἐπισκοποῦντες," *Interlinear New Testament*, 902. Thayer, "ἐπισκοπέω," *Thayer's Greek-English Lexicon*, 242.

131. "ἐπισκοπέω," L&N 1:463.

132. Balcer, "Athenian Episkopos and the Achaemenid 'King's Eye,'" 252.

133. Balcer, "Athenian Episkopos and the Achaemenid 'King's Eye,'" 252–53.

134. Balcer, "Athenian Episkopos and the Achaemenid 'King's Eye,'" 252–54.

came from the highest levels of exercised power in both the Achaemenid and Athenian empires, which seems to have set the example for the role of the *episkopos* in the early church.

In the New Testament, the word ἐπίσκοπος (*episkopos*) refers to the individual(s) fulfilling the role in the First-Century Church of an overseer, and the ἐπίσκοπος was an adaptation of the royal office of the Achaemenid Empire by the Greeks. Ἐπίσκοπος has σκοπος as its root word, and σκοπος means "an observer, a watchman; the distant mark looked at, the goal or end one has in view (Phil 3:14)," combined with the prefix ἐπι, "upon, on, at by, before, against, over."[135] Therefore, an ἐπίσκοπος (*episkopos*) is "an overseer, a man charged with the duty of seeing that things to be done by others are done rightly, any curator, guardian, or superintendent," equivalent for the Hebrew word פָּקִיד (*paqiyd*) occurring in Neh 11:9: "And Joel the son of Zichri was their overseer."[136] To establish a democratic system of government in allied cities, the Delian League commissioned ἐπίσκοποι (*epískopoi*) to accomplish the task.[137] The early church utilized the concept of the overseer from the OT but with the Greek linguistic equivalency, further proving the influence of the Septuagint in Jewish culture. Jesus had left his twelve apostles responsible for continuing his work; therefore, they were the church's first appointed overseers (Acts 1:20). Later, the title of overseer was bequeathed to a position of authority that did not require the holder to be one of the gift ministries, though someone with a gift ministry could also function as an overseer, as well as a minister or elder. Paul entrusted Timothy, who was both an apostle and an overseer, with the charge of all the in-home churches of the metropolis of Ephesus (1 Tim 1:3). Likewise, he also charged Titus with the oversight and care of all on the island of Crete (Titus 1:5). In Acts 20:28, Paul, addressing the leaders in Ephesus, states, "Take heed therefore unto yourselves, and to all the flock, over the which the Holy Ghost hath made you overseers [ἐπίσκοπος], to feed the church of God, which he hath purchased with his own blood." Indicating there was more than one overseer in the metropolis, which most likely included the surrounding areas.[138]

135. Thayer, "ἐπι,"; "σκοπος," *Thayer's Greek-English Lexicon*, 231–36; 579.

136. Thayer, "ἐπίσκοπος," *Thayer's Greek-English Lexicon*, 243, in correlation with "פָּקִיד," BDBG, 824.

137. Rhodes and Markschies, "Episkopos, Episkopoi."

138. References to Ephesus, leadership at Ephesus, and the church—body of believers—at Ephesus are widely understood to mean not only the inhabitants of Ephesus proper but also its suburbs and the region that was directly involved with the city-life, as Ephesus was the first and largest metropolis of Asia under Roman rule. Metzger and

The Ephesian overseers were ordained to their roles by the Holy Spirit. Their duties were to serve the congregation instruction in right living, reproof, and correction to preserve them before God. Just as the apostles performed signs, miracles, and wonders, any person stepping into the role of an ἐπίσκοπος (*episkopos*) has to pray and believe to manifest the power of God unto the household of God (Acts 4:24–31).

In Phil 1:1, Paul wrote, "Paul and Timotheus, the servants of Jesus Christ, to all the saints in Christ Jesus which are at Philippi with bishops (ἐπισκόποις) and deacons (διακόνοις)." Like with the Ephesian church, observing the context of the first chapter of Philippians, Paul exhorts the overseers and deacons concerning the care and maintenance of the church he had established in Philippi. The entire letter of Philippians is the "operations manual" for overseers and ministers alike as it addressed both factions. As these letters circulated among all the churches, the leadership and the believers alike knew the directives and responsibilities. The leadership's relationship with the people they served was to be transparent. Philippians 1:27 declares, "Only let your conversation [conduct, behavior] be as it becometh the gospel of Christ: that whether I come and see you, or else be absent, I may hear of your affairs, that ye stand fast in one spirit, with one mind striving together for the faith of the gospel." The leaders and the people were to operate as a team, a single-minded unit with the same game plan, and that was the gospel of Christ. Further on in the letter, Paul challenged his audience to look to Jesus Christ as their primary example, God's servant (*doulos*) unto humanity (2:5–11). Though Paul could not visit them during his imprisonment in Caesar's palace, he sent the apostle Epaphroditus to teach and guide them (2:25–30). In chapter three, Paul warned them to be vigilant against enemies of the church and to mature in Christ and the hope of his return. Paul directs the leaders at Philippi to replicate his example to their congregation (Phil 4:9). In the closing of chapter four, Paul cites himself as an example that a leader's sufficiency in any situation resides in their dedication to Christ; therefore, God would supply any need they had in life. Paul closed the letter with, "The grace of our Lord Jesus Christ be with you all. Amen" (4:23).

Though Phil 1:1, 1 Tim 3:2, and Titus 1:7 all translate ἐπίσκοπον (*episkopon*), the accusative masculine singular form, or ἐπισκόποις, the dative masculine plural form, as "bishop" via King James English,

---

Coogan, *Oxford Companion to the Bible*, 189; Osborne, *Ephesians*, 3.

"overseer" would be a more appropriate title for this position. Similarly, 1 Pet 2:25 also directly references Jesus Christ as "the Shepherd and Bishop of your souls." Therefore, Jesus is the prime example to anyone stepping into the role of an overseer/bishop that they are responsible before God for the oversight and caretaking of others' souls. An overseer of the church, ἐπίσκοπος (*episkopos*), is defined by their actions as one who serves as a church leader, an overseer, watchman, and superintendent, in charge of God's work, caring for the needs of a body of believers and directing the activities of the membership as their helper and spiritual guardian.[139]

### The Minister

Traditionally, the first deacons of the First-Century Church were Stephen and the other six individuals noted in Acts chapter six.[140] Though Peter and the other apostles never directly named these members of the leadership body "deacons," like Jesus had done when he selected twelve of his faithful disciples to become his apostles, verse two contains the source of the title. Acts 6:2 reads, "Then the twelve called the multitude of the disciples unto them, and said, it is not reason that we should leave the word of God, and serve tables." The word "serve" is διακονεῖν (*diakonein*), a verb form of διάκονος (*diakonos*), and is understood in Greek literature as meaning "to be a servant, attendant, domestic; to serve, wait upon," but regarding its meaning in the context of the Scriptures, "to minister to one; render ministering offices to; to minister, i.e., supply food and the necessaries of life."[141] Someone who fulfills the position of a διάκονος (*diakonos*) is one who serves, taking upon themselves the responsibility to help and care for the needs of believers.[142] The table at which the διάκονος (*diakonos*) served others is God's spiritual table setting before the followers the gospel of Christ. In such a setting, the διάκονος (*diakonos*) is a lowly benevolent servant; still, in the assistance they give the church overseers, carrying out church business, they wield the authority of Jesus Christ with boldness.[143] The title διάκονος (*diakonos*), in conjunction with the ἐπίσκοπος, as found

---

139. "ἐπίσκοπος, ov, ὁ," L&N 1:463, 542.
140. Merkle, "Authority of Deacons in Pauline Churches," 311.
141. Thayer, "διακονεῖν," *Thayer's Greek-English Lexicon*, 137.
142. "διάκονος, ov," L&N 1:541.
143. Merkle, "Authority of Deacons in Pauline Churches," 310–16.

in Phil 1:1, indicates this is no mere servant of physical tables but is an honorific signifying a ministering agent of God's people, subordinate to the overseers.[144] They serve the collective church body as an intermediary stratum with a delegated authority between the overseers and the congregation of the in-home churches.[145] Service to the household of God and bringing others to maturity in Christ are the goals of the ecclesiastical role of the *diakonos*/minister.

As witnessed in the context of Acts chapter six, the congregation of the believers promoted the first seven deacons of the church to the apostles for confirmation. The position of a deacon was lower in rank but assisted the apostles with their ministration. The body of believers chose individuals who had proven themselves capable through the service performed prior to their ordination. In the First-Century Church, a person's ordination to a position or a task did not consist of a ceremony full of pomp, prestige, solemnity, and ceremony like in churches today. Instead, the authorities officiating laid their hands on the person or persons, prayer was said, possibly prophecy pronounced, and sometimes a fast lasting a day might be observed, but the event was simple (Acts 6:6, 13:2–3; 1 Tim 2:7, 4:14).[146] In the early years of the church's development, the deacons assisted the apostles and the overseers in ministering to the believers.[147] Not until much later does one observe deacons/deaconesses leading local church groups. For example, in Rom 16:1, Paul mentions Phebe as a deaconess of the Cenchrean church. In 1 Cor 3:5, Paul refers to himself and Apollos as "ministers [διάκονοι] by whom ye believed." Though Paul operated the gift ministry of an apostle, he served the believers in Corinth in the manner of a deacon, displaying that apostles were ministers but not all minsters were apostles (Col 1:25). The title of a deacon developed into a respected position of authority within the church, but "minister" would seem more appropriate considering the service they delivered to the people. Subordinate to and lacking the judicial authority of an ἐπίσκοπος, διάκονοι led others through their service, while an ἐπίσκοπος served the church by their leadership and oversight.[148] Chapter five of this discourse handles the qualifications for someone to be a deacon/minister. Some other noteworthy individuals who served as

144. Collins, "Deacons," 236.
145. Strauch, *Paul's Vision for the Deacons*, 51.
146. Bradshaw, *Rites of Ordination*, 17–19.
147. Fraser, "Office of Deacon," 13–19.
148. Fraser, "Office of Deacon," 18.

διάκονοι (*diakonoi*)—minsters were Tychicus (Eph 6:21; Col 4:7), Timothy (1 Thess 3:2), and Epaphras (Col 1:7). As the First-Century Church evolved, a standard developed that before an individual could serve the church as an overseer, they first proved themselves as its ministers in an official capacity.

Concerning the duties of a διάκονος (*diakonos*)—minister, many promote similarly to Merkle, who stated that "unlike the overseers or elders, the deacons do not teach as a part of their official duties. Instead, they are qualified individuals who serve the community."[149] Such a statement is an assumption based upon the fact that in 1 Timothy chapter three, Paul does not blatantly state that deacons' responsibilities include teaching. However, in the book of Acts, after the ordination of the seven to their positions of service assisting the apostles, one of the first events recorded was Stephen's discourse boldly proclaiming, correcting, and teaching the temple priesthood concerning the risen Lord and Savior Jesus Christ. Next, another of the seven, Philip expounded the Scriptures concerning Jesus to the Ethiopian eunuch. When Philip asked the eunuch if he understood what he was reading, the eunuch answered, "How can I, except some man should guide me?" (Acts 8:31). The word "guide" means to be a guide, a teacher, to lead on one's way, literally or figuratively to teach another.[150]

In Col 3:16, Paul declared to the whole church, "Let the word of Christ dwell in you richly in all wisdom; teaching and admonishing one another in psalms and hymns and spiritual songs, singing with grace in your hearts to the LORD." Every member of the church was to teach and encourage each other. Paul refers to himself as a minister—*diakonos* of the new covenant, and he was a master teacher (2 Cor 3:6). In 2 Cor 5:17–21, Paul describes how everyone who obtains salvation through Christ is entrusted with the ministry of reconciliation by Christ. It would be impossible to persuade, convert, and reconcile another individual without teaching and imparting some measure of the gospel of Christ unto them. No verse of Scripture restricts teaching only to the church leaders; they are expected to be more adept and knowledgeable, setting the example. Admittedly, the gift ministry of a teacher was bestowed upon only a few elites. Still, when the thousands of converts began meeting house to house, they repeated what the apostles had taught and imitated what

---

149. Merkle, "Authority of Deacons in Pauline Churches," 311.

150. Thayer, "ὁδηγέω," *Thayer's Greek-English Lexicon*, 437; "ὁδηγέω," L&N 1:328.

their leaders did. After the apostles added the seven *diakonoi* to their ranks, the thousands they ministered to still outnumbered the leadership. The church did not yet have the resources of the elders to assist them. Without the development of the level of the οἰκονόμος (*oikonomos*), it would have been impossible for the church to continue as it did. A logical conclusion would be that just as the church promoted the διάκονοι (*diakonoi*) from the ranks of the disciples, so also would they the οἰκονόμοι or stewards (Acts 1:15; 6:1, 7; 9:1,19, 25). There is no recorded event of an οἰκονόμος receiving a laying on of hands, prayers, or prophecy for their placement in a position like with the overseers, ministers, and elders within the First-Century Church; therefore, it should not be assumed to be so. Because the role of an οἰκονόμος—steward did not receive ordination, that does not mean they did not exist or participate in the functions of the church. First Peter 4:10 states, "As every man hath received the gift, even so minister [διακονουντες] the same one to another, as good stewards [οἰκονόμοι] of the manifold grace of God." The early church could not have maintained its unity without the household managers subordinate to and working with the overseers and ministers.

The Jewish people were accustomed to the synagogue environment where anyone could stand up and read from the Scriptures, then sit down to speak, teach, and discuss the matter. Typically, a synagogue had individuals posted as readers of the Torah or the Septuagint, but others were permitted to do so; an example of this occurs in the Gospels in the life of Jesus (Luke 4:17). Upon his conversion, Paul preached Christ in the synagogues, yet without inclusion among the early church's leadership (Acts 9:19–20), and years had passed since the events recorded in Acts chapter two before Peter evangelized to the household of the gentile Cornelius in Acts 10–12. Still, the membership of the early church had remained, by a vast majority, Jewish. To assume that the people simply dropped their Jewish heritage and traditions by the wayside would be ignorant. The OT instructed them to write the words of the word of God down and commit them to memory and then teach their children, and such actions took place in the setting of the family home. The book of Acts serves as an overview of and testifies to the development and the happenings of possibly one percent of the early church through its focus on the apostles and those who directly assisted them.[151] Suppose the

---

151. The possibility exists for divergences from the recorded standard; variance is always a subject for speculation. The primary concern of this study is the documented standards contained within the Scriptures, which should have been the standard for any

Scriptures speak on one incident happening, such as the ordination of the *diakonoi* (Acts 6:1–6), or that an in-home fellowship had a doorkeeper (Acts 12:13). In that case, it is reasonable to conclude that when the situations permitted, all of the First-Century Church operated after such a fashion, due to Paul's expressed teachings on maintaining the unity of the church as a whole (Rom 12:16, 15:6; 2 Cor 13:11; Eph 4:3, 13; Phil 1:27, 2:2).[152] As the church adopted the mode of conducting in-home fellowship meetings from the beginning, the logical conclusion is they adopted the framework from their apostles/overseers, assisted by their ministers—διάκονοι (*diakonoi* [pl.]), and then disseminated teaching and ministering, through the stewards—οἰκονόμοι (*oikonomoi* [pl.]). In maintaining order, the stewards, managing the in-home churches, answered to the ministers, and the ministers assisted and reported to the overseers.

In 1 Timothy chapter three, Paul set forth the church's leadership standards. The bishops and deacons had to prove the quality of their character by how they led their family in the confines of their home. He states, "For if a man know not how to rule his own house, how shall he take care of the church?" (1 Tim 3:5). Considering the structure and operations of the First-Century Church, this was a true statement from a microcosm and a macrocosm perspective. Preliminary to an individual managing a church within their home, leaders would have observed his family members, him in action with his family, and their collective maturity. Likewise, one's family life ought to be evaluated before one's ordination to the stratum of a deacon or bishop. Jesus declared, "He that is faithful in that which is least is faithful also in much: and he that is unjust in the least is unjust also in much" (Luke 16:10). Furthermore, Paul taught that before one could receive recognition as a deacon, they had to prove themselves through having already performed the position's responsibilities without the appointment (1 Tim 3:10). How else might the collective body of believers in a town or city be aware of someone manifesting the qualities of a deacon unless they first served at the home church level? The in-home church provided the necessary proving grounds for service at every stratum of church leadership.

---

who desired to follow the apostles' teachings.

152. Luke, the author of the book of the Acts of the Apostles, stresses that the members of the early church were of "one accord" signifying their unity (Acts 1:14, 2:1, 4:24, 5:12, 7:57, 8:6, 15:25).

## The Elder

In the book of Acts, the category of "elders" was a senior body of leadership associated with the religious and political authorities in Jerusalem (Acts 4:5, 8; 4:23; 6:12). As the early church developed and evolved, they adopted their own council(s) of elders, but the same Greek word, πρεσβύτερος (presbyteros), or a derivative is employed when referencing any such council. The πρεσβύτερος (presbyteros), or sometimes πρεσβύτεριον (presbyterion), in reference to the early church, were respected individuals (as single or as a council) of maturity both in age and wisdom that were able to handle congregational matters that interacted with the surrounding culture(s).[153] Campbell informs, "In the ancient world the elders are those who bear a title of honour, not of office, a title that is imprecise, collective and representative, and rooted in the ancient family or household."[154] After the church developed a locus of operations in Antioch of Syria, Acts 15 records that both the Antioch and Jerusalem churches had a congress of apostles with a council of elders assisting them in the early church's leadership. Acts 15:2–29 records the occurrence of the apostles working in tandem with the elders to resolve an issue with the collective that caused division between the believers. In Paul's letter to Titus, he instructed that elders were to be ordained in every city under Titus's oversight to assist with maintaining order (Titus 1:5).

Stemming from the historical and cultural influences of the Old Testament, the Hebrew people were well-acquainted with the purpose and profit elders provided. The Hebrew people were not unique in their respect and reverence for the elders of their society. Ancient societies were family-oriented and revered the family's elders for their accumulated experience and wisdom. One observes in *The Tebtunis Papyri* that the people consulted with an elected council of elders who oversaw their farming practices in Ancient Egypt.[155] It is no coincidence that Moses selected seventy elders (Exod 24:1–9) from the ranks of the children of Israel because Exod 1:5 declares, "And all the souls that came out of the loins of Jacob were seventy souls." These would undoubtedly have formed the more prominent families within the twelve tribes. When Moses demanded Pharaoh release the people, the elders accompanied him, displaying their support for their leader (Exod 3:18). In Ezra, the elders formed a governing

---

153. "πρεσβύτεριον; πρεσβύτερος," L&N 1:134; 542–43.
154. Campbell, "Elders: Seniority in Earliest Christianity," 187.
155. Grenfell et al., *Tebtunis Papyri*, 103–5.

body for the exiles that returned to Jerusalem (Ezra 5:5, 6:7–14).[156] The elders at the city gates levied judgments of redemption, humiliation, and punishment.[157] As noted previously, the leadership structure of the temple in the Second Temple period included a body of elders. Thus, throughout Hebrew history and culture, individuals honored with the title of "elder" provided wisdom, judgments, and support, commanded authority, received reverence, and assisted with the day's politics.

Nearly every society in the Ancient Near East revered their elders, whether they applied their wisdom and experience in the familial setting or a more social one, such as guiding matters of city and state. In the Ancient Near East, one's elders, the heads of the households who were revered, bore the titles of *zekanim*, *presbyteroi*, *gerontes*, and *seniores*—all of which are generally converted to "elders" in English—but beyond the familial and communal environments, the "elders" later evolved into the titular office of the church.[158] Concerning the elders of the First-Century Church, David Miller argues against Hellenistic influence as the catalyst that led to the development of elders in the early church, citing a lack of evidence.[159] In the early formation of the First-Century Church, with the vast majority of converts being Jewish, Miller finds the synagogue format to be the strongest influencer for the followers of Christ.[160] In the early period of church development, elders are not mentioned until the eleventh chapter of Acts. Paul's instruction to Titus to ordain elders over the believers in Crete to help with the establishing and maintaining order there can be compared with how a body of Jewish elders might initiate a new synagogue (Titus 1:5). However, Miller draws a stark contrast between elders in a synagogue and NT church elders, for church elders may teach while those in a synagogue do not (1 Tim 5:17). Elders in a synagogue bear administrative duties and administer discipline within the ranks of those serving; in the church, elders dispense wise counsel to youths in the congregation.[161] The ordination of elders by Paul and Barnabas in Acts 14:23, after the churches had been initiated and just prior to their departure, has the appearance that the elders were installed to guide and assist those Paul and Barnabas left in charge. Miller concludes that

---

156. Merkle, *Elder and Overseer*, 27.
157. Albertz and Schmitt, *Family and Household Religion*, 398.
158. Elliott, "Elders as Leaders," 686.
159. Miller, "Uniqueness of New Testament Church Eldership," 317.
160. Miller, "Uniqueness of New Testament Church Eldership," 319.
161. Miller, "Uniqueness of New Testament Church Eldership," 322.

the development of church elders, while similar to other cultures, had more aspects that differed, making them unique, just as the First-Century Church was unique and differed from other contemporary religions.[162]

As the First-Century Church developed across Asia Minor amongst gentile cultures and societies, the development of councils of elders within new branches of outreach would have been both practical and profitable. In the Greco-Roman realm, which dominated the region, the πρεσβύτεροι (*presbyteroi* [pl.]) were the revered elders of one's family and clan, and those of the wealthiest and most influential families more often were local community, state, and governmental leaders.[163] In Roman society, the *gens*, or the family, both immediate and one's clan, were a dominant focus of life.[164] The family elders taught their progeny to revere and follow the *Lares*—the gods familiar to that particular family that served as spiritual guardians of the home.[165] When Christians converted the familial elders, or the *paterfamilias*, in most cases, the entire household and possibly even the extended family converted. Such was the case in the conversion of Cornelius (Acts 10:1–11:18), Lydia (Acts 16:11–15), the Roman jailor (Acts 16:25–34), and Crispus the synagogue president (Acts 18:1–11). If enough elders in a town converted to Christianity, the majority of that town would most likely follow. Finally, like with Titus, appointing revered familial and social elders to the church presbytery ensured the church's footing in a town and area.

Like in all of the other positions of guidance and leadership in the church, women could have participated on a council of elders because, in 1 Tim 5:2, the epistle attends to "elder women," and the Greek word employed is the feminine of πρεσβύτερος (*presbyteros*).[166] Considering the context deals with the importance of elder leadership and their guidance for the younger members and that the overarching context of the epistle is the order, qualities, and qualifications of leadership, to simply state that these elders, both men *and* women, referred to in this section of Scriptures, were merely *older* is diminutive of their roles and importance. These women must have provided a noteworthy and profitable service to the church. Ehrman states, "Women may have enjoyed a significant representation among these unofficial early church leaders."

162. Miller, "Uniqueness of New Testament Church Eldership," 327.
163. Campbell, "Elders: Seniority in Earliest Christianity," 184–85.
164. Beard, *Religions of Rome*, 17.
165. Beard, *Religions of Rome*, 30–31.
166. Mounce and Mounce, *Interlinear New Testament*, 811.

He continues, "Women in house-churches appear to have played a much more prominent role than they did in the community at large."[167] Such prominence, especially in light of exemplary women in the church such as Phebe, Priscilla, Junia, Tryphena, and others, should generate the possibility for women who served as elders in the early church community because these notable women, as they aged, could have filled that role. In addition, the elders aided the bishops and deacons by serving in related ministerial capacities within the church (Jas 5:14). In the early church, strict lines of demarcation did not exist; instead, they shared the load of responsibilities and needs. First Peter 5:5 states, "Likewise, ye younger, submit yourselves unto the elder. Yea, all of you be subject one to another, and be clothed with humility: for God resisteth the proud, and giveth grace to the humble." With the "younger" members, possibly younger in age or newly converted, submitting themselves for tutelage from the elders, such practices demonstrate apprenticeships at work within the body of believers and ensure order within the community.[168] Due to such humility, the positions of authority, leadership, and council were liquid-like and malleable to meet and serve the needs of the people, beginning with the topmost, the apostles and elders.

Just as the early church separated from the temple in Jerusalem, it would do similarly with the synagogues in cities across Asia Minor. Paul instructed Titus to "appoint elders [πρεσβυτέρους] in every town" (Titus 1:5 NIV).[169] Titus served Crete as their apostle commissioned to them and in lieu of Paul and as their ἐπίσκοπος, but he was not originally from there; it was his duty to select elders to a council that would advise him.[170] Church traditions regard Titus as a bishop, and the authority bequeathed to him by Paul seems to support the title, though no Scripture calls Titus an ἐπίσκοπος.[171] The dominant view drawn from Paul's address to Titus has been since ἐπίσκοπος is in the singular in Titus 1:7, and he is not directed to appoint any other to the role, by default, he was to be Crete's ἐπίσκοπος; therefore a college of πρεσβύτεροι, each a representative of a town, would assist Titus.[172]

---

167. Ehrman, *After the New Testament*, 429–30.
168. Elliott, "Elders as Leaders," 690–91.
169. Mounce and Mounce, *Interlinear New Testament*, 827.
170. Young, "On ΕΠΙΣΚΟΠΟΣ AND ΠΠΕΣΒΥΤΕΠΟΣ," 142–46.
171. Britannica, "Saint Titus."
172. Young, "On ΕΠΙΣΚΟΠΟΣ AND ΠΠΕΣΒΥΤΕΠΟΣ," 142–44.

The First-Century Church most likely developed its presbytery from the direct influence of the Jewish synagogue and the indirect influence of Jewish culture and history.[173] As the Greek and Roman cultures also revered their elders, eldership within the First-Century Church would have presented a shared social connection with the society surrounding them. The NT does not record the elders exercising oversight of the churches of the Body of Christ like the bishops/overseers, nor are they seen ministering to the physical and spiritual needs of smaller groups like the deacons/ministers, but they do deliver knowledge and judicial disciplines benefiting church members at all levels.[174] The church elders served as a source of wisdom to aid the church's leaders in negotiating social, cultural, and political situations. In addition, the elders were proven, trusted, and honored leaders of families that hosted in-home churches, supported and encouraged weaker believers, and counseled the overseers and ministers of the city where they lived. Within the household code and dynamic that framed the First-Century Church, replacing the temple/synagogue dynamic, a πρεσβυτέρους could serve as a manager of an in-home church. In the letters to Titus and Timothy, the duties attributed to familial and societal elders, both men and women, of guiding and setting examples for the younger members reflect the household codes of conduct.[175] Not only in the first century but into the second, πρεσβύτερος and πρεσβύτεροι did not refer to an office of authority within the First-Century Church but denoted senior members of the community worthy of reverence who contributed as an advisory council.[176]

## The Steward

In Luke chapter sixteen, Jesus told a parable about a rich man who had a servant who was the manager of his household and was wasting his master's money (Luke 16:1–8). The word utilized in the KJV is steward, which in Greek is the word οἰκονόμον (*oikonomon*), a form of οἰκονόμος, which both the NIV and the NASB render as "manager."[177] The οἰκονόμος (*oikonomos*) is "one who is in charge of running a household—manager of

---

173. Lightfoot, *St. Paul's Epistle to the Philippians*, 190–92.
174. Fraser, "Office of Deacon," 16–18.
175. Young, "On ΕΠΙΣΚΟΠΟΣ AND ΠΠΕΣΒΥΤΕΠΟΣ," 144–45.
176. Young, "On ΕΠΙΣΚΟΠΟΣ AND ΠΠΕΣΒΥΤΕΠΟΣ," 146.
177. Mounce and Mounce, *Interlinear New Testament*, 297.

a household, steward" and in addition to that, also, "one who is in charge of, one who is responsible for, administrator, manager."[178] In Hellenistic culture, which influenced the Jewish culture of the day, the δοῦλοι (*douloi*) of the household were subordinate to the οἰκονόμος (*oikonomos*).[179] Luke 16:1–3 exemplifies this position in one of Jesus' parables, the rich man and the steward. In the record, the Greek word employed for "steward" is οἰκονόμος (*oikonomos*), for he was head of the household affairs—his stewardship—οἰκονόμια (*oikonomia*).

In Acts chapter two, the congregation expanded in size and numbers, so the believers started holding meetings in one another's homes. Though the temple at Jerusalem remained the epicenter of Jewish culture, as the fledgling church continued adding people to its numbers and ranks, the in-home church fellowships became the focus of their activities (Acts 5:42). Beginning with the conversion of thousands to the faith on the day of Pentecost in Acts chapter two, the temple in Jerusalem was no longer a suitable place for the gatherings of the early church. Jesus had set a precedent during his ministry of taking his gospel to people's homes. In Acts chapter two, the apostles did likewise. The text bears witness, "And they (all who believed from verses 42–45) continuing daily with one accord in the temple, and breaking bread from house to house, did eat their meat with gladness and singleness of heart" (Acts 2:46). Thus began an evolutionary change for this offshoot of Judaism, from being a temple-based faith to a home-church centered one. The Acts of the Apostles records the transition the First-Century Church made from the style of the temple's organization and hierarchy, or that of a synagogue, to a more flexible home-based organization with a stratified leadership body. As they established more home churches, there would have been a need for a manager for each in-home church. In the culture of that day, an individual who was the head of a household and owned his own property was known as an οἰκονόμος; this cultural significance carried over to the application of the title in the early church.[180] Though they may not have been ordained like a *diakonos* or *presbyteros,* such was the importance and the role of the οἰκονόμος (*oikonomos*).

The early church flourished under the Greek philosophy of democracy, and its congregations expanded and exploded within the home-household environment. Campbell assumes that in a single-family

178. "οἰκονόμος," L&N 1:477; 521.
179. Young, "On ΕΠΙΣΚΟΠΟΣ AND ΠΡΕΣΒΥΤΕΠΟΣ," 144.
180. Goodrich, "Overseers as Stewards," 85–86.

arrangement or if several families were joining together, the situations maintained a degree of informality, and the elder of a household, who already had the respect of its members, took up a natural position of leadership.[181] While the situation Campbell proposed may have occurred, another possibility also exists. In Greco-Roman culture, the person who managed a city under the rule of the Roman Empire was an οἰκονόμος (*oikonomos*). For example, Rom 16:23 mentions "Erastus, the chamberlain of the city." Erastus was the administrator of the city's affairs, an official bearing rank and status who became a close minister and assistant to Paul alongside Timothy (Acts 19:22; 2 Tim 4:20).[182] As Greek culture recognized and respected the authoritative position of the οἰκονόμος (*oikonomos*), there is no cause nor evidence to suggest that the early church would not conduct itself in like manner. Paul presented himself as a manager or steward of God's affairs concerning the followers of the First-Century Church, which he referred to as the "household of God" (1 Cor 4:1; Titus 1:7; Eph 2:19).[183] Likewise, the apostles were the managers/stewards of the collective body of believers of the First-Century Church. After the apostles, next the ἐπίσκοπος (*episkopos*) of a town or region was required to set the example for other leaders as the οἰκονόμος (*oikonomos*) or steward of God's household (Titus 1:7) on a larger scale.[184] The steward of an in-home church, an οἰκονόμος (*oikonomos*), imitated the ἐπίσκοπος (*episkopos*) but on a smaller scale for the believers that met in his home. Therefore, in the early church, individuals appointed to the specific leadership position of managing or conducting the in-home churches were "stewards": οἰκονόμος (*oikonomos*). On some occasions, the one running the in-home church group did not own the house where a particular group of believers gathered. The steward was then responsible for leading an in-home church but without subverting the authority of the family elder or patriarch. Within the household dynamic, there existed the possibility of a πρεσβύτερος leading an in-home church or an οἰκονόμος conducting it with a πρεσβύτερος providing counsel, assistance, and his home for the group of believers to perform their services.[185] The household codes offered a sense of flexibility between socio-religious positions of authority and respect in the First-Century Church that was not available

---

181. Campbell, "Elders: Seniority in Earliest Christianity," 183–84.
182. Goodrich, "Erastus of Corinth," 587–88.
183. Danker, "οἰκονόμος," *Concise Greek-English Lexicon*, 248.
184. Young, "On ΕΠΙΣΚΟΠΟΣ AND ΠΠΕΣΒΥΤΕΠΟΣ," 144.
185. Campbell, "Elders," 184–86.

within the rigidity of the temple format. If the early church brain was the councils of apostles and elders, the in-home church was its beating heart.

In the Greek language, the root of the words οἰκονόμος and its cognates, such as οἰκονόμον, is οἰκεῖος (*oikeios*), which is defined as "belonging to a house or a family, domestic and intimate; belonging to one's household; belonging to God's household."[186] This definition further establishes the οἰκονόμος (*oikonomos*) as the manager of the household church or its steward. For comparison and distinction, a cognate related to οἰκονόμος but of a lower value was the οἰκέτης (*oiketēs*), which was a household servant but was not a manager of the household and was a more restricted position than a δοῦλος (*doulos*).[187] In the culture of that day, a household encompassed more roles than may be accounted for today, such as the nuclear family, servants, slaves, and hired workers.[188] In Acts 10:7, after the angel delivered its message to Cornelius, being obedient, Cornelius commissions two "household servants," οἰκέτων (plural of *oiketēs*) and a loyal soldier, to go find and bring back Peter. He did not send the manager of the servants in his house, but two servants of a lower cast and with less responsibility from his staff. The church of God, with Jesus Christ as its head, is supposed to function like a great household, with various tiers of leadership, positions of service, and parts for each member to play so that it increases with more souls won to it. The code of the household and its implications are essential for one's understanding of the dynamics of how the early church functioned.[189] The household metaphor and imagery are superior to that of the temple and more endearing because they generate a sense of belonging for each person incorporated into the household.

The NT names only a few individuals this study could refer to as stewards in the First-Century Church. In 1 Cor 16:19, Paul mentions Aquila and Priscilla "with the church that is in their house." In the Greek text, the wording is specifically ordered αὐτῶν ἐκκλησίᾳ, "their church," with αὐτῶν as the genitive masculine third-person personal plural possessive pronoun denoting ownership, or in this case, direct responsibility over that group. It is believed that Paul wrote 1 Corinthians from Ephesus, indicating that Priscilla and Aquila were in the vicinity.[190] The Scriptures display they conducted an in-home church wherever they went, from

---

186. Thayer, "οἰκεῖος," *Thayer's Greek-English Lexicon*, 439.
187. Thayer, "οἰκέτης," *Thayer's Greek-English Lexicon*, 439.
188. "οἰκονομέω; οἰκονομία, ας," L&N 1:520.
189. MacDonald, *Pauline Churches a Socio-Historical Study*, 105.
190. Coogan, *New Oxford Annotated Bible*, New Testament, 242.

Corinth to Rome to Ephesus (Acts 18:1–2, Acts 18:24–27; Rom 16:3–5). Then, in Col 4:17, Paul extends his greetings to the Laodicean believers and to "Nympha and the church in her house."[191] Like the passage concerning Aquila and Priscilla, this verse credits the stewardship of an in-home church to Nympha. In Greek, it states αὐτῆς ἐκκλησίαν, with αὐτῆς as the genitive feminine third-person singular personal possessive pronoun indicating it was "her church in her home." Again, a noteworthy woman excelled in a leadership capacity in the First-Century Church. She may have been a widow, and the home was left to her by her late husband, but the context does not indicate whether she was or was not a widow. Nympha's testimony as a leader attests to the importance of women in the early church.[192] Philemon also served the believers by managing a church in his home (Phlm 1:1–2). In the conclusions of Paul's epistles, he often mentions significant individuals and couples who operated in-home churches. According to the apostle Peter, every person who has received the gift of God's Spirit and everlasting life through Christ Jesus is directed to serve/minister to one another and be a praiseworthy steward (οἰκονόμος—oikonomos) of God's grace (1 Pet 4:10). Paul challenged the church of the Corinthian believers to rise in their maturity and responsibility as stewards—οἰκονόμοι (oikonomoi [pl.]) for Christ and God (1 Cor 4:1–2). Paul's letters of Galatians, Ephesians, and Colossians emphasize an οἰκεῖος—household code of ethics, structure, and conduct meant to guide the first century with a cohesive familial unity.[193] This code finds its roots in Paul's illustration of "the one body" in 1 Cor 12, and the epistles of Timothy, Titus, and Peter build upon the code to help ensure the collective church's continuation into the second century and beyond.

Later, in 1 Tim 3:8, Paul writes, "Let the deacons be the husbands of one wife, ruling their children and their own houses well." This verse infers that when possible, a successful family and, most likely, a home-based church were the proving grounds for one who desired to serve as a deacon/minister. In his letter to Titus, under the listing of qualifications for one to become a bishop/overseer, that person would first have served

---

191. This quotation is from the NIV in *The Zondervan Greek and English Interlinear New Testament (NASB/NIV)*, 785, by Mounce and Mounce. The KJV reads, "Nymphas, and the church which is in his house." This would seem to be a translational error as "Nympha"—Νύμφαν is an accusative feminine noun which agrees with the feminine possessive pronoun and "church"—ἐκκλησίαν is also in its feminine form. Both the NIV and NASB recognize Nympha as a woman.

192. MacDonald, *Pauline Churches a Socio-Historical Study*, 105.

193. MacDonald, *Pauline Churches a Socio-Historical Study*, 104–5.

as a "steward [οἰκονόμον] of God" (Titus 1:7). Logic dictates that, excluding rare exceptional occasions, an individual progresses through necessary stages demonstrating proficiency with handling the responsibilities and duties of each level of leadership before promotion from one of lesser accountability to the next with its increased obligations. Just as the management of the home church was a prerequisite for ministers, so was it also essential for the role of the overseers. The described progression was a framework for organizing the First-Century Church collective and provided guidelines that remained flexible to the congregation's needs.

Concerning the previously mentioned household code, the entire body of believers is called the household of faith and the household of God; therefore, every overseer must serve the church collective as God's steward (Gal 6:10; Eph 2:19). Thus, in the later years of the church, a progression of ascendency evolved. First, one demonstrated proficiency with conducting their family and then as manager of a household church—steward. Next, that person could attain the level of a minister and afterward possibly receive promotion to an overseer. To this day, the Greek Orthodox Church recognizes a position bearing a cognitive title within its ranks of leadership: the Economos.[194] The οἰκονόμος (*oikonomos*)—steward would have been the early church's first notable leadership stratum for believers seeking others' examples to follow.

## THE ASSISTANTS AND APPRENTICESHIP LEVELS

The following strata of leaders within the church, namely the *hypēretēs*, *doulos*, and *thyrōros*, were subordinate to all other leaders this study has observed so far, and they should be regarded as assistants, trainees, and apprentices to the gift ministries and the stewards, overseers, ministers, and elders. This discourse has interwoven the illustration of the household throughout its study of each of the strata of leaders, and it is through this illustration that the positions of the *hypēretēs*, *doulos*, and *thyrōros* truly become anchored to the model of the stratified leadership of the First-Century Church. The *hypēretēs*, *doulos*, and *thyrōros* were necessary servant roles in the larger and more prominent households of Jewish and Greco-Roman societies because there were greater numbers of people within a family than traditional average families, even to the point of having servants who cared for the needs of other servants. Even though these

---

194. Orthodox Observer News, "His Eminence Archbishop Elpidophoros."

levels of leadership do not receive the attention in the Scriptures that other previous ones have, the lack of scriptural acknowledgment does not lessen their importance, nor the respect they would have received from church-service attendees because of the service these minor leaders dispensed. These service positions also afforded the overseers, ministers, and church managers specifically dedicated apprentices to train for the ever-expanding body of believers. This study now focuses on the minor leadership roles of assistants, servants, and doorkeepers within the early church.

## The Assistant

The ὑπηρέτης (*hypēretēs*) was an assistant's position, derived from the Greek navy, for the term literally translates from the Greek as "under rower." In his studies of the Greek navy, J. S. Morrison concluded that on a trireme, the *hypēresia*—ὑπηρεσία (plural of ὑπηρέτης—*hypēretēs*) were not enslaved people but freemen and were not only oarsmen but a group that included the helmsmen of the ship.[195] Morrison further relates that the *hyperesia* was a commissioned part of the Greek navy separate from the seamen—*nautai* on a vessel and the two divisions of oarsmen who performed the rowing, the *stratiotai* and the *epibatai*, for unpaid slaves were often used in these positions.[196] Furthermore, in Greek literature from before the advent of Christ and the NT, in the Greek navy, they were comparable with the ranks of the *kybernētai*—helmsmen, *keleustai*—bosun (in charge of the rowers), and others.[197] The naval role of a *hypēretēs* evolved and was adapted to Greek culture to mean an assistant but of a specific kind, one who specialized in their responsibilities, like an aide-de-camp or a commander's staff-officer, and was not a generic servant available for any task.[198]

Later in the Greek literature of the NT, the meaning of ὑπηρέτης (*hypēretēs*) changed, as it is translated into English as an officer, minister, or servant, and whether it was in reference to a king's attendant, an officer of the Sanhedrin, a servant of the synagogue, or a minister,

---

195. Morrison, "Hyperesia in Naval Contexts," 49–50.

196. Morrison, "Hyperesia in Naval Contexts," 52–54.

197. Jordan, "Meaning of the Technical Term 'Hyperesia' in Naval Contexts," 188–89.

198. Jordan, "Meaning of the Technical Term 'Hyperesia' in Naval Contexts," 190.

the word meant "anyone who aids another in any work."[199] This position is a humble one, as the service a ὑπηρέτης (*hypēretēs*) provides is non-specific, but instead whatever the situation requires.[200] In Acts 26, Paul presented his testimony to King Agrippa and related his conversion from a church persecutor to one of its chief promoters. In Paul's monologue of his conversion, he quoted Jesus Christ's instruction: "But rise, and stand upon thy feet: for I have appeared unto thee for this purpose, to make thee a minister and a witness both of these things which thou hast seen, and of those things in the which I will appear unto thee" (Acts 26:16). In this verse, the word "minister," is ὑπηρέτην (*hypēretēn*) is the accusative masculine singular form of ὑπηρέτης (*hypēretēs*): Christ appointed Paul as his personal ὑπηρέτην (*hypēretēn*), an assistant whose duty it was to minister to the master's needs whatever he required.

In 1 Cor 4:1, Paul wrote, "Let a man so account of us, as of the ministers of Christ and stewards of the mysteries of God." The word "ministers" in the KJV is the Greek word ὑπηρέτας (*hypēretas*), the accusative masculine plural of ὑπηρέτης (*hypēretēs*). In that verse, Paul addressed the Corinthian Church, asking each to consider themselves Jesus Christ's personal assistant. In addition to being Christ's ministers, Paul challenged them to see themselves as stewards, οἰκονόμος (*oikonomos*) for God. The 1 Cor 4:1 passage supports the fact that people often served in dual capacities for the early church. In the early days of the church, a clearly defined and strict regimentation of leadership positions did not exist but evolved over time. Still, leaders took upon themselves multiple roles because the supreme goal was the service of God for Christ unto the church. In Acts chapter thirteen, when the church leaders in Antioch commissioned Barnabas and Saul, John Mark was appointed to serve Barnabas and Saul as their "minister" (Acts 13:5). The word "minister" is ὑπηρέτης (*hypēretēs*); John Mark was their assistant, sent to aid them in spreading the Gospel of Christ. In addition to assisting and serving them, John Mark was uniquely positioned to learn from their examples and receive training. Though a ὑπηρέτης was not a glorified position, it was recognized and respected.

The role of the ὑπηρέτης (*hypēretēs*) was widely recognized and respected in the Hellenistic world amongst politicians and the military as well as other types of professionals, who provided aid and assistance to

---

199. Thayer, "ὑπηρέτης," *Thayer's Greek-English Lexicon*, 641–42.
200. "ὑπηρέτης, ου," L&N 1:460.

other official titles such as *oikonomos, epimelētēs, grammateus, archōn, epistatēs,* and *tamias*.[201] Bureaucratically, a ὑπηρέτης (*hypēretēs*) was a minor governmental official who aided a senator or other governmental official.[202] Someone who served as another's ὑπηρέτης (*hypēretēs*) would be treated as their superior's envoy. This immediate assistance to another respected position in society, such as a senator or other role, provided the one serving as a ὑπηρέτης (*hypēretēs*) the opportunity to learn that role's functions and responsibilities so that one day the servant might ascend to the position they once aided.

In Hellenistic culture, the ὑπηρέτης (*hypēretēs*) was distinguishable from the δοῦλος (*doulos*) because the ὑπηρέτης (*hypēretēs*) was free and, in a majority of cases, paid wages for his service; in contrast, the *doulos* did not have a choice, was not paid but instead depended upon the master for all physical needs.[203] In the structure of the early church and for the promulgation of the Christian movement, the ὑπηρέτης (*hypēretēs*) not only assisted but also learned and, in a manner, apprenticed under their superior.[204] The early church did not operate ecclesiastical schools teaching others how to preach their message, establish new churches, and minister to people; rather, leaders such as Paul, Barnabas, and Peter apprenticed followers under them who learned through assisting.

One such individual, Timothy, was recognized throughout the churches of Asia Minor because of his travels alongside Paul. Later, in Paul's epistles to Timothy, Paul addressed him as a capable leader within the church, but in his early years, Timothy filled the role of a ὑπηρέτης (*hypēretēs*). Due to his loyalty to Paul, as evidenced throughout the Scriptures, one could present an argument that Timothy never ceased serving Paul. Therefore, an apostle could have a ὑπηρέτης (*hypēretēs*), and so also could a bishop, a deacon, and a household manager. In theory, if the number of attendees to an in-home church exceeded the capacity of the space or the care of the manager, the situation would necessitate the manager's assistant to become a manager also. Then, one church would become two and, in so doing, generate more positions for others to serve. Through cultural evidence and scriptural passages, one may assume the rest of the various leaders, through the church, trained other members similarly.

201. Harris, "Part I," 35.
202. Collins, "Re-thinking 'Eyewitnesses,'" 451.
203. Mather, "Paul in Acts as 'Servant' and 'Witness,'" 28.
204. Mather, "Paul in Acts as 'Servant' and 'Witness,'" 28.

## The Servant of All

The role of the servant—*doulos* is possibly the most common Greek word for the position of a "servant," appearing over 120 times across the NT. "Slave" was another meaning drawn from this word, and in that culture, men and women were bought and sold as property, for they were slaves.[205] Revelation 1:1 states, "The Revelation of Jesus Christ, which God gave unto him, to shew unto his servants things which must shortly come to pass; and he sent and signified it by his angel unto his servant John." The Greek term employed for "servant(s)" is δοῦλος (*doulos*) and is defined as "a slave, bondman, man of servile condition . . . a female slave, handmaiden," in addition and more importantly because of the scriptural context, "one who gives himself up wholly to another's will."[206] For one to be a partaker of the revelation of Jesus Christ, one was required to be his δοῦλος (*doulos*). The application of δοῦλος (*doulos*) in relation to the church was meant in a figurative sense and based upon a disciple's dedication to serving the church. This metaphorical understanding of δοῦλος (*doulos*) follows the example of Nethinims of the temple (Ezra 7:7). This understanding also connects further back in Hebrew history to the servants, who, upon receiving their freedom, chose to dedicate themselves willingly to their master (Exod 21:2–6). The first usage of the term δοῦλος (*doulos*), in reference to the neophyte church, occurs in Peter's sermon in Acts chapter two. He stated, "And on my servants and on my handmaidens I will pour out in those days my Spirit; and they shall prophecy" Acts 2:18). Both the words "servants" and "handmaidens" are forms of δοῦλος (*doulos*). As believers dedicated themselves to service, they were rewarded with privilege and responsibility.

Jesus' teaching to his disciples dealt with both διάκονος (*diakonos*) and δοῦλος (*doulos*) as varying degrees of depth in one's discipleship. In the tenth chapter of the Gospel of Mark, Jesus taught:

> But Jesus called them to him, and saith unto them, 'Ye know that they which are accounted to rule over the Gentiles exercise lordship over them; and their great ones exercise authority upon them. But so shall it not be among you: but whosoever will be great among you, shall be your minister: And whosoever of you will be chiefest, shall be servant of all.' (Vs. 42–44)

---

205. "δοῦλος, ov," L&N 1:741.
206. Thayer, "δοῦλος," *Thayer's Greek-English Lexicon*, 157–58.

In his lesson, Jesus endeavored to teach them that discipleship meant willfully denying one's interests and risking all for the sake of another's betterment while engaging in lowly service to others to deliver the gospel of Christ to them. Such character mimics the Savior's lifestyle: "For the Son of man came not to be ministered unto, but to minister, and to give his life a ransom for many" (Mark 10:45). As deacons became the next stratum of leaders under the apostles, the humility in their title reflected their willingness to wait on others like servants waited upon their master's dining tables.[207]

Hellenistic society prized freedom and independence as the highest human rights; therefore, as the opposite, slavery was detestable.[208] As an example, Paul claimed that he was a free-born Roman citizen, having dual claims to both Judean and Roman society; his status and his education placed him among the Roman elite (Acts 22:28). Despite his legal Roman and Judean rights, education, and noble heritage, Paul preached that he devoted himself to serving Christ and the church as a δοῦλος (doulos), a devoted servant/slave. In Rom 1:1, Paul calls himself the servant—δοῦλος (doulos) of Jesus Christ, called to be an apostle. Paul was a servant first, and from his faithfulness to that role, he was honored to be made an apostle second. Considering that culturally, a δοῦλος (doulos) was a slave and the property of an owner, in Paul's rhetoric, he utilizes the term to illustrate his relationship with Christ—Paul belonged to Christ.[209] There are occasions in Paul's epistles where the dedication he feels owed to Jesus Christ is like that of an enslaved person who has no choice but the will of his master. Paul would identify himself at least five times in his epistles as a δοῦλος (doulos) of the Lord Jesus Christ (Rom 1:1–2; 2 Cor 4:5; Gal 1:10; Phil 1:1; Titus 1:1). In 1 Corinthians chapter seven, Paul draws out an extended allegory concerning servants/slaves and freemen. He pointedly tells his audience that because Christ's sacrifice paid for their lives, they were to behave as his servants—δοῦλος (doulos), all the while understanding they had been called to be children of the most high God. As a δοῦλος (doulos), Paul voluntarily surrendered his life in service to God, to Jesus Christ as his Lord, and to minister to the believers. He presented his life as a testimony to the church, encouraging them to follow his example and dedicate themselves to serving the Lord, just as he did.

---

207. Kgatle, "Diakonos and Doulos," 76.
208. Kgatle, "Diakonos and Doulos," 77.
209. "δοῦλος, ov," L&N 1:741.

The verb form of δοῦλος (*doulos*) is δουλόω (*douloō*), meaning "to reduce to servitude, enslave, oppress by retaining in servitude, to render subservient."[210] Concerning Jesus' teachings and examples within the church, a δοῦλος (*doulos*) was "a devoted servant or minister, one pledged or bound to serve."[211] Unlike a slave, the dedication and service rendered by a δοῦλος (*doulos*) in the church was of a member's free volition. Mookgo Kgatle related this position was a sign of one's voluntary subjection to endure, to take upon themselves the lowliest duties and lowliest responsibilities in serving others; furthermore, Kgatle stated, "Doulos was a bond slave who served the master without question . . . by recommending that his followers become 'slave of all,' Jesus underlines his ideal of universal service toward others."[212] Metaphorically, when describing one's devotion to God, Jesus, and the church, the use of δοῦλος (*doulos*) described one's positive moral and spiritual relationship in recognition of the price paid for their salvation.[213] A διάκονος (*diakonos*) served a specific function and position of leadership within the church. However, similar to enslaved people in Hellenistic society who served any function their masters required, within the church, disciples who dedicated themselves as *douloi* [pl.] were willing to render whatever service the church needed of them selflessly regardless of hardships or sufferings.[214] The versatility and flexibility exemplified by a *doulos* meant that they could assist any of the other levels and serve any believers within the church. Within their position in the stratified leadership model, a δοῦλος (*doulos*), or more than one, have the potential to meet any need or mode of service required by the church-body public. The overseers, ministers, and elders might call upon a δοῦλος (*doulos*) to care for widows, tend to children, and provide for the safe-keeping of the poor and vulnerable. They become the "Swiss Army knife" of servants with the household of God fulfilling the duties of readers, cantors, food prep, cleaners, heavy labor, and any other subcategory required within the body of believers. In the church strata, the label of a δοῦλος (*doulos*) exemplified one that was dedicated to being a servant of all, fulfilling whatever need might arise.

Within the early church, a δοῦλος (*doulos*) was more than simply someone who attended their meetings; as the connotation of the title

210. Mounce and Mounce, "δουλόω," *Interlinear New Testament* (NASB/NIV), 1047.
211. Mounce and Mounce, "δοῦλος," *Interlinear New Testament* (NASB/NIV), 1047.
212. Kgatle, "Diakonos and Doulos," 79.
213. Kgatle, "Diakonos and Doulos," 79.
214. Kgatle, "Diakonos and Doulos," 79–80.

suggests, it was a member dedicated to serving the collective church body in any function required. The NT utilizes δοῦλος (*doulos*) both literally and figuratively; however, concerning the believers in the First-Century Church, it bears a profound figurative sense of one who had freely relinquished their freedom in service to God, Jesus Christ, and the collective body of the church.[215] Such devotion and dedication exceeded that of a disciple. In following Jesus' example and teachings, how early Christians conducted themselves declared unto all their wholeheartedness and faith (2 Cor 3:1–4; Jas 2:14–17).

Though every Christian who received salvation through Christ owed him their life, not every Christian lived accordingly. A person regarded among the believers as a δοῦλος (*doulos*) of Christ would demonstrate it by their daily conduct, as Paul had described. That individual could have been called upon by any in need of their aid, with the complete confidence that the δοῦλος called upon would deliver to their most total ability. Paul mentions one individual, Epaphras, and praises him as "servant (δοῦλος) of Christ, saluteth you, always laboring fervently for you in prayers" (Col 4:12). The stratum of a δοῦλος (*doulos*) would not have been the same as a disciple, i.e., a disciplined follower, because rather than following along with the Christian movement, their service aided the movement's momentum. As one learned what it meant to be a disciple, they became more dedicated to Christ in service to him and the church. One may almost trace a progression of growth in character examples from the book of Acts, such as Timothy, as believers transitioned from conversion to discipleship to the servanthood of a *doulos* (Acts 16:1; 17:14–15; 18:5, 19:22, 20:4; Rom 16:21; 1 Cor 16:10; 2 Cor 1:1; Phlm 1:16).

A δοῦλος (*doulos*) was not necessarily dedicated to a particular home church or a specific individual like a ὑπηρέτης (*hyperetes*) but was free to serve where needed. Paul often sent his letters to churches and individuals in the hands of a trusted δοῦλος (*doulos*). Examples in Paul's writings of members who were recognized δοῦλοι (*douloi*) within the church were Epaphroditus, Tychicus, Onesimus, and Timothy (Phil 1:1, 2:25, 4:18; Col 4:7–9).[216] Following Paul's example, if a member of the congregation was to ascend the ranks of leadership, they first had to demonstrate themselves as dedicated servants of Jesus Christ and the church: a δοῦλος (*doulos*).

215. Kgatle, "Diakonos and Doulos," 79.

216. Epaphras was a contracted form of Epaphroditus. Thayer, "Ἐπαφρᾶς, Ἐπαφρόδιτος," *Thayer's Greek-English Lexicon*, 229.

## The Doorkeeper

Among household servants, the position of the doorkeeper was considered one of the lowliest in rank, yet still necessary. Doorkeepers, though lowly, were essential for the perpetuation of Greek temples. Two hundred years before the advent of Jesus, Aristides recorded the duties of those who kept the Asclepieion temple; it was the doorkeeper's responsibility to maintain the purity of the entrance, open the doors in the morning, close them at night, and light the sacred candles.[217] In ancient Roman religions, the essential roles included the priest, the sexton, the sacristan, and the doorkeeper.[218] In Greek, Jewish, Islamic, and Christian cultures, the doorways and thresholds into temples, places of worship, and sacred spaces present to the devotee a physical symbolism of a boundary between the secular world and the holy area.[219] The individual charged with faithfully guarding a holy doorway, maintaining the purity of the room that lay beyond, shouldered a critical duty. Hebrews chapter nine compares the Aaronic High Priest, whose duties permitted him entry into the holy of holies within the Tabernacle, and Jesus Christ, who opened unto all who believe in him the holiest of places, spiritual access to God. Their duties appointed both individuals as doorkeepers over their respective sacred thresholds. The high priest could only enter once a year, but his duties also kept all others at bay. Conversely, when Jesus Christ ascended to the holy of holies in the heavenlies, he became the new high priest, granting salvation to all (Heb 10:18–22).

One can trace the role of the doorkeeper back to the OT. The priesthood in Jerusalem employed Levites to maintain and guard the entrances into the temple. In addition, they served as janitors, sweeping the thresholds and collecting offerings from the people who passed through them.[220] In the Hebrew language utilized in the OT Scriptures, there are two words that the English language translates as doorkeeper or porter. The dominant word for porter or doorkeeper/gatekeeper is שׁוֹעֵר (shō'ēr).[221] The OT utilizes שׁוֹעֵר (shō'ēr) and its derivatives no less than thirty-seven times across the scriptures. For example, 1 Chr 9:24 shows that there were porters/doorkeepers stationed at each of the temple's entrances:

217. van Opstall, *Sacred Thresholds*, 118–19.
218. MacMullen, "Perceptible," 42–44.
219. van Opstall, *Sacred Thresholds*, 36.
220. Sanders, *Judaism*, 136.
221. "שׁוֹעֵר," BDBG, 1045.

north, east, west, and south. Second Chronicles 31:14 records, "And Kore the son of Imnah the Levite, the porter toward the east, was over freewill offerings of God, to distribute the oblations of the LORD, and the most holy things." This verse illustrates that the Levite, Kore, stationed at the east-gate temple entrance, oversaw the collection of freewill offerings from the people unto God. In another record, the doorkeepers Berechiah and Elkanah were responsible for protecting the ark of the covenant and ensuring only the high priest approached it on the appointed day (1 Chr 15:18). Another reference lists the king's porters that guarded his sanctuary (1 Chr 9:17–18). Finally, 1 Chr 9:22 declares that King David and Samuel personally ordained the porters responsible for the house of the LORD. Though the position of the doorkeeper may not have been as illustrious as the high priest or others of the Aaronic priesthood, the doorkeeper/porter was respected and held authority.

The more obscure word, הִסְתּוֹפֵף (histowpep), occurs only once in the OT. In Ps 84:10, the Scripture declares, "For a day in thy courts is better than a thousand. I had rather be a doorkeeper in the house of my God, than to dwell in the tents of wickedness." The word "doorkeeper" in Hebrew is הִסְתּוֹפֵף (histowpep), the infinitive form of the verb סָפַף (sāpap), which means "to stand guard at the threshold, to be a doorkeeper," and it indicates a low-level position within the ranks of the temple.[222] In comparison, larger households maintained doorkeepers, sometimes called porters, as did the temple at Jerusalem and the synagogues in the culture of the Palestinian and Mediterranean regions. In the Greek vernacular, this person "who kept the door" was the θυρωρός (thyrōros). The definition of θυρωρός (thyrōros) is "one who guards the door giving access to a house or a building–doorkeeper."[223] In Mark 13:34, in Jesus' parable, the master of the house gave every servant a duty, and he "commanded the porter [θυρωρός]to watch." In that culture, the primary responsibility of the θυρωρός (thyrōros) was guarding the main entryway into the house (Mark 13:34; John 18:16–17).

The θυρωρός (thyrōros) was considered a lowly position among household servants as well as in religious arenas. Yet it was necessary because the porter, or doorkeeper, was responsible for regulating who gained entry to the master's home and who remained outside. The role did not receive the glory that other servants' positions of higher rank

---

222. Baker and Carpenter, "(5605) סָפַף—sāpap," *Complete Word Study Dictionary Old Testamen*, 787.

223. "θυρωρός, ον," L&N 1:521.

garnered. In the record of John 18, when the soldier took Jesus before the high priests and chief priests for his mock trial, Peter had to wait outside. He waited until another vouched for him to the doorkeeper, and then she permitted Peter entry (John 18:16–17). The passage indicates that though the doorkeeper was a woman, and the position among the household servants may have been lowly, the post still commanded respect.

Christian tradition views Jesus as the gatekeeper of heaven and hell and controls access to God (John 10:7–10; 1 Tim 2:5; Rev 3:8).[224] A messianic interpretation of Isa 22:22 is that Jesus possesses the key of the house of David and therefore controls its perpetuity, which is realized in the book of Revelation (Rev 3:7).[225] Therefore Jesus, for the Christian believer, fulfills the role of the θυρωρός (*thyrōros*), as the ultimate doorkeeper. Another Christian tradition is that Peter, as Jesus' successor, keeps watch over the entrance of heaven because Jesus committed the keys of the kingdom of heaven to him in Matt 16:19.[226] Thus, in the Christian faith, to follow after the Savior, to imitate him even if only symbolically as a doorkeeper to a church here on earth, would be considered an honor.

The in-home churches enlisted the use of doorkeepers when available. In Acts 12:13, Peter went to the house of a local church after his release from prison, and Rhoda, the doorkeeper, answered his knocking. Rhoda is the only person named in the NT whose duty was serving as a doorkeeper or porter. Eusebius bore witness to the position of the doorkeeper as an active role in the church in the middle of the third century.[227] However, the scant writings and inscriptions concerning Christianity, from the end of the first century until Eusebius sometime in the third, do not mention doorkeepers or porters in church activities. Yet because the position and the duties performed by doorkeepers were established by OT, the Jewish temple and synagogues, from which Christianity evolved, and because the role re-emerged in Christianity in the third century, it is logical to conclude that, when available, the role of the doorkeeper existed within Christianity through the years in between.[228]

All posts of service and leadership within the early church were voluntary and undertaken because individuals felt compelled to give and serve others because that was the example and teaching of their Lord,

224. van Opstall, *Sacred Thresholds*, 189.
225. van Opstall, *Sacred Thresholds*, 193.
226. van Opstall, *Sacred Thresholds*, 192.
227. Eusebius, *History of the Church*, 282.
228. Burtchaell, *From Synagogue to Church*, 272.

Jesus Christ. It is reasonable to conclude that if a member of the congregation of believers, a disciple, desired to serve the church actively, the doorkeeper would have been the entry-level service position. Their duties, much like in the synagogues, would have possibly included the admission of those attending their meetings, the collection of offerings, and perhaps any janitorial details. Such a service position placed a devotee in direct contact with the manager of the in-home church and the assistant, which provided increased opportunities for influence, observation, and learning. This position provided a disciple with a dedicated opportunity in a home church to serve others while maneuvering themselves to be close to more mature believers. The doorkeeper's position would place an individual in continual contact with the home church manager, their assistant, possibly elders, and others who devoted themselves to the service and ministration of the body of Christ. As long as the churches remained in peoples' homes, these positions were essential to the early church for maintaining order and organization, followed by the apostles' examples of humility in service.

## THE LORD'S PERSONAL ATTENDANT

The eighth and final possible leadership position within the First-Century Church is also the most obscure. The title is the Greek word θεράπων (*therápōn*), and the New Testament utilizes it only once in its whole text. Richard C. Trench, in his volume *Synonyms of the New Testament*, lays this word alongside δοῦλος (*doulos*), διάκονος (*diakonos*), οἰκέτης (*oikétēs*), and ὑπηρέτης (*hypēretēs*) as equivalent words, all bearing relatively similar meanings–servant.[229] Yet θεράπων (*therápōn*), appearing only in Heb 3:5, lacks the frequency and commonality of use with which its siblings are employed. Frequently, when a word in Hebrew or Greek is only used once within a text, as a hapax legomenon, it carries special significance. Still, interpreters may have difficulty finding the most accurate meaning because of its infrequency. Through the eons, translators have often bound more mysterious words with similar terms for ease in their rendering. But, if the standard is upheld that every word within the Word of God was given with holy intent and purpose and that its author, God, was neither flippant nor wasteful in his choices for expressing his heart, then the words utilized must not be handled irreverently as so much flotsam

---

229. Trench, *Synonyms of the New Testament*, 30.

and jetsam (2 Pet 1:20–21). Therefore, the immediate context of the singular usage must be analyzed. The testimony of Hebrews asserts:

> Wherefore, holy brethren, partakers of the heavenly calling, consider the Apostle and high priest of our profession, Christ Jesus;
> Who was faithful to Him that appointed him, as also Moses *was faithful* in all His house.
> For this *man* was counted worthy of more glory than Moses, inasmuch as he who hath builded the house hath more honor than the house.
> For every house is builded by some *man*; but he that built all things *is* God.
> And Moses verily was faithful in all His house, as a servant for a testimony of those things which were to be spoken after;
> But Christ as a son over His own house; whose house are we, if we hold fast the confidence and the rejoicing of the hope firm unto the end. (Heb 3:1–6)

The focal passage of this subsection of Scripture directly juxtaposes Moses with Jesus Christ for comparison and contrast, and it bears a quotation from Num 12:7. This study will consider the implications of the etymology of the word θεράπων (*therápōn*). In Greek culture, there is a particular and unique purpose to the role of a θεράπων (*therápōn*), which deepens one's understanding regarding the author's message in this passage. A precise knowledge of these three points is necessary for a clear understanding of the word and its usage in the scriptures of Hebrews.

The comparisons and contrasts of Jesus Christ to Moses and Jesus Christ's ministry to Hebrew traditions and beliefs within the book of Hebrews were intended to win over those faithful and dedicated to the Mosaic law and its practices. It also speaks to the completion of those ways, mandates, and traditions, which were dangerous to those who had become institutionalized by them and were dependent upon them for their way of life and being. The primary difference between Jesus and Moses: Moses was one of the most humble and privileged men in history to the extent that he held the words of the Word of God to which he was entrusted in his hands and cared for it with his being until his last day. He was privileged beyond measure to have seen "the hinder parts" of Yahweh (Exod 33:17–23) and to be so intimate with him that Moses talked with God "mouth to mouth" (Num 12:8), which exceeded the status of "friend of God," attained by Abraham (Isa 41:8), but he was left behind. Jesus Christ, not only a faithful vessel but also an emanation and incarnation of the Logos recorded in John 1:1–17, still lives on to this day, a testament to the life in the words of the Word of God, thus showing the superiority of one man over the other. Yet Jesus humbled himself unto the example of Moses, and both men rendered complete selflessness in utter devotion to Yahweh first and then the care of his people next. As a result, Moses is awarded the praise of "My servant Moses . . . faithful in all mine house" (Num 12:7), and this exceeds the glory of Solomon, who was "chiefest among ten thousand" (Song 5:10). Then in Heb 3:5 the Scripture states that "Moses verily was faithful in all his (God's) house as a servant—θεράπων (*therápōn*)." Through his faithfulness, Moses earned the title of Yahweh's personal attendant.

From the mouth of Moses, he prophesied that God would raise a prophet like himself, and the testimony of Hebrews declares Jesus as that promise brought to fruition (Deut 18:15–18). The first verse of Hebrews chapter three entitles Jesus as the apostle and high priest. Hebrews 3:2 states, "Who (Jesus) was faithful to him (God) that appointed him, as also Moses was faithful in all his (God's) house." The Scripture says that Jesus' faithfulness was equal to Moses', and thus, he is also worthy of the title of θεράπων (*therápōn*). Then, the author ups the stakes because verse six accounts for Jesus' status as God's son. In a household, the master's children are not required to do anything concerning that household's care, maintenance, and ministration: the children are above the servants. Yet, Jesus Christ placed himself voluntarily as a servant unto all: first during the law administration as a servant unto all God's servants, and next in the grace administration as a servant and mediator unto all who would believe to become children of God. This verse witnesses the fulfillment of the role established with Moses, then completed by Jesus, and the greater honor bestowed upon Jesus. Those so zealous for the laws and traditions handed down to them from Moses would have to square themselves with this truth.

The word θεράπων (*therápōn*) means "an attendant, servant: of God, spoken of Moses discharging the duties committed to him by God," and it is an equivalent for עֶבֶד (*'ebed*) in Hebrew occurring in the OT.[230] In the Scriptures of the Old Testament עֶבֶד (*'ebed*) has many applications from a general slave, a king's servant, messengers, ordinary soldiers, and worshipers of God.[231] Certain Scriptures from the book of the prophet Isaiah,

---

230. Thayer, "θεράπων," *Thayer's Greek-English Lexicon*, 289.
231. "עֶבֶד," BDBG, 713–14.

which have been interpreted as messianic, utilize the word עֶבֶד (*'ebed*) when speaking about the LORD's servant—the Messiah.[232] For example, Isa 42:6–7 states, "I the LORD have called thee in righteousness, and will hold thine hand, and will keep thee, and give thee for a covenant of the people, for a light of the Gentiles; to open the blind eyes, to bring out the prisoners from the prison, and them that sit in darkness out of the prison house." When interpreting this passage in light of the promised Messiah, its fulfillment occurs in Luke 2:30–32. In Isa 42:1, as immediate context for verses six and seven, this individual, to whom the LORD is pledging himself by the mouth of his prophet, the Scripture states, "Behold my servant," and servant is עֶבֶד (*'ebed*). This particular servant—עֶבֶד (*'ebed*) was "an ideal servant chosen and endowed with the divine Spirit to be a covenant of Israel and a light of the nations ... bearing the sins of all as a lamb and a trespass offering" (Isa 52:13–15; 53:10–11).[233] The *'ebed* of Isaiah, God's servant par excellence, finds equivalency in the θεράπων (*therápōn*) of Hebrews chapter three.

The verb form of θεράπων (*therápōn*) is θεραπεύω (*therapeuō*), which is rendered "to adore (God) or to relieve (of disease), cure, heal, worship; θεραπεύω (*therapeuō*) primarily signifies 'to serve as a *therápōn*,' an attendant."[234] From θεραπεύω (*therapeuō*) comes the word θεραπεία (*therapeia*), meaning "attendance (spec. medical, i.e., cure), healing, and household; *therapeia* primarily denotes a household, a place where one's render constant care and attention."[235] The English word "therapy" is from this Greek word, θεραπεύω (*therapeuō*). Therefore, the one ministering service—θεραπεύω (*therapeuō*), would be dispersing warmth, healing, comfort, and attention to those in need, especially those in her household. Thus, building an understanding from its lexical sources, a θεράπων (*therápōn*) was a humble, cherished attendant who is devoted to and adores his lord, the highest in respect and stature of all the master's servants; one who is responsible for an entire household—seeing to and caring for the ministration of the needs of the family and the body of servants: a dispenser of attention, cures, healing, and warmth.

As the word θεράπων (*therápōn*) is used only once in Scripture, necessity requires one to observe how it is used in Greek literature and

---

232. Strong, "עֶבֶד," *Strong's Exhaustive Concordance of the Bible*, 201.
233. "עֶבֶד," BDBG, 714.
234. Strong, "θεραπεύω," *Strong's Exhaustive Concordance of the Bible*, 115.
235. Strong, "θεραπεία," *Strong's Exhaustive Concordance of the Bible*, 115.

culture and then overlay that understanding with the scriptural use. According to P. A. L. Greenhalgh,

> There remains in Homer one relationship-term *among the aristocracy* which by definition seems to indicate a servant-master relationship and which by context often implies economic dependence *combined* with a potential leadership status above that of the chief's apparently non-dependent fellow-nobles and even kinsmen—a position of leadership second only to that of the chief himself, and derived directly from him. This term is *therapon*.[236]

In his study, Greenhalgh referenced the *Iliad* by Homer, dated to the eighth century BC, in which the θεράπων (*therápōn*) was both the devoted personal attendant and the ritual substitute who replaced his master. Achilles appointed his cousin and close childhood friend, Patroclus, as his θεράπων (*therápōn*), "one whose service was not constrained, but the officious ministration of love."[237] In the example of Achilles and Patroclus, as the *therápōn*, Patroclus prepared a meal for Achilles and his guests and waited upon them out of devotion to Achilles. Later, when Patroclus donned Achilles' armor and led the Myrmidons into battle, it is said that his ways, commands, and movements so imitated those of Achilles the soldiers could not discern that it was not Achilles whom they were following. As the ultimate show of his devotion, Patroclus died in the service of his master.[238] The Greek gods were incapable of dying; therefore, it was incumbent upon their *therápontes* (pl.) to do so for them. When a Greek commander died in battle, the people understood the event as a physical representation of a spiritual reality. That commander was regarded as taking the place of the particular deity to whom they were devoted. Likewise, in their temples, the high priest was to be so devoted to the god they served that they became the physical representation for the people of that god whom they had come to worship. God-Yahweh, incapable of dying himself, placed the responsibility upon his son Jesus, appointing him as his θεράπων (*therápōn*), with the promise of the resurrection for surrendering his life for humanity's redemption.

An example of this cultural belief occurs in Acts 14. When the miraculous healing of the crippled man at Lystra took place, the people

---

236. Greenhalgh, "Homeric Therapon and 'Opaon,'" 81–90.
237. Trench, *Synonyms of the New Testament*, 31.
238. Nagy, "Achilles and Patroklos as Models for the Twinning of Identity."

compared Paul and Barnabas to the deities of Mercury and Jupiter. In verse 11, it reads: "And when the people saw what Paul had done, they lifted up their voices, saying in the speech of Lyconia, 'The gods are come down to us in the likeness of men.'" "In the likeness," in Greek, is one word: ὁμοιωθέντες (*homoiōthentes*), the aorist, nominative, masculine plural verb form of ὁμοιόω (*homoioō*) and it means to make like, liken unto, to compare, to resemble, to assimilate, to become similar.[239] Paul and Barnabas had already been among the people, and presumably, their appearance looked nothing like the statues of Jupiter and Mercury because they had not said anything about the two men before the miracle. So, what was it that the people were drawing into comparison? The supernatural works produced were not of men but could only be attributed to an identity associated with power more significant than that of the mortal, finite, impotent man. The spectators, unfamiliar with the true God whom Paul and Barnabas served, attributed the miracle to the deities they were familiar with. In the Greek culture, only an individual so wholly devoted to his god could draw upon such power—a θεράπων (*therápōn*)—and the audience would regard the θεράπων (*therápōn*) with the same reverence as the deity being represented. Therefore, the Lyconians, within their beliefs, claimed Barnabas and Paul to be the *therápontos* of Mercury and Jupiter.

In all of the records concerning the First-Century Church, the title of θεράπων (*therápōn*) was not used for anyone living. The use of this title in Hebrews about Moses and Jesus Christ is, in a posthumous sense, awarded to them for having dedicated their lives to living for God and making known his Word and will until their last breath. This study theorizes that the author of Hebrews utilized this unique title to provide a goal for all other overseers, ministers, and elders within the household. Proverbs 29:18 states, "Where there is no vision, the people perish." Paul spoke of a leader's service to God's people like an athlete running a marathon (1 Cor 9:24–26; Phil 2:6; Heb 12:1). Nearing the end of his life, in a letter to Timothy, he wrote, "I have fought a good fight, I have finished my course, I have kept the faith" (2 Tim 4:7). In the following verse Paul described how he was looking forward to being rewarded by Jesus Christ with "a crown of righteousness" (2 Tim 4:8). Paul had a goal in mind

---

239. This understanding presented for ὁμοιωθέντες was derived from comparing the definition for "ὁμοιόω." Thayer, "ὁμοιόω," *Thayer's Greek-English Lexicon*, 445, with Mounce and Mounce, "ὁμοιόω," *Zondervan Greek and English Interlinear New Testament (NASB/NIV)*, 517, 1124.

throughout his ministry of service: to become as Christ-like as possible. By describing Moses and Jesus as *therápōntes* of God, Paul communicated his concept of ultimate service and dedication to other believers; he provided them a goal, a pole star for them to navigate their lives. Ministers and leaders of Christian churches in modernity would do well to live their lives with the objective of attaining the title of θεράπων (*therápōn*). The individual may then assess their own life throughout it by asking the question, "When I am through, when my ministry is over, and my service has ended, would those whom I have served regard me as and possibly award me with the title of a θεράπων (*therápōn*) of my Lord Jesus Christ and my Heavenly Father, God? When I stand before His throne, will He say, "Job well done?"

Jesus Christ, the son of God, encapsulates the ministry of the θεράπων (*therápōn*): a servant of selfless humility and dedication, devoted to becoming the living example of his heavenly father unto all who would believe. Jesus spoke what God wanted him to say and moved as God directed him to move. In carrying out the will of God, he ministered healing wholeness and life unto all who would receive and believe in him to the degree that he could claim "The Father, and I are one," "he who hath seen me hath seen the Father," and "not my will but thine be done." Paul declared, "Let this mind be in you, which was also in Christ Jesus" (Phil 2:5). People perform at their best when they have a clear goal they are working to achieve, even if they never see it fulfilled. While Hebrews appears to present the θεράπων (*therápōn*) as a posthumous award, to entitle a living individual with it would be at the discretion of an assembly of overseers, ministers, and elders. The level of the θεράπων (*therápōn*) is the ultimate goal for any person with Jesus as their Lord.

In all of the New Testament, only Moses and Jesus received the title of God's θεράπων (*therápōn*). This level of faith, believing, and faithfulness is the highest echelon of spiritual maturity displayed in all of Scripture. The Bible speaks on several occasions that believers should grow to their full capability in Christ, but for many, striving to become Christ-like may be too lofty a goal (Matt 5:48; Rom 12:2; Phil 2:5; Col 1:28). However, there are two other possible candidates after Jesus, who served as prime examples of selfless service to the household of God. There may be cause for the nomination of different individuals, but the Scriptures present a weightier amount of evidence for these two than any others. As tradition has it, these men served God, the Lord Jesus Christ, and the church up to their death, thus following the Lord's example of the ultimate sacrifice.

They are the apostles Peter and Paul, but for their humility, neither dared to appropriate the title of θεράπων (*therápōn*) for themselves, but they both served as the Lord's personal attendants. These two men presented themselves to the believers of the First-Century Church as examples to be followed in the place of the absent Christ. The examples of their imperfect lives may continue to encourage people everywhere who desire to live worthy of their Lord's praise and legacy.

## Peter as Jesus' Personal Attendant

One of the first to follow and learn from Jesus Christ, though he stumbled along the way, Peter emerged as the first leader of the early church with his revelatory sermon on the day of Pentecost in Acts chapter two. Peter was a witness to the miracles Jesus wrought, and he had been present at Jesus' transfiguration (Matt 17:2; Mark 9:2). Jesus promised Peter the "keys to the kingdom of heaven" (Matt 16:19). Jesus charged Peter as his right-hand man with leading his followers after his departure: "Feed my lambs . . . take care of my sheep . . . feed my ewes" (John 21:15–17).[240] Jesus also prophesied to Peter, "When thou shalt be old, thou shalt stretch forth thy hands, and another shall gird thee, and carry thee whither thou wouldest not" (John 21:19). Verse nineteen is often interpreted to explain eighteen—that Peter would be crucified just like Jesus—but it is not without disagreement.[241] This study acknowledges the discussions, debates, and arguments from both for and against the authorship of the Petrine epistles.[242] This study accepts the epistles of 1 and 2 Peter as delivered by the apostle because the available evidence outweighs the controversy; the early church received them, and 1 and 2 Peter reflected the times and culture in which they were transcribed.[243] The epistles deliver a testimonial

---

240. This passage was quoted from the Lamsa Bible, because it illustrates more clearly Jesus' directive for Peter to oversee and pastor the young, the adult, and the aged members of his flock in his absence.

241. McDowell, *Fate of the Apostles*, 60–64.

242. Best, "1 Peter," *Oxford Companion to the Bible*, 584–85.

243. According to David L. Bartlett, all arguments against the authenticity of the Petrine authorship are founded upon the timing of Peter's death, the reference to Paul's writings in the text, and that Peter was not so educated in the Greek language as occurs in the text: Bartlett, *Hebrews, the General Epistles, and Revelation*, 667. A lack of exposure, and experience with the Greek language is mere assumption, when culturally the Greek language dominated the Hellenistic empire, and the Septuagint had existed in circulation in synagogues for close to three hundred years prior to Peter's life. The

of Peter preaching and teaching the church as an eyewitness for Christ until his last days (1 Pet 5:1).

The Petrine letters aim to continue the church beyond Peter's lifetime. Within them, Peter presented fundamental concepts the church needed, and at the center was their salvation in Christ and their hope in his promised return (1 Pet 1:2–5). First Peter 1:1 addresses its audience as "the strangers scattered throughout Pontus, Galatia, Cappadocia, Asia, and Bithynia, elect according to the foreknowledge of God through the sanctification of the Spirit." The intention for the epistle of 1 Peter's circulation among the in-home churches of Anatolia and Asia Minor is evidenced by listing those specific cities. The Greek word for "strangers" in this verse is rendered "pilgrims" in 1 Pet 2:11: παρεπίδημος (*parepidēmos*), which is defined as "one who comes from a foreign country into a city or land to reside there by the side of the natives; hence stranger, sojourning in a strange place, a foreigner; in the New Testament a metaphor in reference to heaven as the native country, one who sojourns on earth: so of Christians."[244] They were all one body through their salvation in Christ and, therefore, collectively looking toward the same hope of the promise of Christ's appearing unto them at his return (1 Pet 1:7, 13). The message of the second chapter of 1 Peter stresses the believers' extraordinary and unique identity because of salvation and the examples made of their lives to others in the culture around them.

Both 1 and 2 Peter address their audience similarly, highlighting their spiritual identity in Christ, adding a sense of continuity between the two letters. The audience Peter was writing to could have been exiled believers due to Roman persecution but also, in the sense of their spiritual identity, they were exiles because this world was no longer their home. Jesus had taught his disciples that just as the world's societies rejected him, they would refuse his followers. Therefore, there was no home for Jesus and his followers in this world. Peter expounded on his audience's identity in Christ, their salvation in Christ, and their hope for the future because of all Christ had accomplished and will accomplish. He wrote, "Praise be to the God and Father of our Lord Jesus Christ! In his great mercy, he has given us new birth into a living hope through the

---

exact occurrence of the time and place of Peter's death is unknown and what has been accepted is based upon speculative traditions; ref.: McDowell, *Fate of the Apostles*, 56. He also points to insufficient data to support theories in which Peter could not have been exposed to Paul's writings: McDowell, *Fate of the Apostles*, 59.

244. Thayer, "παρεπίδημος," *Thayer's Greek-English Lexicon*, 488.

resurrection of Jesus Christ from the dead and into an inheritance that can never perish, spoil, or fade. This inheritance is kept in heaven for you" (1 Pet 1:3–4 NIV). Furthermore, any physical afflictions endured reflect the sufferings of Jesus, encouraging them to follow Jesus' example (2:20–21). This exhortation echoes that of Jesus from John 15:19, "If ye were of the world, the world would love his own: but because ye are not of the world, but I have chosen you out of the world, therefore the world hateth you." Peter, of course, was well known to them, and he could have utilized his own life and experiences, but instead, he guided his audience to follow after and devote themselves to Christ just as he had.

In these letters, Peter fulfilled part of the duty Jesus called upon him to "feed my sheep." At that time, Peter classified himself as an elder, for he had been leading the church for many years and was an older man (1 Pet 5:1). Peter referred to Jesus Christ as the "living stone disallowed" and then extended his metaphor, involving his audience in by saying, "Ye also, as lively stones are built up a spiritual house" (1 Pet 2:4–5). In verses six and eight, Jesus is the "chief corner stone" and the "stone of stumbling," which are quotations from Isaiah (8:14, 18:16). He directed the church to look toward and follow after Jesus, who is "the Shepherd and Bishop of your souls" (2:25). Then in chapter 3:18–22, Peter delivered a coruscating and necessary message illustrating the Christian's salvation designed to ennoble the Christian's identity, knowledge, and belief in what God wrought for them through Christ. Chapter four addresses the believers' conduct, behavior, and reputations among each other and the unbelieving world around them, similar to Paul's address in Ephesians chapter four. Finally, in chapter five, Peter closed the letter by addressing the leadership and instructing them to "feed the flock" and "neither as being lords over God's heritage, but being ensamples to the flock" (5:2, 3).

In the introduction of the letter of 2 Peter, he calls himself Jesus' servant (*doulos*) and an apostle (*apostolos*) "to them that have obtained like precious faith with us" (1:1). He provides a testimony of his ministering to them and others and encourages his audience in virtuous and godly behaviors (1:2–8). Next, Peter speaks of the imminent end of his life: "knowing that shortly I must put off this my tabernacle," and that the church must continue while keeping Peter and his teachings in their remembrance (1:14–15). In chapter two, he warns the believers against following false prophets and teachers (2:1–3). Chapter three acknowledges that they are all seeking the return of Christ and God's judgment but that such events are in God's hands (3:1–8). In verse 10, he tells his audience, "The day of the Lord will come as a thief in the night," which was corroborated by the gospels of Matthew and Luke as well as by Paul in Thessalonians (Matt 24:42–44; Luke 12:37–40; 1 Thess 5:2). In the closing verse of chapter three, Peter encourages their faithfulness: "We look for a new heavens and a new earth" (v. 13) and reminds them to exercise diligence (v. 14), study Paul's epistles (vs. 15–16), and continue growing in the grace and knowledge of Jesus Christ (v. 18).

These epistles of Peter provide a testimony of the apostles as a witness for his Lord, Jesus Christ, until his last days. Their composition shows that he desired no glory for himself but taught believers to follow Jesus' example and hope for his return. His messages on how the believers were to minister to each other focused on the shepherd's analogy, which Jesus had taught Peter. Peter quoted the Scriptures often in the epistles, and the gospels and Paul's epistles echo his encouragements, reminders, and lessons to the church. Peter gave all he had to the church in service to God and Jesus, just as Jesus had done. Peter provided himself as a substitute that others could see in place of the absent Christ, who they could not, and fulfilled the commission received from his Lord. Such a testimony promotes Peter's candidacy as a *therápōn* of Christ to the church.

## Imitating Christ: Paul, the Lord's *Therápōn*

The apostle Paul was born in the free city of Tarsus, the capital of Cilicia, known for its Greek educational and philosophical schools.[245] Educated as a youth in Jerusalem to be a Pharisee like his father before him, he studied under the renowned doctor of the Law, Gamaliel, the elder (Acts 5:34; 22:3; 23:6; 26:5; Phil 3:5).[246] In his own words, Paul's zeal for the Law drove him to obtain letters of authority to arrest the followers of Jesus Christ to stand trial for heresy (Acts 8:3–4, 9:1–2, 21:20; Gal 1:14). Paul's salvation and conversion to join the variant of the Jewish faith he had persecuted required no less than the intervention of Jesus Christ (Acts 9:1–6). According to his testimony to King Agrippa, Jesus appointed Paul as his minister (*hypēretēs*) and witness to spread the gospel (Acts 26:16).

Paul rose through the ranks of the early church, proving himself to the apostles, elders, and believers, first in Damascus, then Jerusalem, where Barnabas testified of Paul's conversion (Acts 9:27). He served the

---

245. Thayer, "Ταρσός," *Thayer's Greek-English Lexicon*, 615.
246. Thayer, "Γαμαλιήλ," *Thayer's Greek-English Lexicon*, 108.

church alongside Barnabas when they took relief from the believers in Antioch back to Jerusalem (Acts 11:25–30). Acts 13:1–2 documents Paul's service as a prophet/teacher in the church and his commissioning as an apostle to spread the gospel of Christ in Syria, Greece, and Asia (Acts 14:14). Paul became known as the apostle unto the gentiles, taking the gospel of Jesus across Asia Minor, Greece, and into Caesar's palace (Acts 18:6; 19:10; Rom 11:13; Gal 2:7; Phil 1:13; 1 Tim 2:7; 2 Tim 1:11).

This study utilized Paul as an example, with nearly every title of leadership researched and described except for a few. Through the research, one finds Paul to have served the church not only as an apostle but also as a teacher/pastor, an evangelist, and a prophet (one who speaks for God). Though he may never have been overtly entitled as an evangelist or pastor, there is strong evidence in his letters and the book of Acts showing his performance in those ministries. Next to an apostle, he identifies himself most frequently as Christ's δοῦλος (*doulos*). In his study on Paul's self-identification, David M. May states, "Paul is even more explicit regarding his self-identity: 'Think of us in this way, as servants of Christ and stewards of God's mysteries' (1 Cor 4:1).[247] In that verse of Scripture as covered before, "servants" is the plural form of the word δοῦλος (*doulos*), and "stewards" is the plural of οἰκονόμος (*oikonomos*). He states in Col 1:25, "Whereof I am made a minister (διάκονος), according to the dispensation of God which is given to me for you, to fulfil the word of God."[248] Paul presents himself as God's ministering servant, the manager, within the administration of his household. Yet, in humility, Paul thought of himself as "less than the least of all the saints," so that no service rendered unto the church was beneath him, but all was for the glory of God (Eph 3:8).

As an apostle of Jesus Christ, Paul endured many hardships. He suffered greatly, yet his response was, "By the grace of God I am what I am: and his grace which was bestowed upon me was not in vain; but I labored more abundantly than they all" (1 Cor 15:10). In Acts 14:19, Jews from Antioch and Iconium that pursued Paul, assaulted him, stoning him to death, but by a miracle, he was brought back to life, and he continued in service to God and the church. In 1 Corinthians, he tells his audience,

---

247. May, "Servant and Steward of the Mystery," 470.

248. "Dispensation" is οἰκονομίαν—*oikonomian*, the accusative feminine singular form of οἰκονομία—*oikonomia*: "administration, management of a household or household affairs." Thayer, "οἰκονομία," *Thayer's Greek-English Lexicon of the New Testament*, 440.

"Be ye followers of me" (4:16) and "Be ye followers of me, even as I also am of Christ" (11:1). "Followers" could be better understood as imitators. By revelation through the grace of God, Paul was permitted to put himself as the church's example for how to live, as Jesus Christ had. Jesus was no longer the visible example for the church like he had been for his disciples during his earthly ministry. Instead, Paul had become their living example: "Imitate me and my ways, just as I imitate Christ." In his letter to the Galatian Church, Paul described how he had so dedicated himself to Jesus that he no longer lived for himself; it was as if he had crucified himself with Christ to permit Christ to live through his physical form (Gal 2:20). Finally, writing to his former apprentice, Timothy, who had become a church bishop, Paul described the imminence of his last days. "I have fought a good fight, I have finished my course," Paul says, "I have kept the faith" (2 Tim 4:7). He was a faithful manager of the household of God (Eph 2:19). Paul confidently gave his entire life to preaching the gospel of Christ, ministering to the church, promoting other leaders, rendering his life a transparent example of what it meant to "let this mind be in you, which was also in Christ Jesus" (Phil 2:5). Like Peter, the testimony of Paul's life recorded in the Scriptures secures his candidacy as a *therápōn* of Christ and an example for the church.

## CONCLUSION

According to the design of 1 Cor 12:27–28, the leadership of the First-Century Church successfully guided the collective body of followers through acute discernment, judgment, wisdom, and guidance, with the proficiency of an experienced helmsman at the wheel of a seafaring vessel. Through an investigation of the Scriptures, this study first presented the two differing bodies of leadership: the gift ministries—those charismatically guided by the Spirit of God—and those who ordained, elected, and selected to various administrative leadership roles within the First-Century Church. The spiritually energized gift ministries are apostles, prophets, evangelists, and pastor-teachers (or pastors and teachers), and together with and following after Christ, form the church's foundation. Striving together with them are the appointed positions of the *therápōn*, *episkopos*, *presbyteros*, *diakonos*, *oikonomos*, *hypēretēs*, *doulos*, and *thyrōros*, which this study refers to as the stratified leadership body of the First-Century Church.

Before shifting focus to display the organization and structure of the stratified leadership body, this study presented a brief but detailed analysis of the gift ministries for contrast and comparison and to aid in defining and understanding their counterpart-appointed leadership roles. Then, this study engaged in a thoroughly biblical, cultural, and social-scientific exposition of those eight elected and appointed leadership positions. Examples provided displayed how specific roles functioned as the primary appointed leadership. In contrast, others served as assistants and apprentices to them, but all worked for the service of the public body. In an organized fashion, the First-Century Church leaders followed Jesus' example of "the greatest leader is the greatest servant," displaying a willingness to do whatever was necessary for the good of the church body in service to the Lord and the will of God. Jesus Christ is the preeminent one, the chief cornerstone setting the orientation for the household of God. The apostles, prophets, evangelists, pastors, and teachers energized through the holy spirit by God and subordinate to the Lord Jesus form the structure's foundation.

Upon that foundation stand, in order, the church's overseers, ministers, elders, and stewards, each stratum interlocking and supporting the next. The overseers set the pace for the collective church and delegated authority and responsibilities to the ministers; both received counsel and wisdom from the church elders. The stewards managed the in-home church groups on a smaller-scale setting, endeavoring to imitate their overseers' service to the collective. After those layers, and with their guidance and support, the assistants/apprentices, the church's servants—δουλοι (*doulos* [pl.]) and the doorkeepers served the household. The final leadership position investigated by this study was the *therápōn* exemplified by the lives of Moses and Jesus Christ. The presentation of this role in Hebrews sets it forth as the ultimate goal for anyone who strives to give their whole life in service to God and his household. These functions all serve the household of God as the stratified leadership body, capable of systematically delivering the gospel of Christ to disciples, believers, and neophytes anywhere outreach may take root.

# CHAPTER 5

# The Perpetuation of the Church

AFTER JESUS' ASCENSION AND the initiation of his church by the apostles, thirty to forty years passed, but the return of the Lord, which they eagerly anticipated, had not transpired (Acts 1:6–11; 1 Thess 4:15–18). Both Peter and Paul sensed the imminent cessation of their lives and the termination of their services to the church. The continuation of the church from one generation of leadership to another became essential for maintaining the gospel of Christ movement until the Lord's return. The letters of 1 and 2 Timothy, Titus, and 1 and 2 Peter served to guide the church after its first generation of leaders were gone.[1] Paul provided related guidelines and directives to his two apprentices and successors, Timothy and Titus, on how they should appoint others to leadership roles within the church. Peter also stressed in his epistles that the church would continue beyond his lifetime.

The epistles of Peter and Paul do not mention all eight levels that form the stratified leadership model studied; the lack of attention does not discredit the presence of the lesser levels. They are only inferior concerning the attention received and the degree of responsibility and reverence

---

1. There is an ongoing disputation and debate as to whether Paul's epistles to Timothy and Titus and the epistles of Peter to the Asiatic churches were, in fact, authored by the apostles to whom they are credited. The burden of proof falls upon those seeking to discredit the legitimacy of these letters, for far more tradition, time, and evidence supports their veracity, but that is a study for others to carry out. This discourse accepts and supports these letters as the legitimate Scriptures of God written by these men or at least dictated to their amanuenses. These letters are essential, for they contain the codification of the church's leadership structure to be committed to a second generation of faithful believers and beyond. Note 2 Pet 1:20–21; 3:16.

they hold. Because it had been proven effective, the followers of Christ were to adapt and replicate the stratified model the church had developed wherever new in-home churches sprang up. In 1 Cor 12:14–27, Paul addressed the subject of "the one body" and how no person in the body of Christ—the believers of Jesus' true church, the Church of God—was of any less importance than any other, but that all need each other. Likewise, the lesser levels of the *hypēretēs*, *doulos*, and *thyrōros* were equally necessary due to the aid they delivered, the training they received, and that future leaders would be drawn from these strata. In addition, the epistles of Timothy stress the household model, both literally and metaphorically; therefore, one may conclude that just as the *hypēretēs*, *doulos*, and *thyrōros* were component parts of the household structure, they should also be considered as structural and functional positions of the stratified leadership model of the First-Century Church. The epistles of Timothy, Titus, and Peter focus upon the leadership strata of the *episkopos*, *diakonos*, and *presbyteros*, with inferences to the *oikonomos* because they bear the greater weight for their responsibility, direction, and example before the body of the church.

This chapter analyzes the standards prospective leaders need, according to Paul and Peter, detailed in those epistles to ensure the church's perpetuation. The epistles to Timothy contain references to five of the eight leadership roles studied, as do the epistles of Peter, while the epistle to Titus bears witness to three of them. Timothy and Titus were Paul's apprentices, whom he commissioned to lead the churches of Ephesus and Crete. It is advantageous to know who these two men were and understand the relationships they had fostered under Paul's training. The instructions in those letters were crucial to the continuation of the First-Century Church in the second century and beyond. They also pay attention to women's functions within the church structure. This chapter will continue to explore the inclusion of women within church leadership as capable counterparts to men. All of the roles find space and function within the guidelines of the familial household. The first generation of church leaders never intended for the movement to end with the passing of their lives. One of Paul's final postulations to Timothy stated, "And the things that thou hast heard of me among many witnesses, the same commit thou to faithful men, who shall be able to teach others also" (2 Tim 2:2). These epistles provide the diagram for the church's perpetuation unto further generations.

## PAUL'S INSTRUCTIONS TO TIMOTHY

The first letter from Paul to Timothy addresses him as Paul's "true child in the faith," expressing how Timothy had adhered not only to Paul's instruction to take charge of the leadership and the in-home churches in Ephesus but also Timothy's faithfulness to the teaching and training he received from Paul (1 Tim 1:1–3). Bearing the oversight of the metropolis of Ephesus, Timothy may also have held the responsibility for the surrounding region, seeing as Ephesus has been recognized as a conglomerate mother church, made up of several local in-home churches and including other nearby towns such as Magnesia, Smyrnia, and Tralles.[2] Paul stated that he left Timothy in Ephesus, that "thou mightest charge"—he was to maintain order and to announce and command what must be done (1 Tim 1:3).[3] While the Scriptures do not award the title of overseer to Timothy, the level of authority required implies it, as do Paul's statements concerning Timothy's ordination.[4] Verse 18 speaks of prophesies laid upon Timothy, which could be attributed to his ordination as an overseer in the church. In 2 Tim 2:7, Paul tells Timothy to "stir up the gift of God which is in thee by the putting on of my hands," referring directly to and confirming Timothy's ordination. The phrase at the tail of this verse also supports the idea that Timothy was an overseer, "that thou by them (the prophecies) mightest war a good warfare." The NIV and NASB present this phrase as "fight the good fight."[5] However, "mightest war" could be better rendered as "lead others on a campaign," and "good warfare" is the "genuine battle."[6] Paul often referred metaphorically to the struggle with the spiritual realm with militaristic terms (2 Cor 10:4; Eph 6:10–18).

---

2. Osborne, *Ephesians*, 3. In addition, Ignatius's letters to the churches of each these of these specific towns indicates that, by the time of his oversight, their membership had grown, requiring his attention for their specific needs. Ignatius's oversight over multiple towns serves as plausible evidence that he had imitated another leader before himself, most likely Timothy, thus supporting this hypothesis. Lightfoot, "Epistles of S. Ignatius," 42–75.

3. "παραγγέλλω," L&N 1:426.

4. Paul's epistle to the Philippians (KJV) opens with "Paul and Timotheus, the servants of Jesus Christ, to all the saints in Christ Jesus which are at Philippi, *with the bishops and deacons*." The word "with" is σύν and is utilized in passages where one is "to be associated with one to whom some action has reference," states Thayer, in addition, had Paul intended to convey that the bishops and deacons were of a higher rank or status than himself or Timothy, he would have used the preposition καὶ instead of σύν. Thayer, "σύν," *Thayer's Greek-English Lexicon*, 598–99.

5. Mounce and Mounce, *Interlinear New Testament*, 806.

6. Thayer, "στρατεύῃ, στρατείαν, στρατεύω," *Thayer's Greek-English Lexicon*, 590.

For reference, Harold Hoehner renders Eph 6:12 as stating, "Because our struggle is not against flesh and blood, but against authorities, against the cosmic potentates of this darkness, against spiritual beings of wickedness in the heavenly realms."[7] In 2 Tim 2:3, Paul encourages Timothy to have the endurance of a soldier, but his statement refers not to any common soldier but a "champion of the cause of Christ."[8]

Paul's challenge for Timothy to stand apart as a champion for Christ, from a particular vantage, relates to the role of the *therápōn* studied in the previous chapter.[9] In the ancient world, occasions would arise in warfare where armies would agree to select a singular individual to bear the responsibility for the battle's outcome. This individual would have been the best, the bravest, and the mightiest of all the soldiers in that particular army. That soldier would serve their entire military force by substituting himself in place of them. An example of this situation was recorded in the seventeenth chapter of 1 Samuel, where David and Goliath faced one another. Likewise, in the Greek understanding of the *therápōn*, that individual represented, as a substitution, one of their gods here in the physical world. As a half-Greek and half-Jew of Lystra, Timothy's heritage and culture on his father's side could have exposed him to the Greek concept of the *therápōn* (Acts 16:1). He would have probable awareness of the history of King David from his mother's side. As Heb 13:23 mentions "our brother Timothy," it is highly likely that he read the epistle and knew of its usage of *therápōn* concerning Jesus Christ. People often need heroes to inspire them, to light the fire of desire within themselves, and to rise and become a better, more mature version of themselves. Paul challenged Timothy to become Christ's champion, leading his people just as the Lord would have done. In essence, he was to become Christ's physical representative, who the people could see, who takes charge and leads the church for Christ, who they could not see.

The book of Acts introduces Timothy as a disciple of the church, "well reported of by the brethren," whom Paul takes on his sojourn through the cities in Galatia, establishing the churches they visited (Acts 16:1–6). Timothy was a disciple with a good reputation who caught the attention of the apostle Paul. Paul took the young man under his wing,

---

7. Hoehner, *Ephesians*, 573.

8. Thayer, "στρατεύωτης," *Thayer's Greek-English Lexicon*, 590.

9. The Septuagint specifically utilizes θεράπων for the Hebrew word עֶבֶד when speaking about Moses in Num 12:7; Josh 1:2, 8:31, 33 and in Sap 10:16 ["Wisdom" in the Apocrypha]. Thayer, "θεράπων," *Thayer's Greek-English Lexicon*, 289.

exposed him to the duties of a servant (*doulos*) of Christ to the church, and adopted him as his assistant (*hypēretēs*), for Paul calls Timothy his "workfellow" (Rom 16:21). In 1 Cor 4:17, Paul calls Timothy "my beloved son, and faithful in the Lord." Timothy's dedication to ministering to and for Paul and his faithfulness in the gospel of Christ deeply endeared him to Paul. Timothy earned Paul's confidence, so he sent the young man abroad as his emissary (1 Cor 16:10). Second Corinthians 1:19 bears witness that Silvanus and Timothy were commissioned to their evangelical detail preaching Christ.[10] In the absence of schools to teach theology and conduct as the Pharisees operated, the early church utilized the master-apprentice construct to significant effect. Paul apprenticed several men during his ministry, but his top students, arguably, were Silas, John Mark, Titus, and Timothy. In 1 Thess 3:2, Paul calls Timothy "our brother and minister," and the word minister is διάκονος (*diakonos*), indicating he had received his ordination.[11] In Phil 1:1, Paul gives Timothy equal billing as "the servants (*douloi*, [pl.]) of Christ with himself unto the leadership of the church at Philippi," which shows he became a man of renown in the First-Century Church. Likewise, the introduction of 1 Thess gives Timothy (Timotheus) and Silas (Silvanus) equal billing with Paul, and the entire epistle speaks in the third person plural "we," throughout it, which would seem to establish the two younger men in sharing the same authority with Paul, "as the apostles of Christ" (1 Thess 1:1, 2:6; 2 Thess 1:1). In 1 Cor 4:17, Paul sent Timothy in his stead with the necessary authority to admonish the entire body of believers—all the in-home churches there—at Corinth of Paul's teachings concerning the gospel of Christ. Christianity bases its tradition for assuming Timothy became a bishop/overseer of the church on Paul's epistles to Timothy. Though he is never overtly called an *episkopos*, the context shows his authority over the Ephesian Church (probably multiple towns), his authority to ordain other leaders, and Paul's challenge for him to become the church's prime example as a champion for Christ (1 Tim 1:3).

Concerning the subject of ordination from a purely biblical perspective, there were only three leadership roles that individuals were ordained to perform publicly. These were the overseers, ministers, and church

---

10. The book of Acts records "Silas," accompanying Paul on his journeys, yet in Paul's letters, he names "Silvanus," (Acts 15:22–40; 16:19, 25–29; 17:4–15; 2 Cor 1:19; 1 Thess 1:1; 2 Thess 1:1). Thayer, "Σίλας," is a contraction of the name "Σιλουανός," *Thayer's Greek-English Lexicon*, 575.

11. Thayer, "διάκονος," *Thayer's Greek-English Lexicon*, 138.

elders (not to be confused with the familial or social status of an elder). In the KJV, the word "ordained" occurs only once, in Acts 14:23: "And when they (Paul and Barnabas, who were apostles) had ordained them elders in every church." In the Greek text, "when they had ordained," is χειροτονήσαντες, which the NIV and NASB render as "when they had appointed"; however, that word could be better understood to mean "to vote by stretching out the hand; to create or appoint by vote; one to have charge of some office or duty; to elect, appoint, create by show of hands."[12] Another form of this verb appears in 2 Cor 8:19, speaking of another unnamed leader, accompanying Titus to Corinth, "who was also chosen of the churches to travel with us." The Scriptures do not say this, but many have thought the verse to refer to Luke; however, "chosen" is χειροτονηθείς. A group of in-home churches selected that individual—possibly a vote was cast in his favor—to accompany Paul. In his epistle to Titus, Paul states for him to "ordain elders in every city," but the Greek word for "ordain" is different; in this reference, it is καθίστημι: "to appoint one to administer an office."[13] Both terms account for honor and authority conferred to individual(s) by an election or administration outside themselves. Therefore, while ordination in the NT is not what it has become in modernity, the believers did have a means of selection and differentiation of individuals, which conforms after a fashion to the ordination of a person to a position of leadership and authority.

The NT does not have a passage declaring a specific ceremony that one may point to as an official ordination process. The Scriptures do bear witness to events that signify and conform to ordination. Acts 1:24-26 tells that prayers and voting were involved in Matthias's promotion to the ranks of the apostles, which the Scriptures refer to with three titles: "bishoprick"—ἐπισκοπήν; "ministry,"—διακονία; and "apostleship"—ἀποστολῆς. When, at the apostle's directions, the body of believers selected the seven ministers who were appointed to "serve—διακονεῖν under the apostles and over the public body of followers; the chosen individuals were designated, having met the necessary criteria, the apostles prayed over them and laid their hands upon them" (Acts 6:1-6). When the Holy Spirit called out Paul and Barnabas, the leaders present performed a fast,

12. "Χειροτονήσαντες," is the active aorist nominative form of "χειροτονέω." Thayer, "χειροτονέω," *Thayer's Greek-English Lexicon*, 668.

13. Thayer, "καθίστημι," *Thayer's Greek-English Lexicon*, 314. See also Luke 12:42, "shall make ruler"; Acts 6:3, "we may appoint"; and in Heb 2:7, "didst set him," which concerns the authority God bestowed to Jesus Christ.

prayed, and laid their hands on the two men as part of their commissioning (Acts 13:3). Concerning the man Timothy, in 1 Tim 4:14, Paul writes, "Neglect not the gift that is in thee, which was given thee by prophecy, with the laying on of the hands of the presbytery." Paul reiterates this in 2 Tim 1:6 by encouraging Timothy to stir up that same gift. Based upon the context of other Scriptures involving the installation of an individual to a leadership role, which also included prayers, prophecy, laying on of hands ceremonially, and election by other leaders or similar, the conclusion arrived at is that Timothy received an ordination. In addition, Paul directed Timothy to make his life an example in both word and deed; therefore, in the most straightforward understanding, Timothy could not be an example to another of an overseer if he had not served as one himself (1 Tim 4:12). These instances exemplify what ordination consisted of in the era of the First-Century Church.

The codification of standards for the leadership roles of the church takes center stage in the epistles of Timothy, Titus, and Peter. In addition, Paul compares the structure of the greater Christian community to a familial household.[14] He introduced the subject of "the household of faith" in Gal 6:10 and then elaborated upon it as "the household of God" in the book of Ephesians (Eph 2:19). God—the Father—designed what fatherhood is, and Eph 3:15 states that of him, "the whole family in heaven and earth is named." The familial terminology strengthens the cohesion of the community's members, instills a sense of communal identity, and provides an atmosphere of belonging. The household ideals and illustrations (husbands and wives, older members with younger ones, masters and servants) Paul presented in the church epistles are strengthened in the Pastoral Epistles.[15] Within the framework of the household of God, the overseers (ἐπίσκοποι) were first in authority, the ministers (διάκονοι) second, and subordinate to them were the stewards (οἰκονόμοι) followed by the servants (δοῦλοι).[16] In Timothy, the elders, male and female (πρεσβύτεροι, πρεσβύτεραι), were to be revered and respected like elder fathers and mothers of the family (1 Tim 5:1–2).[17] Such ideals aided the continuation of the early church after the first generation of leaders faded away. Many organizations flourish while their original leaders are present. Once they are no longer a guiding presence, those

---

14. MacDonald, *Pauline Churches a Socio-Historical Study*, 207–09

15. MacDonald, *Pauline Churches a Socio-Historical Study*, 208.

16. Young, "On ΕΠΙΣΚΟΠΟΣ AND ΠΠΕΣΒΥΤΕΠΟΣ," 143–44.

17. Young, "On ΕΠΙΣΚΟΠΟΣ AND ΠΠΕΣΒΥΤΕΠΟΣ," 143.

organizations flounder; some wither and die out, and new leaders may completely transform others. The organization of standards and guidelines in the pastoral epistles ensured the early church's perpetuation beyond its first generation of leaders. The letters 1 and 2 Timothy bear the most significant quantity of those guidelines that apply to the overseers, ministers, and elders.

## Bishops/Overseers

Paul instructs Timothy on an individual's qualifications to become an overseer, ἐπίσκοπος (*episkopos*), of the church in 1 Tim 3:1–7. Paul states, "This is a true saying, if a man desire the *office of a bishop* (overseer) he desireth a good work" (1 Tim 3:1).[18] An overseer was to be irreproachable, a "husband of one wife" who controlled their desires and emotions, was sound-minded, resisted the immoderate use of alcohol, was modest, generous to guests, and skillful in teaching the Word of God (v. 2). Before a person could answer the call to serve the church as an overseer, they already had to be accomplished and proficient at teaching the Scriptures to others. Where would a person have the opportunity to cultivate the practical experience necessary? Logically, in their time spent serving as a household manager, a minister, and possibly as an assistant to another overseer. Verse three bears a second warning against potential alcoholism and adds that an overseer was not to be a fighter or of a contentious, quarrelsome personality. In addition, overseers were not to be greedy, desirous of bribes, or coveting the things of others (v. 3).

    The overseer's stratum was more spiritually mature than that of the minister in their spirituality, experience, and expertise with the Scriptures; they were also above the elders in their spiritual responsibilities and stature.[19] An overseer had to have his household in order; as the church meetings were widely held in the home, such implies that an overseer would have successfully conducted an in-home church (vv. 4–5). The NASB states, "If a man does not know how to manage his own household, how will he care for the church of God?" (v. 5). Finally, an overseer was not to be one of the newly converted, a neophyte believer; still they needed to have a good report, reputations, and have proven themselves

---

    18. "Office of a bishop," according to Mounce and Mounce is "ἐπισκοπῆς"— *episkopēs*, the genitive feminine singular noun form of "ἐπίσκοπος," Mounce and Mounce, *Interlinear New Testament*, 808.

    19. Condon, "Church Offices," 74–8, 84.

amongst the faithful believers and other leaders, which takes time, work and service to the church. One earns the trust of others over time, not overnight, and the proving stage for an overseer was as a minister.

## Deacons/Ministers

Paul then turns his attention to the qualities necessary for one to qualify to serve the church as a minister, διάκονος (*diakonos*). The appellation of διάκονος is utilized as a formal title alongside ἐπίσκοπος as demonstrated in Phil 1 and 1 Tim 3.[20] As the stratum of the minister was a proving ground before one might graduate to the level of an overseer, many of the attributes Paul lists are those required of an overseer. For example, "Deacons, likewise, are to be men worthy of respect (grave, venerable), sincere, not indulging in much wine, and not pursuing dishonest gain (dirty money, bribery). They must keep hold of the deep truths of the faith with a clear conscience" (1 Tim 3:8–9 NIV).[21] The duties of a minister were different than those of an overseer, and though they were subordinate to the overseers, they should not be regarded as the overseer's assistants, for they were also distinct from the *hyperetes*.[22] Instead, the agency of the διάκονος—minister was initially as an agent-spokesperson for the apostles (in their absence) and an attendant for the people, who acted as a "go-between" or intermediary, and later evolved into an intermediary for the ἐπίσκοπος—overseer and the οἰκονόμος—steward.[23]

In verse ten, Paul states that candidates for the minister's position were required to prove themselves to the church through ministrations, serving others after the fashion of a minister/deacon. The NT never states if such service were to have been in an official capacity, such as a *hyperetes* or *doulos* or some other fashion of apprenticeship, or in an unofficial capacity before receiving their promotion. Utilizing the appointment of the seven ministers in Acts 6 and of Timothy in Acts 16, a person first garnered a positive reputation amongst the believers for their willingness and abilities to serve others. In the early years of the First-Century Church, most likely, individuals took responsibility for themselves as

---

20. Strauch, *Paul's Vision for the Deacons*, 27.
21. "Deacons" in this Scripture reference is the nominative, masculine plural form for "διάκονος, διάκονοι," Thayer, "διάκονος," *Thayer's Greek-English Lexicon*, 138.
22. Fraser, "Office of Deacon," 17–18.
23. Merkle, "Authority of Deacons in Pauline Churches," 314.

independent reactions to the needs of others. Many years after positions of authority had evolved within the collective church body, a mode of apprenticeships would be expected based on the surrounding culture. However, such does not eliminate some individuals' independent service actions.

Paul's statement, "Let these also first be proved" (1 Tim 3:10), aligns with the standards for the selection of the first seven ordained ministers (Acts 6:1–6). They had proven themselves to the congregation before ever receiving honors or a title. Before a man could receive ordination as a minister, his wife had to have a character report that matched his (v. 11). In accord with Paul's earlier teachings from 1 Cor 11 and 1 Cor 14, and the pastoral epistles continued his exhortations for wives to be subordinate to their husbands.[24] One may recognize a bolstering of this marital standard from the first epistle of Corinthians to his teaching in Ephesians until becoming a codified standard for the leaders in the letters of Timothy and Titus. Like the overseers, the ministers were to be married, with one wife, keeping an orderly household. How a couple conducted their family and their household, and it is no slight stretch to include a household church, was the primary means by which they gained a glowing reputation among the believers of their town (v. 12).

The letters to Timothy do not mention the position of the home church manager, the steward—οἰκονόμος (*oikonomos*). Still, Paul repeatedly stresses the importance of familial relationships and their witness to the church. Margaret McDonald promotes that the Pauline epistles of Timothy and Titus advance and further establish the household codes from his earlier church epistles.[25] Furthermore, she states, "Exhortations concerning church leaders demonstrate the close connection between one's position in the household, one's behavior with respect to that position, and eligibility for office. The role of the bishop is closed to those who are not model householders" (1 Tim 3:4–5).[26] The leadership was expected to have an open and transparent relationship with the congregation, as would exist if they all dwelt under the same roof. The root word for οἰκονόμος: οἶκος (*oikos*), meaning "an inhabited house; any building whatever: the palace, the house of God, the tabernacle; any dwelling place," is utilized several times.[27] This word, οἶκος (*oikos*), appears in 1

---

24. MacDonald, *Pauline Churches*, 105.
25. MacDonald, *Pauline Churches*, 207–10.
26. MacDonald, *Pauline Churches*, 210.
27. Thayer, "οἶκος," *Thayer's Greek-English Lexicon*, 365.

Tim 3:4–5 in reference to the overseers' homes and in 3:12 referring to the ministers' houses. First Timothy 3:15 mentions the proper behavior for the believers "in the house [οἴκῳ] of God."[28] As the Greek text presents things as "οἴκῳ Θεοῦ," it could be translated as "God's household," further strengthening the household codes witnessed in these epistles.

This research established earlier in chapters three and four that the home church and the leadership stratum of the *oikonomos* were essential to the Christian movement of the first century. Culturally speaking, the title of οἰκονόμος is more prevalent among the tombstones, honorary inscriptions, and dedications in remembrance of household servants/slaves.[29] Young concludes, "It is hardly surprising that Θεοῦ οἰκονός would acquire authority and be seen as representing God."[30] If the home lives of those who would be ministers and overseers were so crucial and integral to their character as leaders, so were their developed and proven abilities and reputations as successful household-church managers. Though not mentioned in the Timothy letters, the stratum of the *oikonomos*—stewards, is either assumed or implied because that level would have served as a developmental stage for individuals who would later become the church's ministers and overseers. Paul states, "A deacon must be the husband of one wife and must manage his children and his household [οἴκων] well. Those who have served well gain an excellent standing and great assurance in their faith in Christ Jesus" (1 Tim 3:12–13 NIV). A deacon/minister first serves his family, then his household, then the church, with each level increasing his aptitude as a leader for Christ.

When one looks past the KJV English, verse eleven proves controversial. The KJV reads, "Even so must their wives be grave." However, the New Oxford Annotated Bible reads, "Women likewise must be serious, not slanderers, but temperate, faithful in all things."[31] The disagreement between the versions is because, in Greek, this verse reads as follows: Γυναῖκας ὡσαύτως σεμνάς, μὴ διαβόλους, νηφαλίους, πιστὰς ἐν πᾶσιν.[32]

---

28. Other usages of "οἶκος," appear in 1 Tim 5:4; 2 Tim 1:16; 4:19; Titus 1:11; 1 Pet 2:5; 4:17.

29. Young, "On ΕΠΙΣΚΟΠΟΣ AND ΠΠΕΣΒΥΤΕΠΟΣ," 144.

30. Young, "On ΕΠΙΣΚΟΠΟΣ AND ΠΠΕΣΒΥΤΕΠΟΣ," 144.

31. For another comparison, the footnote from the NIV states, "*Their wives.* The Greek for this phrase simply means 'the women' and therefore could refer to (1) deacon's wives, (2) deaconesses, or (3) female deacons." 1 Tim 3:11, ff. NIV, 1839. It is not known what difference the NIV points to by referring to "deaconesses" and "female deacons," for presumably they are the same.

32. Mounce and Mounce, *Interlinear New Testament*, 809.

Γυναῖκας (*gynaikas*), a noun, is the accusative feminine plural form of γυνή (*gyné*), which is utilized universally across the NT for "a woman of any age, whether a virgin, or married, or a widow."[33] The women mentioned in verse eleven could be either the wives of the deacons or single women who became deaconesses in their own right. The KJV assumes that the usage of γυναῖκας in the passage alludes to the wives of the deacons, who would then become the wives of the bishops once their husbands attained that level. Yet, the Scriptures are silent, providing no instructions concerning the responsibilities of concerning the elders and bishops' wives. Paul instructs the collective body of the believers that wives are to be subordinate to their husbands (Eph 5:22–24; Col 3:21). So why would it mention deacons' wives and leave out the wives of the other two levels? Therefore, upon the logic that Paul would not provide specific instructions for deacons' wives and not those of the elders and bishops, the usage of γυναῖκας in verse eleven refers to single women in the collective church body who were promoted to the level of a deacon.

The information provided by the New Oxford and the NIV presents the possibility for women to become church deaconesses like Phebe, mentioned in Rom 16:1. As the collective church increased in numbers and the number of in-home churches within its structure, changes evolved within the responsibilities of leadership positions. Romans 16:1 bears witness that Phebe was the servant—διάκονος for the church of Cenchrea, which was an important port located approximately five miles west of the metropolis of Corinth. The Scriptures utilize "church" for groups of various sizes; due to the population of Cenchrea and its importance to the economy of Corinth in that period, it would be an underestimation to assume this reference intended a singular in-home church. Instead, under Paul's oversight, it is more likely that Phebe was responsible for the entire body of believers of the town of Cenchrea, however many in-home gatherings that may have accounted for. The Scriptures' testimony of Phebe was as a respected deaconess who ministered to the believers as an extension of Paul's ministry.

There exists a difficulty in understanding whether the writers of the NT meant "wife" or "woman" when they utilized both γυνή and γυναῖκας in the text, for there is no absolute assignment to either word, but instead, they remain interchangeable. Louw and Nida relate, without presenting a definitive rule, that "the contexts normally indicate clearly

---

33. Thayer, "γυνή," *Thayer's Greek-English Lexicon*, 123.

which meaning of γυνή is involved."³⁴ Therefore, utilizing the context as the discerning factor, understanding the "women" of verse eleven as "the wives of the deacons" bears the most weight (1 Tim 3:11). The greater significance of including women in this passage shows they were essential to the movement promoting the gospel of Christ. The *Didascalia Apostolorum* provides evidence that the position of the deaconess held importance and authority within the church collective in the early centuries preceding the formation of the Roman Catholic Church. The purpose of the deaconess appears to have been the managing of the single women of the church, for it states, "The ministry of the widows is downgraded and a ministry of deaconess introduced in order that women's ministries might come within episcopal control."³⁵ This statement also bears witness to two other factors that relate to the organization of leaders in the NT: that women operated notable roles of service and leadership within the church collective and that the widows of the congregation maintained importance and usefulness since being mentioned several times in the NT (Acts 6:1, 9:39–41; 1 Cor 7:8; 1 Tim 5:3, 11, 16; Jas 1:27). First Timothy 5:10 speaks concerning a widow, known for good deeds, ministering to others within the church, such as lodging strangers (travelers), washing other's feet (presumably at their meetings), and aiding those in affliction and distress, and the text presents these actions as "good works" to be emulated by others. Though their specific positions of service within the First-Century Church are difficult to identify with exactness, what is evident is women were valuable in varying modes within the early church and beyond.

### Elders

In 1 Tim 5, Paul then focused his attention on the elders' roles within the church. In recalling the testimony of Acts 14:23, by that time in the church's history, they practiced the ordination of elders (πρεσβύτερος— *presbyteros*) in every church, where available.³⁶ These revered individuals were older people than the average within a body of attendees, who served the church as responsible and authoritative counselors "in matters

---

34. "γυνή, αικος," L&N 1:119.

35. Stewart-Sykes, *Didascalia Apostolorum*, 152.

36. Πρεσβύτερος (*presbyteros*) in this verse reference is in the accusative masculine plural adjective form, which describes both the person and their function within the church. Mounce and Mounce, *Interlinear New Testament*, 518.

of socio-religious concerns both in Jewish and Christian societies."[37] The NT never states whether there was more than one elder per church or only one. Likewise, the NT does not stipulate how many elders served in each town or metropolis where in-home churches occurred.[38] When 1 Tim 4:14 speaks of the charismatic gift (presumably a gift ministry, as Timothy had already received salvation many years prior) imparted to Timothy at his ordination accompanied by prophecy, those who laid their hands on him were a council of elders. The Greek word utilized in that reference is πρεσβυτερίου (*presbyteriou*), which is the genitive neuter singular noun form of πρεσβύτερος, indicating a singular group of elders.[39] The NT uses πρεσβυτέριον in Luke 22:66 and Acts 22:5 for the council of elders that served the temple, but πρεσβυτερίου in 1 Tim 4:14; each of these usages of πρεσβύτερος resembles a senate of elected politicians.

The lack of details and limitations for forming a council of elders in the early church permits considerable flexibility in interpreting its application. In a town with several in-home churches, a singular minister, but no overseer, each church might submit one elder to serve on such a council, whose job was assisting the local minister. In such an arrangement, those elders may have been the steward—*oikonomos* of an in-home church, or they could have served with an *oikonomos* also counseling that person. A council of elders could have also similarly assisted a church overseer, except if the body of individuals elected to such a senate represented a larger number of in-home churches, their number would also have been larger. There is no mandate restricting church eldership to only the aging leaders of the church, nor does it exclude those who may have been familial or social elders from serving in the capacity of church presbyters. The lack of directions leaves the congregation flexible for adaptation to their needs. Also, the focus of the letters of Timothy, Titus, and

---

37. "πρεσβύτερος," L&N 1:134, 542–43.

38. Likewise, Paul's greeting to the Philippian believers addresses deacons and bishops in the plural sense of both words (Phil 1:1). The lack of specificity leaves readers with the possibility of more than one overseer and minister per city or that the introduction was meant to address not only Philippi but also the surrounding towns and immediate territories. Without explicit instructions from the Scriptures, both vantages are valid. As Christianity developed, the apostolic fathers set down specific rules and traditions so that the people accepted only one bishop/overseer per city/territory, presumably based upon Timothy's oversight for Ephesus and Titus's for Crete.

39. "πρεσβύτερος," L&N 1:134, 542–43; corroborated with Mounce and Mounce, *Interlinear New Testament*, 811.

Peter remains on directing leaders of the First-Century Church. Therefore, if other NT writings do not attend to elders regarding their social and familial sense, then most likely, the believers would have followed the cultural behaviors of the period. According to Young, in the period estimated between the first and fourth centuries, the bishop appointed the presbyters as an advisory council, which aided the bishop and the deacons.[40] Therefore, one could logically conclude that a panel of elders could have similarly assisted overseers and ministers in the First-Century Church.

First Timothy 5:1–2 concerns the church elders, both men and women, stating they were to be revered and treated like one might their father and mother. Within the functioning strata of the household-church arrangement, the elder men were expected to teach, counsel, guide, and provide examples to the youthful men and the same with the elder women unto the young women (1 Tim 5:1–3).[41] The elder women were expected to coach the younger ones in the roles of dutiful wives and successful mothers.[42] The close mentoring of one generation to the next reflected the cultural practices of the day and helped ensure a transfer of values within the congregation while furthering its unity.

Regarding individuals who possibly previously served the church as leaders but that had aged into the role of the elders, verse 17 declares, "Let the elders that rule well be counted worthy of double honour, especially they who labour in the word and doctrine." "Rule" in this verse is related to "rule, ruleth, and ruling" found in 1 Tim 3:4, 5, 12, all sharing the same base but as different forms of the word προΐστημι (proïstēmi).[43] Another possible rending of this form of προΐστημι could be "who have been serving"; thus, verse 17 would read, "Let the elders who have been serving well be considered worthy of double honor."[44] The latter half of this verse, "They who labour in the word and doctrine," could also be more accurately stated as "those who are laboring hard at preaching and

---

40. Young, "On ΕΠΙΣΚΟΠΟΣ AND ΠΠΕΣΒΥΤΕΠΟΣ," 145.

41. MacDonald, *Pauline Churches*, 209.

42. Despite the fact that such ethics reinforces other established biblical ideals related to marriage and family, MacDonald views the mentoring of younger women in this fashion as "an attempt to eliminate women from leadership positions." MacDonald, *Pauline Churches*, 209.

43. "Rule" in verse 17 is "προεστῶτες," the masculine plural active nominative perfect participle verb form of "προΐστημι." Thayer, "προΐστημι," *Thayer's Greek-English Lexicon*, 539–40.

44. Mounce and Mounce, *Interlinear New Testament*, 813.

teaching."⁴⁵ This verse indicates that while elders were not mandated to excel at teaching and preaching the Scriptures, those who exerted themselves were due twice the honor compared to those who only advised and provided wise counsel. Not all aging believers became "church elders," and to restate something said previously: while apostles, prophets, pastors, teachers, overseers, and deacons, as they aged, would become elders of the church, not all who were elders had served in such leadership capacities. Therefore, the ones who had served the church collective after that fashion were remarkable.

## Servants

Finally, in 2 Tim 2:24, Paul addresses the position of "the servant (δοῦλος—*doulos*) of the Lord," which Timothy, by his life and conduct, was to exemplify for the church. Throughout Paul's writings, teaching, and preaching, including how he described his relationship with the Lord Jesus Christ, he encouraged others to devote themselves to Jesus as his servants and as the servants of God (Rom 6:22; 1 Cor 7:23; 2 Cor 4:5). As a successor to the apostle Paul (1 Cor 4:17; Phil 2:19–22), Timothy needed to be a pacesetter for the church, striving to be a champion for Christ (2 Tim 2:3–4), who was a strong husbandman (2:6), to study avoiding actions and attributes of ungodliness (2:16–17) and exerting himself as God's workman (2:15). Timothy was to become worthy of God's honor (2:20–21) and to "flee youthful lusts, but follow after righteousness, faith, charity, peace, with them that call on the Lord" (2:22).⁴⁶ All of the aforementioned qualities lead up to Paul's exhortation concerning a servant (*doulos*) of the Lord. By the context, one had to earn the title of *doulos* through their actions displaying dedication and loyalty. Clearly, in the First-Century Church, for one to be esteemed, the Lord's *doulos* was not a light matter.

The positions of assistants and doorkeepers do not make an appearance in the pastoral epistles. They should not be counted out or assumed to be eliminated. Paul states in 1 Tim 3:15, "But if I tarry long, that thou mayest know how thou oughtest to behave thyself in the house of God, which is the church of the living God, the pillar and ground of the truth."

45. Mounce and Mounce, *Interlinear New Testament*, 813.

46. Paul trained several young men to become leaders for the church collective, with the exception of possibly Titus, only Timothy received glowing reports like these across Paul's epistles, including the benediction of 1 Tim 6:13–21.

In reading these letters, one should never forget the influence of the Greco-Roman culture that surrounded the Christ movement as it grew and evolved. In addition, Paul's letters, the four canonical Gospels, and the book of Acts present the cultural and doctrinal context that supports the directives of the letters of Timothy, Titus, and Peter. When Paul wrote in 1 Cor 4:1 from the perspective of an all-inclusive "we," he proclaimed that others outside the church should logically conclude, upon witnessing the lives of Christians, that they are the assistants of the Lord Jesus Christ and household managers for God, he meant that standard should apply to all believers everywhere. The early church leaders utilized the master-apprentice relationship to train others to perform the roles necessary within the church. Assisting a minister or an overseer allowed one to learn that position up close and personally. The fact that the temple at Jerusalem, Jewish synagogues, and other religious structures utilized doorkeepers, as did the Christian church in Rome circa the third century AD, proves that position's value and presence.[47] The testimony of the pastoral epistles displays an increased focus on the more influential leadership roles in the early church, for they set the pace and bore the responsibilities for overseeing all the others.

Paul frequently utilized agricultural metaphors concerning instructing and nurturing maturation in the followers of Christ. He states in 2 Tim 2:6, "The husbandman that laboureth must be first partaker of the fruits."[48] A "husbandman" was a land worker, a tiller of the soil, a vinedresser, or a farmer; he produced crops, whether he raised grains, fruits, or vegetables.[49] In ancient cultures, one often planted a whole piece of fruit or produce and not merely the seeds to reproduce another plant of the same kind; hence, the husbandman had to partake of the fruit himself. Metaphorically, before a leader in the early church could expect the believers to produce spiritual qualities resulting from the doctrines taught to them, they needed a living example from their teachers. In the opening chapter of Romans, Paul stated that he wanted the believers in Rome fully aware of his purpose for visiting them; spiritually speaking, his visitation would aid their maturation and fruitfulness (Rom 1:13). Crops require tending, nurturing, maintenance, and patience to grow to maturity. Also, one could not scream at, browbeat, or abuse crops with an expectation

---

47. Eusebius, *History of the Church*, 282.

48. For other examples see also: Rom 6:21–22; 7:4–5; 1 Cor 9:7; Gal 5:22; Eph 5:9; Phil 1:22; 4:17; Col 1:6.

49. Thayer, "γεωργός," *Thayer's Greek-English Lexicon*, 114.

that they might develop expediently. In 1 Cor 3:6, he states concerning the congregation's development, "I have planted, Apollos watered; but God gave the increase." Then he explains, "For we are labourers together with God: ye are God's husbandry" (1 Cor 3:9). The teachings of a false apostle, pastor, overseer, or minister will not produce results reflecting the gospel of Christ, and their followers' lives' will bear the produce (Gal 6:7-8). Every other leader who follows Paul's example, desiring to emulate his ways and means, is therefore accountable to their congregation for presenting themselves as a living example, and their teaching, instruction, and tutelage aids the believers to become spiritually mature in the gospel of Christ. As he wrote in Gal 6:9-10, "And let us not be weary in well doing: for in due season we shall reap, if we faint not. As we have therefore opportunity, let us do good unto all men, especially unto them who are of the household of faith."

Paul's instruction for Timothy to teach others, thereby ensuring the perpetuation of the church, bookends chapter two. In 2 Tim 2:2, he commanded Timothy, "And the things that thou hast heard of me among many witnesses, the same commit thou to faithful men, who shall be able to teach others also." Such a mandate for Timothy would have been a reinforcement of Paul's directive to the Philippian leaders, "Those things, which ye have both learned, and received, and heard, and seen in me, do: and the God of peace shall be with you" (Phil 4:9). Paul made his life an open display for others to duplicate. While Timothy received direct instructions to make his own life an example in word and deed, there should be no room to doubt that others whom Paul trained, like Titus, Silas, John, Mark, and others, would have received the exact instructions. Leaders in the First-Century Church were expected to exemplify what they promoted in their teachings. In 1 Cor 4:1-2, according to Paul, stewards of God's mysteries were required to be faithful, and the Greek words for "stewards" were forms of οἰκονόμος (*oikonomos*).[50] As household managers for the church, people had opportunities to prove their faithfulness in serving others before becoming deacons/ministers, and they also were afforded opportunities to teach the believers who gathered in their homes. Then, in 1 Tim 2:24, Paul stated to Timothy that the Lord's servant δοῦλον (*doulon*) needed to be skillful in teaching.[51] Thus,

---

50. In 1 Cor 4:1 "stewards," is "οἰκονόμους," the accusative masculine plural form of οἰκονόμος, and in verse 2, "stewards" is the demonstrative masculine plural form, "οἰκονόμοις," Mounce and Mounce, *Interlinear New Testament*, 649.

51. "Δοῦλον," the accusative masculine singular form of "δοῦλος." Mounce and

from the second chapter, one should understand the importance of the leadership level of the *doulos* to the other more mature leadership positions. The believer grew in maturity and faithfulness, learning from others via mentoring and apprenticeships how to teach the gospel of Christ. The level of the household manager was the proving ground before one was elevated to that of the minister. Then, after proving one's maturity, earning his excellent report in the church, and displaying his developed aptitudes and expertise, that servant, that *doulos* of the Lord, received his ordination with prophecy and laying on of hands to become an overseer of the church.

## The Controversy of Women in the Ministry

The third chapter of Timothy, containing the duty codes and prerequisites for overseers and ministers within the household of God, contextually stands on Paul's edicts and instructions in the second chapter, and in the second chapter lies a problematic verse of Scripture concerning women. First Timothy 2:12 states, "But I suffer not a woman to teach, nor to usurp authority over the man, but to be in silence." Christian churches have utilized this verse and 1 Cor 14:34 like a *Malleus Maleficarum* upon women for years. In the twentieth century, denominations began debating whether women should be allowed to teach and lead in congregations. All believers and followers of the Lord Jesus Christ have a duty to speak his gospel and teach each other (Col 3:16). Deacons/ministers should develop the ability to teach the Scriptures to grow in maturity and become overseers who are expected to be proficient in teaching. Then what about women speaking the Word of God and deaconesses teaching in the church? Titus 2:3 directs women to teach that which is good according to God's Word. One cannot truly minister to others without delivering God's Word, for it is written, "He (God) sent his word and healed them and delivered them from their destructions" (Ps 107:20). Junia, of Rom 16, could not have achieved notoriety amongst the apostles without the ability to articulate and expound the gospel message with alacrity. In Acts 18:24–28, Apollos, who was eloquent and "mighty in the Scriptures," was taken in by Aquila and Priscilla, and together, they "expounded unto him the way of God more perfectly." This husband and wife team together taught this well-educated man God's Word. If Priscilla

---

Mounce, *Interlinear New Testament*, 821.

had not done some of the teaching, the verses might have said something about her keeping silent. What of the prophetess Anna, in Luke 2:36–38, who spoke to any seeking redemption about Jesus Christ? Or, Philip's four daughters who prophesied to the apostle Paul, which their message most likely was corroborated by Agabus in Acts 21:8–11? Women have been speaking out in the name of the LORD and speaking for him, carrying his message since Miriam, the sister of Moses, and before her. So, either there is a contradiction in the Scriptures, or there exists a mistranslation, a misunderstanding within the English rendering of 1 Tim 2:12.

In the immediate context of the second chapter surrounding verse twelve, Paul discusses men's and women's behaviors within the body of the household. He does not address them as husbands and wives in 1 Tim 2:8–11, like in the fifth chapter of Ephesians, which contextualizes the marriage relationship. Still, he does mention the first married couple, Adam and Eve, and childbearing in verses thirteen through fifteen; the marriage relationship seems implied. First Timothy 2:8 addresses "men pray everywhere." The word "men" is ἄνδρας (*andras*), the accusative plural masculine form of ἀνήρ (*anér*), which by definition is "a man, a male" but is rendered in English as "a man; a husband; a betrothed or future husband."[52] "Women," in verse nine, is γυναῖκας (*gynaikas*), again and as before, the accusative feminine plural form of γυνή (*gyné*), which could be interpreted as a woman that was single of marriageable age, married, or a widow.[53] Since the context moves the reader from men and women to Adam and Eve and then to overseers and ministers who were expected to be married (ch. 3), one should understand, in light of 1 Cor 7, the marriage relationship is a prime example of maturity within the believers of the body of Christ (Eph 5). Paul exhorted single followers and disciples to excel in the service of the Lord, but there was some expectation that they would eventually couple up and marry. The verses of this chapter of Timothy, when compared to Eph 5 or 1 Cor 7, do not provide overt marriage context, confining ἄνδρας and γυναῖκας solely to the marriage arrangement; neither is the husband-wife relationship excluded. Therefore, 1 Tim 2:12 must apply to unmarried and married women. Thomas R. Schreiner produced an interpretation of the passage surrounding this particular verse, describing the debate on women teaching and leading as polarized between the complementarian and egalitarian positions on

---

52. Thayer, "ἀνήρ," *Thayer's Greek-English Lexicon*, 45.
53. Thayer, "γυνή," *Thayer's Greek-English Lexicon*, 123.

the subject.[54] He interprets 1 Tim 2:12 to govern all women everywhere in the church. However, the orientation of this study promotes that both positions, complementarian and egalitarian, have merit but that the truth of the situation lies in a balance between the complementarian and the egalitarian and refraining from forcing one to pick a side.

The complementarian position regarding 1 Tim 2:12 is that the apostle Paul prohibited women from "teaching Christian doctrine to and exercising authority over men."[55] This understanding represents a long-standing tradition in Christian dogma that follows, preaches, and imitates much the same. The majority of modern English versions of the Bible reflect this dogma in their renderings with some minor variance. Most scholars and theologians look to the immediate context of verses thirteen and fourteen for confirmation, which put forth that God formed Adam first and Eve second. Thus, the complementarian platform promotes men as dominant and women as subordinate, and women are not permitted to teach or lead in Christian churches. They often support their position by referring to Eph 5:22–24, which emphasizes that husbands and wives have different complementary roles in marriage and that wives should submit to their husbands in all things. They also cite 1 Cor 14:34, "Let your women keep silent in the churches," as additional reinforcement. The complementarian platform then extends the husband-wife arrangement to the rest of the body of Christ, prescribing that all men and women should align themselves in the same fashion.

The egalitarian position promotes that men and women are equal before God because God is not a "respecter of persons," meaning he does not favor one above another simply because they are a particular race of people or male versus female (Acts 10:34; Rom 2:11; Col 3:25). Galatians 3:28 is another favored Scripture, for it states regarding the new covenant and baptism of Christ: "There is neither Jew nor Greek, there is neither bond nor free, there is neither male nor female: for ye are all one in Christ Jesus." If God does not grant favoritism, then people should not either, and women should potentially have the same rites, abilities, and privileges as men. The egalitarian position unilaterally promotes that to deny women the same opportunities as men to lead a congregation, to teach, and to obey the inspiration of the Holy Spirit is an injustice.[56]

---

54. Köstenberger and Schreiner, *Women in the Church*, 171–219.
55. Köstenberger and Schreiner, *Women in the Church*, 293.
56. Köstenberger and Schreiner, *Women in the Church*, 160–61.

First Tim 2:12 is perhaps one of the most polarizing verses of Scripture; with numerous exegetical studies, it is still hotly contested among scholars. Concerning this verse's difficulty, Jamin Hübner writes, "1 Timothy 2:12 has played a defining role in the Christian debate about the role of women in ministry, especially in American evangelicalism."[57] If church traditions are negated and feminist bias suspended, the crux of the argument between these two factions rests upon one's perception, interpretation, and translation of the word αὐθεντεῖν. The KJV renders αὐθεντεῖν pejoratively as "usurp authority," the ESV presents αὐθεντεῖν in a positive light as "exercise authority," and endeavoring to take a neutral stance the 2011 NIV proffers "assume authority." The factor that the occurrence of αὐθεντεῖν in 1 Tim 2:12 is its solo usage in all of the NT or the Septuagint is what makes understanding αὐθεντεῖν difficult—it is a hapax legomenon—elevating the significance of the term and the message of the verse.[58] Linda Bellville presents αὐθεντεῖν as bearing a purely negative meaning and message because she cites that the only other available biblical use, which is found in the apocryphal text, the Wisdom of Solomon 12:6, translates αὐθεντεῖν as "murder."[59] Schreiner, advocating for the complementarian interpretation of 1 Tim 2:12, decries the significance of the hapax legomenon as revealing a distinct meaning differing from the more commonly used term, ἐξουσιάζειν.[60] Upholding the standards of this study previously set forth: every word within the Word of God was given with holy intent and purpose, and the uniqueness of the linguistic idiom, hapax legomenon, merits a careful, diligent investigation of this term αὐθεντεῖν (*authentein*). As long as the Holy Bible is perceived and believed to be the Word and will of the creator, God, entrusted to humanity, then when these Holy Scriptures were committed to written form, they were initially perfect, without flaw, error, or contradiction (1 Pet 1:20–21; 2 Tim 3:16–17). Therefore, any perceived contradictions must be due to misunderstanding, mishandling, and misinterpretations that came with later redactions of the original texts. If no difference in meaning existed

---

57. Hübner, "Revisiting the Clarity of Scripture in 1 Timothy 2:12," 99.

58. Bellville, "Lexical Fallacies in Rendering Αὐθεντεῖν in 1 Timothy 2:12," 317. Schreiner, "Interpretation of 1 Timothy 2:9–15," 195.

59. Bellville, "Lexical Fallacies in Rendering Αὐθεντεῖν in 1 Timothy 2:12," 321; Apocrypha, *New Oxford Annotated Bible*, 86.

60. The verb ἐξουσιάζειν does not appear in the Scriptures, but forms of it do, such as in Luke 22:25: "And *they that exercise authority upon* [ἐξουσιάζοντες] them are called benefactors." See also 1 Cor 6:12: "But I will not *be brought under the power* [ἐξουσιασθήσομαι]" and twice as "power"—ἐξουσιάζει in 1 Cor 7:4.

between αὐθεντεῖν and ἐξουσιάζειν, or any of its cognates, then why would the author utilize it? When an author uses a different word semantically, the message must bear some variance in intent and meaning from the norm. Truth is always simple. Hübner promotes that 1 Tim 2:12 must be interpreted and understood according to the hermeneutical principle that one must interpret an obscure passage in light of those verses of Scripture that speak clearly and plainly on the same subject.[61]

Schreiner's testimony follows in lockstep with conservative Christian dogma and tradition regarding support for the complementarian platform. He acknowledges but quickly dismisses studies performed by other theologians who argue, based upon the culture of that period, that Paul's instructions to Timothy were meant only to quell a feminist movement of some kind, such as advanced by Catherine Kroger or Sharon Gritz.[62] By analyzing the immediate context, he dispenses Andrew Perriman's proposal that verse twelve could be parenthetical.[63] Schreiner promotes that Paul's directive to the First-Century Church was universal, elevated men as superior to women, and unilaterally "prohibited women from teaching and exercising any authority over men."[64]

In his exposé of 1 Tim 2:12, Andreas J. Köstenberger delves into the grammar and syntax of the verse to illuminate its intent. Contrary to the egalitarian position that 1 Tim 2:12 focuses upon "women's negative exercise of authority," Köstenberger does not find that the verse utilizes αὐθεντεῖν (*authentein*) with negatory feeling or implication in addition to its meaning and that Paul's message should "be understood nonpejoratively."[65] At the foundation of his essay is the premise that "mandates that the two activities indicated by διδάσκειν and αὐθεντεῖν ἀνδρός must be, in Paul's consideration, either both positive or both negative; yet it also addresses in more detail the relationship between the two infinitives.[66] Köstenberger's analysis of the syntax of the verse is precise and essential to this study: 1 Tim 2:12 has a negated finite verb οὐκ ἐπιτρέπω—"I do not permit (I suffer not)"; its subject is γυναικί—"a woman," governing the infinitive verbs διδάσκειν—"to teach,"—and αὐθεντεῖν—"to exercise authority," connected by the coordinating

61. Hübner, "Clarity of Scripture in 1 Timothy 2:12," 99.
62. Köstenberger and Schreiner, *Women in the Church*, 175.
63. Köstenberger and Schreiner, *Women in the Church*, 189.
64. Köstenberger and Schreiner, *Women in the Church*, 192–95.
65. Köstenberger and Schreiner, *Women in the Church*, 125–26.
66. Köstenberger and Schreiner, *Women in the Church*, 127.

conjunction οὐδέ—"or" and their object ἀνδρός—"over a man," then the contrasted adversative ἀλλά—"but" with the infinitive εἶναι—"to be" and the prepositional phrase ἐν ἡσυχίᾳ—"in quietness" serving as a predicate adjective.[67] He states that 1 Tim 2:12 is a case where two positive activities exist: "to teach" and "to have authority" joined by the coordinating conjunction "or," but a negative verb "I do not permit" prohibits their exercise. In Köstenberger's experience and the course of his study of this verse and others like it, for the majority of occurrences in the NT, such is the pattern: a finite negative command governing two infinitive positive verbs with a coordinating conjunction.[68] In Greek, the possibility also exists for a finite negative, with two infinitive negative verbs, with a coordinating conjunction; however, this is less common, but not a coordinating conjunction between an infinitive negative verb and an infinitive positive verb.[69] Because αὐθεντεῖν is a problematic word to understand within the verse, Köstenberger chooses to understand it in light of διδάσκειν, which he states, "When used in an unqualified way in the New Testament, it denotes an activity that the writer views positively and that should be rendered 'to teach.'"[70] Köstenberger's conclusion concerning 1 Tim 2:12, while allowing for the possibility of the pejorative interpretation, rests with absolute "I do not permit a woman to teach or to have (or exercise) authority over a man," without any allowance for exceptions to the rule.[71]

Belleville takes issue with the changes and revisions in the *Greek-English Lexicon of the New Testament and other Early Christian Literature*, revised and edited by Frederick W. Danker (BDAG). She puts forth that as of 1979, the BDAG "defined αὐθεντέω as 'have authority, domineer τιός (over someone),'" but that in the 2000 revised edition, "domineer" was removed to eliminate the negative connotation, a change based upon studies conducted by George Knight and Leland Wilshire.[72] Wilshire concluded that for 1 Tim 2:12, αὐθεντεῖν should be "to exercise authority over."[73] Belleville continues to promote that, due to the association with Wis 12:6, αὐθεντεῖν delivers a negative message, and to reinforce her

67. Köstenberger and Schreiner, *Women in the Church*, 128.
68. Köstenberger and Schreiner, *Women in the Church*, 131.
69. Köstenberger and Schreiner, *Women in the Church*, 132–33.
70. Köstenberger and Schreiner, *Women in the Church*, 160.
71. Köstenberger and Schreiner, *Women in the Church*, 159–60.
72. Belleville, "Lexical Fallacies in Rendering Αὐθεντεῖν in 1 Timothy 2:12," 319–20.
73. Wilshire, "TLG Computer and Further Reference to ΑΥΘΕΝΤΕΩ in 1 Timothy 2:12," 120–34.

position, she cites Euripides, *Trojan Women*, in which αὐθεντων is translated as "murderous."[74] She objects to the argument that διδάσκειν [to teach] and αὐθεντεῖν [to usurp authority] must be in agreement—both positive or both negative—in the phrase "I suffer not (do not permit) a woman to teach, nor to usurp authority," because they are verbal nouns, and "they do not form a natural progression of related ideas or move from general to particular."[75] In her conclusion, Belleville advances that women are only prohibited from teaching and leading within the church if their attitudes and behaviors involve exercising dominance over men, and she calls upon NT scholars to reevaluate how the texts translate αὐθεντεῖν.[76]

Concerning αὐθεντεῖν (*authentein*) in 1 Tim 2:12, it is the present infinitive active tense of the verb αὐθεντέω (*authenteō*), formed by the combination of the demonstrative pronoun αὐτος—self and ἔντεα—arms, and is defined as "one who with his own hand kills either others or himself; one who does a thing himself; or one who acts on his own authority; to govern one, exercise dominion over one."[77] Concerning αὐθεντέω, Danker defines it as "one who takes matters into one's own hands; exercise authority over" and that this verb functions in a directive manner.[78] Louw and Nida define αὐθεντέω as "to control in a domineering manner–'to control, to domineer' . . . often expressed idiomatically, for example, 'to shout orders at,' 'to act like a chief toward,' or 'to bark at.'"[79] Al Wolters admits that "a series of scholarly studies have sought to show that the rare verb αὐθεντέω means something other than 'have authority' (as in the NRSV), while others have countered by defending this widely accepted rendering." But he continues to state, "Most scholars now agree that αὐθεντέω has to do with the exercise of authority in some way."[80] In his study of αὐθεντέω, he endeavors to maintain neutrality between the egalitarian and complementarian camps. Wolters, citing the two uses available closest to Paul's in Timothy, promotes that αὐθέντης in Euripides, *Supplices*, and the usage found in Wis 12:6, are homonyms, like

---

74. Belleville, "Lexical Fallacies in Rendering Αὐθεντεῖν in 1 Timothy 2:12," 322.
75. Belleville, "Lexical Fallacies in Rendering Αὐθεντεῖν in 1 Timothy 2:12," 335.
76. Belleville, "Lexical Fallacies in Rendering Αὐθεντεῖν in 1 Timothy 2:12," 339–41.
77. Thayer, "αὐθεντέω; αὐτος," *Thayer's Greek-English Lexicon*, 84; 85.
78. Danker, "αὐθεντέω," *Concise Greek-English Lexicon*, 61.
79. "αὐθεντέω," L&N 1:474.
80. Grenz and Kjesbo, *Women in the Church*, 71.

an ear of corn and an ear on one's head.⁸¹ The phrase in Euripides, *Supplices* reads: καὶ μὴν ὅπου γε δῆμος αὐθέντης χθονὸς, which presents δῆμος αὐθέντης as a "master of the city," and master as a reasonable rendering for αὐθέντης in that context.⁸² Wolters explains that "master" is more logical and rational when one considers that Christians and gnostics would refer to Jesus Christ as αὐθέντης—master, not murderer.⁸³

In the Greek and Hebrew languages, the purpose of a hapax legomenon as a figure of speech occurring in a particular Scripture is to cause that Scripture in which it appears to stand out and apart from the rest of the text for didactic reasons. To gain attention through a stark measure of difference from the norm; otherwise, there is no cause to present such a variance within the corpus. A few examples of other hapaxes occurring in the NT can be found in 2 Tim 2:15, "rightly dividing," 2 Tim 3:16, "given by inspiration of God," 2 Pet 1:20, "interpretation," and Jas 1:21, "engrafted." In 2 Tim 2:12 αὐθεντεῖν (*authentein*) is just such a hapax legomenon, a signpost to the reader that something different, a break from the normal, a paradigm shift is present, and one should pay attention. From the context of the preceding verse, one observes Paul's break from traditional Jewish customs, which forbade women from typical education and learning, instead encouraging women to increase their knowledge of the Scriptures.⁸⁴ "Let the women learn in silence (quiet, stillness) with all subjection (obedient subjection)" (1 Tim 2:11). Next is Paul's use of αὐθεντεῖν when ἐξουσία (*exousia*) is the dominant term for "authority," across the NT. Schreiner puts forth that Paul utilizes ἐξουσιάζω and κυριεύω to say "exercise authority," rather than the single-use αὐθεντεῖν; however, he dismisses this significance without so much as a second glance.⁸⁵ Danker puts forth that the combination of αὐθεντέω with διδάσκω, as in 1 Tim 2:12, results in a command and can be interpreted as "tell a man what to do."⁸⁶ Köstenberger, however, promotes a positive message within the verse due to the more frequent uses of διδάσκειν throughout the NT with a positive context about them, but this does not follow the purpose of a hapax legomenon, nor does his logic follow the fact that the negative finite verb οὐκ ἐπιτρέπω initiates

81. Köstenberger and Schreiner, *Women in the Church*, 73.
82. Paley, "Supplices," 1:442.
83. Köstenberger and Schreiner, *Women in the Church*, 73.
84. Köstenberger and Schreiner, *Women in the Church*, 187.
85. Köstenberger and Schreiner, *Women in the Church*, 195–96.
86. Danker, "αὐθεντέω," *Concise Greek-English Lexicon*, 61.

and governs the sentence as a whole.[87] With οὐκ ἐπιτρέπω as a negative finite verb and observing διδάσκειν and αὐθεντεῖν negatively, the prohibitive message of the verse is unified and intensified. This study, therefore, favors a combination of the meaning and understanding promoted by Louw and Nida with the analysis performed by Al Wolters. Αὐθεντεῖν should be interpreted as seizing or assuming control for oneself, giving orders to another person, to be a master over others in a domineering authoritarian fashion.[88] Αὐθεντεῖν then illustrates the negative attitudes of one who desires to be a leader/master over another that is contrary to the teachings previously reviewed in this study from Jesus (ch. 3) and Peter and Paul (ch. 4), which espoused leadership, direction, and guidance through loving care and selfless service.

Suppose one chooses to promote the dominant interpretation of 1 Tim 2:12, as presented by the complementarian position that women have no right nor place to teach, instruct, or lead men. This interpretation causes this verse of Scripture to contradict the rest of the Scriptures concerning women active in the First-Century Church presented previously in this study. The unilateral promotion of the egalitarian perspective is not entirely correct, either. In marriage, Eph 5 is clear the wife is subordinate to the husband as the proper order, but it also states in the same context, "Submitting yourselves one to another in the fear of God" (Eph 5:21). Paul also makes an example of Adam and Eve in Tim 2:13–15, and then in chapter three, he discusses the proper order for overseers and ministers to assume the appropriate leadership of their households. First Peter 3:1–7 also describes the husband-wife relationship, stating that wives are to be subject to their husbands and that husbands must bestow honor to their wives, and both are to be unified "as heirs together of the grace of life." Consider, together with these Scriptures, 1 Cor 14:32–35: the women mentioned are the prophets' wives, and rather than causing a scene in public and bring disgrace to their husbands—the prophets—the wives of the prophets should keep silent and hold their peace (Luke 20:26) until they are at home. For the wives to restrain themselves in the public forum, with their husbands present, prevents bringing disgrace to their husbands, the prophets, and finds agreement with the women learning in silence (quiet, stillness) with all subjection (obedient subjection).

---

87. Köstenberger and Schreiner, *Women in the Church*, 125–26.
88. "αὐθεντέω," L&N 1:474. Köstenberger and Schreiner, *Women in the Church*, 73.

Next, considering the grammatical rule governing διδάσκειν and αὐθεντεῖν: they must be either both positive or both negative because they are joined by the coordinating conjunction οὐδέ—"or."[89] Following the logical progression, because αὐθεντεῖν is a hapax legomenon, expressing a negative understanding of "assuming, exercising authority" apart from ἐξουσιάζω, then διδάσκειν must also represent a negative message. The first chapter of 1 Timothy presents examples of negative teachings contrary to the gospel of Christ. In addition, Paul reminds Timothy how Eve promoted to Adam thoughts, actions, and sentiments that were contradictory to God's commands unto them, and rather than countermanding his wife, Adam willfully gave in to her lead (1 Tim 2:13–14). Deepening the understanding of οὐδέ in 1 Tim 2:12, Philip B. Payne states that the syntactical form of two concepts conjoined by οὐδέ as a single prohibition and then contrasted by ἀλλά—"but" in the same statement, only occurs twice in the NT (the other is 2 Thess 3:7–8); thus the amplified rarity within the verse loudly calls attention to its message.[90] As διδάσκειν and αὐθεντεῖν are conjoined by οὐδέ, they are an example of the figure of speech, *hendiadys*, meaning two words—in this case, infinite verbs—are utilized to express a singular idea, thought or concept; one action is therefore represented as the two verbs reinforce one another.[91] Payne states, "Paul typically uses οὐδέ to join together expressions that reinforce or make more specific a single idea."[92] Therefore, any interpretation of 1 Tim 2:12 to convey a prohibition of two separate activities does not agree or conform to the proper utilization of οὐδέ by Paul across his epistles.[93] Payne concludes:

> Interpreting 1 Tim 2.12 as a single prohibition of women teaching combined with assuming authority over men fits its context perfectly. This prohibition fits with the central concern of 1 Timothy, false teaching. Teaching combined with assuming authority is by definition not authorized. This is exactly what false teachers were doing in Ephesus.

This study further advances Payne's conclusion by adding that αὐθεντεῖν—"usurp authority" should be understood as "seizing or

---

89. Köstenberger and Schreiner, *Women in the Church*, 127.
90. Payne, "1 Tim 2:12 and the Use of οὐδέ," 245–46.
91. Bullinger, *Figures of Speech Used in the Bible*, 657; 671.
92. Payne, "1 Tim 2:12 and the Use of οὐδέ," 236.
93. Payne, "1 Tim 2:12 and the Use of οὐδέ," 244.

assuming control for one's self to dominate and command others." After the introduction, the context of 1 Timothy chapter one wholly deals with prohibitions against erroneous doctrines and those individuals who utilized their teachings and persuasive words to persuade, defile, and rule or dominate others to lead them away from the gospel.[94] Payne states, "The false teaching described in 1 Tim 4.7 as 'old wives tales' (NSRV) deceived women in particular (cf. 2 Tim 3.6–7)."[95] Therefore, women who do not lead others astray, spread heresy and false teachings, or subvert the authority of established leaders but instead teach and lead others within the public body of believers in accordance with the examples and directives of the established overseers, ministers, and elders, are acceptable and permitted to do so.

While women are particularly prohibited, according to 1 Tim 2:12, from usurping authority and exerting dominion through false teachings, anyone serving the Lord Jesus Christ should equally obey Paul's mandate. Recall that Jesus commanded, "Ye know that the princes of the Gentiles exercise dominion over them, and they that are great exercise authority upon them. But it shall not be so among you" (Matt 20:25–26). Peter also instructs those in charge not to act like "lords over God's heritage" (1 Pet 5:3). Leaders, those in charge, according to the Scriptures, provide loving, firm, confident direction, counsel, and guidance to and for the followers of the Lord Jesus Christ. First Timothy 2:12 prohibits the polar opposite leadership style within the household of God that Paul promoted in 1 Cor 12:27–28.

Paul tells wives twice to submit themselves to their husbands (Eph 5:22; Col 3:18), and again, he utilizes the example of Adam and Eve (1 Tim 2:13–14) to illustrate the godly order from the Scriptures, which is specific to the marriage relationship. Within that relationship, the wife is to be a credit to the husband and bring glory to him; likewise, he builds her up, and the two are to work together as a team (1 Cor 11:7–11), bringing glory and praise to God. For all others within the body of the household of God, outside of or independent of the marriage relationship, Paul directs the congregation that their conduct and deeds should be performed out of love (1 Cor 16:14) and "that ye submit yourselves unto such, and to every one that helpeth with us, and laboureth" (1 Cor 16:16). This passage says nothing about obeying only men, or that women

---

94. Payne, "1 Tim 2:12 and the Use of οὐδέ," 247.
95. Payne, "1 Tim 2:12 and the Use of οὐδέ," 247.

may not lead; "everyone" includes any person, male or female, young or old, who aided Paul in spreading the gospel of Christ and ministering to followers of the First-Century Church.

Any interpretation of 1 Tim 2:12 must agree with all other Scriptures and not follow any fashion that generates contradictions. One must comprehend the syntax of 1 Tim 2:12, paying particular attention to its features that separate it from others, such as the negative finite verb οὐκ ἐπιτρέπω that governs the verse; its hapax legomenon, αὐθεντεῖν; the pair of conjoined infinitive verbal nouns, διδάσκειν, and αὐθεντεῖν; the figure of speech *hendiadys*, and the syntactical form of two concepts combined by οὐδέ into a single prohibition and contrasted by ἀλλά. Each piece of grammatical evidence works to produce a prohibition against anyone, but especially women, utilizing false, heretical teachings to usurp men of their leadership roles, order them about, or "tell them what to do," especially their husbands, and to seize power for themselves, dominating others. Paul prohibited the wives of the leadership from teaching others to take over their husband's rightful authority, and any questions they might have were to be handled in private to prevent any loss of face for their husbands in public. Women of the First-Century Church, like Priscilla, Junia, and Nympha, taught and led others with a loving example, not one of dominance, in accord with the men guiding the church body. Therefore, men and women within God's household have equal potential for leading and teaching others. Still, that potential is to be exercised in submission to one another in love and accordance with godly order as ordained and organized within the collective church body.

First Timothy does not prohibit women from teaching or leading others within the assemblies of the household of God, nor does it contradict the many clear verses of Scripture that tell of women serving and leading at the various levels within the First-Century Church. It does prohibit women from exerting dominion over men, and especially within the marriage relationship, the wife is not to usurp her husband's authority. In the marriage relationship, the wife follows the husband's loving lead, and he, in all humility, receives her input and insight. Within the collective body of the church, no leader should exert dominion over any other person, for this is contrary to the examples of Jesus Christ and his apostles and the Scriptures. All have equal opportunity before God to serve him and his people according to the harmony and order presented in his word.

## PAUL'S INSTRUCTIONS TO TITUS

The epistle of Paul to Titus bears a similar purpose to his letters to Timothy: the establishment of leaders in a new church and the continuation of the Christian community in Paul's absence. Titus had been another of Paul's notable young apprentices, and like Timothy, he became Paul's envoy and a second-generation leader within the collective church. Paul mentions Titus for the first time in 2 Cor 2:13 and speaks highly of the comfort Titus brought him and other believers in chapter seven. In 2 Cor 8:23, Paul refers to Titus as his "partner and fellowhelper." When Paul returned from one of his missionary sojourns to Jerusalem with Barnabas, Titus accompanied them (Gal 2:1). Like Timothy, Titus's relationship and service with Paul afforded him the apostle's mentorship so that Paul felt confident in the younger man's abilities, and placed him as an ambassador to the people on the island of Crete. Christian church tradition refers to Titus as the bishop for the island of Crete, though there is no overt scriptural reference for support.[96] Paul addressed Titus in the introduction of the epistle as "mine own son after the common faith," displaying how endeared to the apostle he was (Titus 1:1). Then Paul proceeded to lay out his directives for the establishment and continuation of the church.

### Elders

In the letter to Titus, Paul begins with the appointment of elders, πρεσβυτέρους—*presbyterous* (pl.), in every city that Titus visited, which was a different tact than the instructions to Timothy (Titus 1:5). If elders are understood to be the patriarchal heads of prestigious families who wielded clout and influence in their communities, there is a logical conclusion to Paul's directive.[97] Through the conversion of an elder fitting that description, Titus would most likely win over the whole household and gain a home to conduct services. Then, by appointing that elder to a council assisting Titus, he would gain influence in the community, and both advantages would propel the Christian movement there in Crete. The lists of attributes required of elders and bishops are very similar between Tim 3 and Titus 1. Just like with the directives in Timothy, in Titus, an elder of the church needed to be, without reproaches or accusations,

---

96. Smith, *Smith's Bible Dictionary*, 701–2.
97. Campbell, "Elders of the Jerusalem Church," 513.

a husband to one wife (Titus 1:6). An elder was required to be a successful father of obedient children who were also converted to the faith and without accusations of debauchery or rebelliousness (v. 6). Thus, the elder's family, known in the community, proved his worth to the church.

In Titus 2, Paul charges the elder men and women with the responsibility of teaching the younger ones proper conduct and candor (2:2–6). Such a pairing of elders with younger members for influence and tutelage bears evidence of apprenticeships in action within the church body. Specifically, the elder women were to instruct the younger women to be successful wives and keepers of the home (2:4–5). Without a successful family and house, there could not be a flourishing church in the home—it began with the family unit. Paul directs Titus to lead the way with the example of his life and character that demonstrated all the previous necessary qualities of the leadership roles (vv. 7–8). Such instructions mirror those sent to Timothy, and thereby, the two reinforce each other.

## Bishops/Overseers

In Titus 1:7, following Paul's description of the elders, comes the bishops/overseers' criteria, and like the elder, an overseer had to be blameless.[98] Still, the Scripture states specifically, "A bishop [overseer] must be blameless as the steward (οἰκονόμον—*oikonomon*) of God" (v. 7). The overseers proved their values to the church as household managers first: that they were not greedy, hot-tempered, or drunkards (v. 7). They also had to have a reputation based upon their hospitality toward others and their self-control; a lover of good things and people, who holds fast to God's Word, able to teach it and thwart the opposition (vv. 8–9). These verses reflect not only the attributes that needed to be evidenced by the individual's lifestyle but also the duty code required for the positions within the church.[99] In addition, the comparison of the roles of the ἐπίσκοπος to οἰκονόμος also connects with the spiritual metaphor of household management and service within God's household (Eph 2:19; 1 Tim 3:15).[100]

---

98. There should be no confusion concerning the elders—πρεσβυτέρους (v. 5) and the overseer—ἐπίσκοπον (v. 7), as the subject has changed categories within the topic of leadership. Chapter four of this research work previously established the differences between elders and overseers, and stressed the necessity of avoiding confusion by accurately distinguishing between the two titles.

99. Goodrich, "Overseers as Stewards," 78.

100. Goodrich, "Overseers as Stewards," 82–83.

Similar to Paul's instructions in Timothy, the importance of the stratum of the household church manger, or οἰκονόμος, was essential to one attaining the position of an overseer.

The Epistle of Titus does not mention the minister's leadership stratum despite how essential it was in the letters to Timothy. This generates the question of why this leadership role was ignored for Titus's instructions but attended to in Timothy's. There is a void concerning scholarly sources that address this issue. A logical hypothesis may be that the two men, Timothy and Titus, received the same training from Paul, and Titus may have been informed of and read Timothy's letters. Then, why would Titus's letter differ from those of Timothy? A plausible conclusion that answers both questions could be that Paul seldom repeated the same instructions but rather expected his letters to be passed amongst the followers, thereby keeping the "like-minded" and unified with the same teachings (Col 4:16; 2 Tim 4:13), and therefore the uniqueness and differences in the letter to Titus were a direct result of the needs of the people on Crete.[101] The description and pattern for starting a new community church in a new town are similar to the method Jews employed for establishing a new synagogue.[102] Some scholars presume that the church was stabilizing and becoming a recognized institution within the Roman Empire; therefore, the moral code described in both Timothy and Titus reflected the sociocultural standards around the Christian communities and the conglomerate church's adaptation to them.[103] In the Greco-Roman society present in the first century, lists of virtues required and vices prohibited for occupations were commonplace.[104] Paul's instructions to Timothy and Titus charged them with ordaining church leadership, which set the proper examples for believers spiritually and socially.

Though the Scriptures never refer to Titus as an apostle, like Timothy, the authority bestowed upon him by Paul to appoint and ordain elders, overseers, and deacons in new communities is evidence that, as an extension of Paul's apostolic ministry and his successor in faith, Titus may have been one also. In his letter, Clement communicates similarly that the chain of command proceeded from God to Jesus to the apostles (1 Clem 42.2).[105] Clement states concerning the apostles, "So preaching

---

101. Mowry, "Early Circulation of Paul's Letters," 73–86.
102. Burtchaell, *From Synagogue to Church*, 293.
103. Merkle, "Are the Qualifications for Elders or Overseers Negotiable," 174.
104. Goodrich, "Overseers as Stewards," 78–80.
105. Lightfoot, *Apostolic Fathers*, 22–23.

everywhere in country and town, they appointed their firstfruits, when they had proved them by the Spirit, to be bishops and deacons unto them that should believe" (1 Clem 42.4).[106] Apostles were the spiritual authorities responsible for establishing new leadership—overseers, ministers, and elders—in the Christian communities that sprang up in new areas. The examples and doctrines, with minor variations, remained valid from the Christian church of the first century and carried over into the second century.

## The Duty Codes for Overseers, Ministers, and Elders

The epistles of Timothy and Titus provide lists of qualities prerequisite in an individual's life prior to attaining the leadership positions of overseer, minister, or elder in service to the church body. Such lists, duty codes, were commonplace in Hellenistic culture for military officers and politicians because these codes held the person serving in such a role accountable to those they served.[107] An individual found guilty of violating the duty codes of his position could be removed from his role of authority. Likewise, one may compare them to the overseers, ministers, and elders of God's household. Paul directed all believers to submit to each other out of a sense of humility and reverence before God (Eph 5:21). Thus, though ἐπίσκοποι, διάκονοι, and πρεσβύτεροι, led the congregations of the First-Century Church, they bore accountability to the people they served to live up to the duty codes of the pastoral epistles, lest they be brought before the church and removed from authority. Furthermore, in light of the household metaphor, in antiquity, before a servant would have been promoted to a level of oversight within a household, it was required they prove themselves first as a capable and trustworthy steward—οἰκονόμος within the household.[108]

It is profitable for this study to present the duty codes of an ἐπίσκοπος, διάκονος, and πρεσβύτερος side-by-side for comparison to display the uniform standards the church body could expect from their leadership. An overseer—ἐπίσκοπος is to be "blameless" (1 Tim 3:2; Titus 1: 7), as is a minister—διάκονος (1 Tim 3:10), and likewise the elder—πρεσβύτερος (1 Tim 5:7; Titus 1:6). This quality of "blamelessness" does not mean that the individual is without fault or does not make mistakes but rather has

---

106. Lightfoot, *Apostolic Fathers*, 23.
107. Goodrich, "Overseers as Stewards," 77–78.
108. Goodrich, "Overseers as Stewards," 85–87.

impeccable character, is not vulnerable to public censure, and that morally and ethically a leader must be irreproachable and inculpable.[109] They needed to have a sound mind and were not to be violent nor susceptible to excessive intoxication (1 Tim 3:2–3, 8; Titus 1:5–7). Each is not to practice polygamy, i.e., "husband to one wife": the πίσκοπος (1 Tim 3:2), the διάκονος (1 Tim 3:12), and the πρεσβύτερος (Titus 1:6). An overseer is required to be skillful in teaching the Scriptures (1 Tim 3:2; Titus 1:9). While teaching is not a requirement for an elder, Paul states that the servant of the Lord must also be apt to teach and that elders who labored in the word and teaching were worthy of double honor (1 Tim 5:17; 2 Tim 2:24).

Unlike the overseers and elders, the duty codes do not overtly state anything concerning the deacons/ministers teaching the people, but it is implied. An overseer must have proven his aptitude and adroitness for teaching the Scriptures before ever ascending to the role. Where else would such skill have been developed if not as an assistant to an overseer, a steward of an in-home church fellowship, or as a deacon/minister? This study has already established that the role of a διάκονος was the proving ground for the position of an overseer (1 Tim 3:8).[110] The overseer would delegate authority and tasks to be performed to their subordinate διάκονος, who then served the people as an agency of ministration for their ἐπίσκοπος.[111] Deacons/ministers were to have a firm grasp of the mystery of the faith and operate with "great boldness in the faith which is in Jesus Christ" (1 Tim 3:11, 13). Such an inherent quality would have manifested in actions and speech (2 Cor 8:7). In addition, deacons/ministers could not be "double-tongued"—speaking differing or contradictory doctrines to people, not addicted to alcohol and not greedy for "filthy lucre"—dishonest gain (1 Tim 3:8).[112] It was expected that overseers, elders, and ministers would have proven themselves successful by maintaining an exemplary family life and raising children who were faithful to God and his Word; this is not achieved without the parents teaching their children well (1 Tim 3:4–5, 12; Titus 1:6). This way the context implies that the deacons/ministers would have been experienced in teaching God's Word because they were required to conduct themselves in like manner to their overseers.

109. Thayer, "ἀνέγκλητος," and "ἀνεπίλημπτος," *Thayer's Greek-English Lexicon*, 44.
110. Fraser, "Office of Deacon," 19; Campbell, "Elders: Seniority in Earliest Christianity," 186.
111. Merkle, "Authority of Deacons in Pauline Churches," 315–16.
112. Strauch, *Paul's Vision for the Deacons*, 25.

Overseers, ministers, and elders had to have their households in order, including any church functions and fellowships conducted in their homes, which required them to extend hospitality to others (1 Tim 3:2, 12, 5:1–8; Titus 1:5–8). These three factions of leaders could not be guilty of pursuing wealth accumulated by shameful means (1 Tim 3:3, 8; Titus 1:5–7). They needed to prefer God's will over their own, reigning in their passions and desires and becoming examples to the people they served. The leaders owed it to the people they served to present their lives with such transparency that the believers would have had no doubts that their overseers, ministers, and elders operated as envoys of the Lord Jesus Christ. These duty lists permitted the congregation of the First-Century Church to hold their leadership accountable before men and God. These qualities had to be present in the lives of overseers, ministers, and elders of the First-Century Church to the degree that no one in the congregation or outside of it could question their integrity and moral character.

## PETER'S LETTERS TO THE CHURCHES IN ASIA

The introduction of Peter's first epistle addresses the "strangers" scattered to the five churches located east and north of Paul's ministry and beyond the region of Palestine. "Stranger" is παρεπίδημος (*parepidēmos*) and means "one who comes from a foreign country into a city or land to reside there by the side of natives; hence a stranger; sojourning in a strange place, a foreigner."[113] Some interpret this reference to signify Jews of the diaspora (Jas 1:1), exiled after Jerusalem's destruction in AD 70.[114] Another metaphorical interpretation of "strangers" understands that having received salvation, including a place in the heavenlies upon the return of Jesus Christ (1 Thess 4:17), the Christian believer is no longer a citizen of this world (Eph 2:5–6), and therefore is a sojourner on earth.[115] Concerning the first epistle, the New Oxford Annotated Bible states, "The letter addresses a critical situation in the lives of the addressees, who once participated in the social and cultural life of their communities, but since their conversion to Christ have become marginalized and abused."[116] The goal of the Petrine letters was the continuation of the church in the face of

---

113. Thayer, "παρεπίδημος," *Thayer's Greek-English Lexicon*, 488.
114. Bartlett, "1 Peter," 668.
115. Thayer, "παρεπίδημος," *Thayer's Greek-English Lexicon*, 488.
116. New Testament, *New Oxford Annotated Bible*, 394.

adversity, and the subjects addressed within its Scriptures handle several situations, not the least of which is the prevention of marginalization, which had the potential to emerge within the church as well as in society external to it.

The first chapter opens with an introduction addressing the members of the five churches, reminding them of their salvation in Christ (vv. 18–23), which provided them with a new life and hope for their future (vv. 24–25). Chapter two encourages the believers to reject and throw away the behaviors found in society that are contrary to their new spiritual nature so that they might become the spiritual household and "holy priesthood" for God and Jesus Christ (vv. 1–5). The author affirms their state, status, and suitability for the audience before God to dispel any sense of alienation, marginalization, and abandonment they might have within (v. 9). The phrasing employed in the first two chapters, such as "elect according to the foreknowledge," "holy nation," and "peculiar people," indicates a separation and distinction from the unbelievers of the day and reinforces the community of God's household (1 Pet 2:5, 9).[117] Then 1 Pet 2:25 states, "For ye were as sheep going astray, but are now returned unto the Shepherd and Bishop of your soul." "Bishop"—ἐπίσκοπον in this verse is the same as in 1 Tim 3:2 and Titus 1:7 and refers to Jesus as the ultimate overseer, which all others serving the church in such a capacity look to as their example (1 Pet 2:21). Louw and Nida state, "Though in some contexts ἐπισκοπή has been regarded traditionally as a position of authority, in reality the focus is upon the responsibility for caring for others."[118] All church overseers should strive to exert the same care for their people, just as Jesus did and does for the whole church.

The unity of the whole church as a familial-style household is of the utmost importance in the Petrine epistles. John Elliott details that the word translated into English as "priesthood," ἱεράτευμα, communicates a "collective force" more like an organized army or artisans' guild and that their particular "election" is "the central and unifying concept of the passage."[119] Today, one might refer to such an organization of select people as a cultic society. The language Peter employs to describe the believers connects their particular community as God's household via the covenantal formula to the household of Jacob in Exodus.[120] First Peter 4:9

117. Elliott, "Elders as Leaders in 1 Peter," 683.
118. "ἐπισκοπή," L&N 1:463.
119. Elliott, "Elders as Leaders in 1 Peter," 684.
120. Elliott, "Elders as Leaders in 1 Peter," 685.

encourages believers to bestow hospitality to each other, the same quality attribute required of overseers in 1 Tim 3:2 and Titus 1:8, reinforcing a person's sense of belonging to the household. Then verse ten states, "As every man hath received the gift, even so minister (διακονοῦντες) the same one to another, as good stewards (οἰκονόμοι) of the manifold grace of God." "Minister" is an active verbal form of διάκονος, and "stewards," οἰκονόμοι, is the plural form of οἰκονόμος.[121] Verse eleven declares that if any man ministers (διακονεῖ—*diakonei*), they should do so with the ability supplied by God. First Peter 4:7–11 provides direction and encouragement to strengthen the community against adversity.[122] The various strata of leaders—overseers, ministers, and stewards/managers—are needed to set the pace, to set the example, to support, comfort, maintain, and bring together the believers, lest they become "like sheep gone astray."

In 1 Pet 5:1–3, Peter addresses the elders (πρεσβυτέρους; see Titus 1:5) of the churches, including himself also as an elder, charging them with "feeding the flock," "taking the oversight," and "being examples." Concerning this passage, Elliott states, "These elders were not simply persons older in age, but senior in households (and all likelihood seniors in longevity as believers) who, because of their prestige and status in the household churches of which they were the household heads, were recognized and respected leaders of their respective household churches."[123] This passage in Peter is similar to the exceptional elders who were worthy of double honor (1 Tim 5:17). Based upon the duties Peter charged these elders with, they most likely had, in their personal histories, served the household churches in various leadership roles such as overseers, shepherds/pastors, ministers, and others. As was observed in Timothy, not all church elders performed this way, as they were not required. Like Paul's writing, Peter exhorted the younger members of the churches to submit themselves to these elders (v. 5).[124] In doing so, the younger members could learn from their elders and possibly apprentice themselves to these more experienced and seasoned veterans.

Peter's utilization of the shepherd and sheep illustration in 1 Pet 2:25 recalls Jesus' teaching from the tenth chapter of John. If the canonical

---

121. "οἰκονόμος," L&N 1:477, 521.

122. Elliott, "Elders as Leaders in 1 Peter," 682.

123. Elliott, "Elders as Leaders in 1 Peter," 685.

124. The writings of Peter and Paul are interrelated and support one another; Peter referenced Paul's letters, and there is evidence that Peter utilized the epistles of Romans and Ephesians in 1 Peter. Robertson, *Word Pictures in the New Testament*, 607–8.

gospels were not yet available, then Peter would have had, besides his memories, only the recitation of Jesus' teachings by other faithful followers to provide context. Through either method, due to the lack of detailed explanation in 1 Peter, the author assumes his audience will understand the illustration's deep meanings. Jesus' teaching regarding the good shepherd, a metaphorical reference to himself, recalls Ps 23, "LORD is my shepherd . . ." which illustrated God as a merciful, loving, tender, and beneficent protector of his people. Jesus took on the role of the shepherd for his followers, which Peter directed the church leaders to emulate.

When shepherds of the Orient led their flocks from the sheepfolds, away from the city, to graze in the open fields, they did so by uttering unique high-pitched calls, each shepherd having their particular vocalization to which the sheep responded and followed after.[125] John 10:3 states that the porter/doorkeeper [θυρωρός—*thyrōros*], who stood guard at night, opened the door to the sheepfold so Jesus might call them and lead his sheep out to pasture.[126] Jesus said the sheep heard the voice of their shepherd, for he called them by name, he went before them, and "the sheep followed after him: for they knew his voice" (John 10:3–4). The overseers and ministers who serve as pastors within and over the entire church do so in lieu of the great shepherd, Jesus Christ (Heb 13:20), and they should imitate his methods from the Scriptures. In doing so, they would "sound like" Jesus to the best of their ability. Therefore, when they call the congregation's members, the people should have no hesitation but respond dutifully to their calls.

The sheep and the shepherd enjoyed a symbiotic relationship. The sheep received nourishment, care, tending, and protection, while the shepherd also nourished and harvested wool for clothing and profited from them in the marketplace. Referring to Jesus metaphorically as the "shepherd and bishop of your souls" draws out a twofold relationship of dependency and obedience from the Christian believer to Jesus Christ. As bishop/overseer, the believer has submissively entrusted their soul, evidenced by faith, belief, and confessions, to Jesus as their protector. As shepherd/pastor and provider of one's salvation, the believer is sworn to follow after and obey Jesus, just as sheep do their shepherd.

In the NT, those who read the English versions will read "pastor" and "shepherd" as separate words, but in the Greek they are the same:

---

125. Freeman, *Manners and Customs of the Bible*, 428–29.
126. Robertson, *Word Pictures in the New Testament*, 225.

ποιμήν.[127] If one serves the church as a pastor, then the claim is they have committed themselves to and act on behalf of the great shepherd. They follow his precepts and have devoted themselves to the congregation's members' care, tending, and protection. Not only was Jesus the central figure whom the followers of the First-Century Church all rallied about (like sheep to their shepherd) for their salvation and relationship to God, but he also was the one who granted them access to a higher and greater spiritual power, as evidenced by Jesus' miracles and those wrought by his devotees. Jesus' loving, tender care for his devoted followers and his compassion for others in need compelled people to follow after him. He instructed his disciples and apostles in word and deed to follow his example, and as he loved and cared for people, they should do the same. Peter states, "For even hereunto were ye called: because Christ also suffered for us, leaving us an example, that ye should follow his steps" (1 Pet 2:21). Therefore, all pastors of the household of God are entrusted in similitude with Jesus to care for the members of the congregation: spiritually feeding, sheltering, binding up wounds, and nurturing one lovingly to maturity. Likewise, the followers of God's household should follow after and willingly heed the words and wisdom of those serving as pastors. Believers, faithful to the gospel of Christ, especially those in leadership positions, in recalling their Lord's example, Peter directs to extend themselves selflessly in service to one another.

## The Duty Codes for Overseers, Ministers, and Elders

Peter spoke of three primary qualities leadership should exemplify in 1 Pet 5:1–4. Verse two declares they should "feed the flock of God which is among you, taking the oversight thereof, not by constraint, but willingly." In Greek, "feed the flock" is ποιμάνατε τὸ ἐν ποίμνιον, which could be rendered as "shepherd the flock." To "shepherd" carries a deeper intent and meaning than to say "feed," in relating the relationship between a leader and their people, utilizes the entire analogy of the shepherd with his sheep. The following phrases describe how and in what manner one should act as a shepherd with their people. They are to exercise oversight, not because it is their duty or job, but voluntarily because doing God's will is most important (1 Pet 5:2). Verse two continues to state that leaders of his church are not to be motivated by money obtained through dishonest

---

127. Thayer, "ποιμήν," *Thayer's Greek-English Lexicon*, 527.

shameful means and deeds; instead they are to present themselves with a cheerful readiness in their soul, eager to serve God and his people. Peter's use of "filthy lucre" in verse two parallels Paul's statements in 1 Tim 3:3, 8, and Titus 1:7. Lastly, in verse three, Peter instructs leaders not to lord over, domineer, or menacingly assert themselves against God's people entrusted to their care; those in charge are to lead and motivate others by their proven examples of service.

The qualities that Peter presented reflect the teachings imparted by Jesus. In John chapter ten, Jesus referred to himself as the good shepherd and declared three qualities by which his sheep recognized him. In verse nine, he stated that he was "the door" and "if any man enter in (through him) he shall be saved." Symbolically, he was telling his audience that he was the doorkeeper of salvation (John 14:6), and beyond those who passed through and entered in the kingdom of God, would not want for anything of the true life, one's spiritual life in relationship with God.[128] Following in his stead, those in leadership capacities are entrusted with bringing people the gospel of Christ and leading them into salvation. In John 10:11, Jesus promised and prophesied that he would sacrifice his life for his devoted followers. Likewise, church overseers, ministers, and elders should willingly open their lives and minister to others from the same heart with which Jesus sacrificed himself doing God's will. Elliott points out that the Petrine epistles bear no reflection of the hierarchical institution that would develop in the second century and beyond, and the leadership Peter described resembled "under-shepherds" rather than "office-holders."[129] Therefore, toward the close of the first century, the leaders of the church collective were ministering in a pastoral fashion rather than lording over others as officers. Thirdly, Jesus stated that he knew his sheep and was known by them, which implied they shared an intimate relationship (John 10:14). Such was not unlike that of a shepherd with his sheep, for the sheep knew the shepherd's voice, his calls, and language, his bodily communications, and even his particular smell. Through up-close, personal, proven, and trustworthy relationships and examples of service, God's leadership persuades, motivates, and guides his people into living according to his ways. If modern leaders ingrained these qualities of Jesus and Peter, they would indeed pattern their ministries after the great shepherd.

---

128. Robertson, *Word Pictures in the New Testament*, 226.
129. Elliott, "Elders as Leaders in 1 Peter," 689.

## CONCLUSION

In summation, the apostles intended for their epistles of Timothy, Titus, and Peter to inform the following generations of believers of the requirements and qualifications of those entrusted with leading God's people. This chapter conducted brief overviews of Paul's acolytes, Timothy and Titus. Timothy's life and history in the church exemplify a young man who rose through varying levels of service and leadership for others to learn from. The perspectives on the varied leadership strata were provided, as seen through the lens of these epistles. The controversy of 1 Tim 2:12 concerning women teaching and leading in congregations was examined, and the position of this study is that the Scriptures do not prohibit women from teaching or leading others within the assemblies of the household of God. The subject of ordination concerning overseers, ministers, and elders was reviewed. This study also looked into illustrations of the husbandman and the shepherd for how the leaders were supposed to handle their followers to ensure they could achieve maturity in Christ.

The concept of the whole church conglomerate functioning as a household received reinforcement in Peter's and Paul's letters. In addition, the authors stressed the need to maintain unity among all the followers, like a family. Overseers, ministers, and elders were entrusted with leading others through the rightly divided and fully instructed Scriptures to a complete and accurate knowledge of salvation through Jesus Christ (2 Tim 2:15; 3:16–17). They should be willing to lay down their lives in selfless service for their people. The relationship cultivated between leaders and their congregation should be both intimate and transparent, ethically and morally speaking. The community could also reciprocate and aid the minister or overseer from succumbing to temptations (for they are as fallible as any other). Caring service attending to the believers' needs from not one but all levels of available leadership was required to uphold the unity of the churches. They all shared in duties, while humility, care, charity, and concern for others were the bywords of the believers. The overseers, ministers, elders, and household church managers provided examples and tutelage necessary to withstand external opposition, adversity, and internal strife and division. The directives of the apostles Peter and Paul instructed the next generation of leadership for the church's perpetuation unto further generations.

# CHAPTER 6

# Conclusions

CHAPTER ONE BEGAN BY introducing a growing problem within Christianity today: the rampant decline of attendance and memberships within Christian churches. Discovering a solution to this problem served as a catalyst that spurred on the research within this work. The issue of declining attendance also presented the question, Is modern Christianity a reflection of the ways and means by which the disciples of Jesus Christ communicated and evangelized the gospel of Christ in the first century? This chapter introduced the thesis for this study: God's design for leadership, presented in the Scriptures and promoted by the apostles in the early church, was a stratified model, different and superior to the hierarchical models of the temple cult and synagogue of the Second Temple era, which could adapt to suit any size congregation without sacrificing the personal attention needed by its followers. This study's research produced a practical service-oriented leadership model that emphasizes the members of its constituency, which was proven successful in the New Testament. While the model benefits Christian churches worldwide, it is a pragmatic blueprint that any organization could potentially adapt and replicate.

Chapter two presented the current state of research concerning leaders' positions of authority within modern Christianity. It illustrated a challenging question regarding modern Christianity: have the preachers, teachers, believers, and followers of today's churches merely accepted, repeated, and promulgated traditions over scriptural lessons and veracity? An example is the use of the word "office" in relation to those positions of authority and its basis within church traditions. The chapter reviewed the apostolic fathers' writings and compared them to the NT Scriptures to determine whether it had been during their time when certain traditions, practices, and confusion began that blurred perceptions regarding leaders' roles. The leadership roles of *episkopos, presbyteros, diakonos, doulos, hypēretēs, oikonomos,* and *thyrōros,* which are levels of leadership contributing to the stratified leadership model, were introduced. These positions, which are present in the pages of the NT, are not all discussed in the apostolic father's writings. In the writings of the apostolic fathers, only *episkopos* (bishop), *presbyteros* (elders/presbyters), and *diakonos* (deacons) received the attention, and those writings presumably established church traditions that shaped perceptions and understandings concerning those titles. Finally, chapter two provided an overview of the research performed in modernity concerning the leadership positions of the early church in the NT.

Chapter three focused on comparative analyses of the temple at Jerusalem leadership models, Jewish synagogues, and Roman temple cult formats. Similarities between those hierarchical structures and Christian churches of modernity were presented. This study reviewed the historical context of the Second Temple period to gain a scope of the religious and political environment from which the First-Century Church emerged. Then, this work investigated the paradigm of Jesus' example and the blueprint he left with his followers to expose the differences between it and traditional Christianity. Understanding the differences between the movement Jesus led and inspired and how it broke from religious traditions were foundational to the First-Century Church and its followers. The illustration of the shepherd and its importance to the culture of that day was reviewed due to Jesus' usage of the metaphor in his teachings. This work observed the husbandry metaphors in NT Scriptures. Jesus' doctrine of ministering service without regard to oneself, in an "all others first" fashion, overturned the typical administrative model for exerting governance and management of people. Finally, after the ascension of Jesus Christ, the initiation of a new church movement in his name and how the first generation of leaders implemented their Lord's teachings were reviewed.

Chapter four assessed the differences between bishops—ἐπίσκοποι (*epískopoi* [pl.]), elders—πρεσβύτεροι (*presbyteroi* [pl.]), and deacons—διάκονοι (*diakonoi* [pl.]) and the significance these differences presented. This study analyzed the roots of the stratified model of leadership found in 1 Cor 12:27–28, expending effort to understand the hapax legomenon of κυβερνήσεις (*kubernēseis*) found therein. The charismatic factions of leaders that comprised the gift ministries were studied first to form a baseline with which to compare and contrast with the ordained ministries. Whether or not the gift ministries of apostles, prophets, evangelists, pastors, and teachers are available in the modern era was discussed. The ordained leadership roles were analyzed, understanding that while ἐπίσκοπος (*episkopos*), πρεσβύτερος (*presbyteros*), and διάκονος (*diakonos*) have dominated scholarly attention, those functionaries received aid, support, and assistance from the οἰκονόμος (*oikonomos*), ὑπηρέτης (*hypēretēs*), and δοῦλος (*doulos*). The last of the roles studied was the most obscure, that of a θεράπων (*therápōn*). This chapter of the study also reviewed issues concerning bishops, elders, and deacons and confusion between the three roles in the church.

The chapter delivered detailed and defining research on the eight levels of the stratified leadership model. Sociohistorical and grammatical analyses were performed on each role, beginning with the ἐπίσκοπος (*episkopos*). Following the order in which they developed in the early church, this study reviewed the διάκονος (*diakonos*) and their purposes: to render service to the household of God and bring others to maturity in Christ. Jesus initially set the standards for any διάκονος, for he stylized service unto others; then Paul declared of himself that he was a minister—διάκονος of the New Covenant, setting an example for the church. The elders—πρεσβύτεροι (*presbyteroi*) were a senior body of leadership associated with the religious and political authorities in Jerusalem, as well as in towns throughout Greco-Roman society, which the early church adopted later to assist and counsel the overseers and ministers. Without lessening the importance of elders within the church, this work highlighted distinct differences between overseers, ministers, and elders, proving they were not the same. Next, the study focused upon the οἰκονόμος (*oikonomos*) or the role of the in-home church manager, also referred to as a steward from the Scriptures. Culturally, the head of a household who owned the premises of his house was known as an οἰκονόμος. Spiritually, the church is compared to and expected to function like a household, for it is called "the household of God" (Gal 6:10; Eph 2:19). The Scriptures challenge every recipient of the gift of God's Spirit and everlasting life in Christ to serve/minister as a steward/manager (οἰκονόμος—*oikonomos*) of God's grace (1 Pet 4:10).

Next, this study examined the assistants and apprenticeship levels of the ὑπηρέτης (*hypēretēs*), δοῦλος (*doulos*), and θυρωρός (*thyrōros*). These roles within the stratified leadership model might be viewed as minor or lesser when compared to the overseers, ministers, and elders, but for the assistance they provided, they were necessary to the church. The usages in the NT for δοῦλος (*doulos*) were prevalent, while those for ὑπηρέτης (*hypēretēs*) and θυρωρός (*thyrōros*) were scarce and easy to overlook. Socio-cultural analyses were performed for each of these. The ὑπηρέτης (*hypēretēs*) served as a direct assistant to any stratum of leadership. Jesus appeared to Paul on the road to Damascus and appointed him as the Lord's ὑπηρέτης (*hypēretēs*), and in Acts 13, when Barnabas and Paul set off on a missionary journey, they took John Mark with them as their assistant. Upon studying the position of the δοῦλος (*doulos*), what was discovered was that a δοῦλος was a devoted servant or minister, someone pledged or bound in service to another, and when in reference to the church, their dedication was voluntary. The apostle Paul declared that he had devoted himself, as a δοῦλος, to the Lord Jesus Christ. Within the household of the First-Century Church, the δοῦλος did not have a fixed assignment or rigid structure for their duties. Instead, one could find them attending to whatever services might be needed, making them the most versatile and flexible of all the roles. The lowliest of all the positions within the strata of leadership, the beginner's position, and yet still one of responsibility and therefore importance to the church, was the doorkeeper, or θυρωρός (*thyrōros*). This position held a long tradition and usefulness within the religions of Palestinian and Mediterranean regions. Temples, synagogues, and prominent families all employed doorkeepers, sometimes called porters. Yet the person who attended to the post of the doorkeeper still commanded the respect of all who entered. In a figurative sense, all who have received salvation through Jesus Christ have been granted access to God's throne room; therefore, Jesus acts as God's doorkeeper guarding the way in (John 14:6).

Finally, the most obscure leadership role in the early church was the position of the θεράπων (*therápōn*) or personal attendant. Other than Jesus and Moses, no other individuals in the Bible were called a θεράπων (*therápōn*), yet all revered their examples. Understanding and assessing this role required understanding its use in Greek culture and comparing it to Moses and Jesus. A θεράπων (*therápōn*) was the highest in respect and stature of all the master's servants, the one who was responsible for an entire household—all the family members and servants alike.

In the Greek culture, for the gods to die was an impossibility; therefore, their θεράπωντές (*therápōntes* [pl.]) took upon themselves the honor and responsibility of dying in service for their respective deities. In comparison, it is an impossibility for God—*Yahweh* to perish, but salvation for all humanity demanded a sacrifice, and Jesus willingly laid down his life as that sacrifice (Heb 12:2). After Jesus Christ and Moses, this study considered two other individuals, Peter and Paul, who possibly could deserve the title of θεράπων, posthumously. This theorization aims to inspire others so they might give themselves wholly in service to the Lord Jesus Christ for others, even to the extent of one's last breath, so that the gospel of Christ might continue for other generations of believers.

In chapter five, the subjects of concern were the epistles of Timothy, Titus, and Peter, the transition of leadership from the first generation of the church to their successors, and the design for the continuation of the church beyond them into future generations. The chapter presents a brief overview of the lives of Timothy and Titus and discusses their service and apprenticeship under Paul. In addition, this study handles the controversial verse of Scripture concerning whether or not women may teach and lead within the church: 1 Tim 2:12. The chapter also covers duty codes for overseers, ministers, and elders, which the collective believers of the household were to know and then to hold their leaders accountable.

In the letters to Timothy, the stratum of the ἐπίσκοπος—the overseer is assessed by the apostle first, followed by the διάκονος—the minister, and then thirdly, the position of the πρεσβύτεροι—the elders is handled. One may hypothesize this order to be due to the responsibilities and spiritual authority within the early church. Paul declares the conduct of one's household to be a prerequisite for both the ἐπίσκοπος and the διάκονος. In the epistle of Titus, an elder was a respected head of a family, known in their community, with obedient children who also had been converted to the faith. An overseer or minister first serves his family, then his household, then the church, with each level increasing his aptitude as a leader for Christ. As these positions should have already been serving the church prior to their ordination to the roles of authority, it is only logical to expect that they must have served as successful in-home church managers or stewards—οἰκονόμοι. The πρεσβύτεροι were older than average attendees who served the church as mature counselors to the other members of the church, especially its overseers and ministers. Paul's directions to Titus differed in that Titus should ordain elders in every city before setting overseers and ministers in place. This study concluded that

Titus was likely familiar with Paul's instructions to Timothy, so repeating those tenets was unnecessary; only the differing necessities needed to be addressed. Paul instructed Timothy and Titus to install leaders who would set proper spiritual and social examples for the believers.

The purpose of Peter's address to the five churches of Asia was to ensure the perpetuation of the church beyond his lifetime. Peter initially reminds his audience of their salvation in Christ, who he calls "the Shepherd and Bishop of your souls" (1 Pet 2:25). The believers were to emulate Jesus' example and minister to each other just as Jesus had done. Anyone in a leadership role, such as an overseer, was expected to act accordingly. He instructed faithful ministers and stewards to lead their people via extending hospitality to those of the household of faith and strangers and unknown guests (1 Pet 4:8–10). Like Paul, Peter encouraged the church's unity through the household metaphor applied to the body of believers. Peter focuses on the relationships between the church elders and younger members, enabling them to work together. In Peter's letters, the elders were to tend the flock of God's people, take up the oversight, and portray the proper example that others were to follow. The more youthful members were to submit to the older ones, and the elders were to teach and guide the younger ones just like in a household. Peter's and Paul's directives in their letters were for preserving the unity in the church and ensuring it carried on to further generations of believers.

## APPLICATIONS FOR MODERNITY

This discourse aims to present the Christian community with a solution to the plight of their departing, detached, disassociated, and disenfranchised members. With his own life, Jesus set the example for all who follow after him in the Great Commission: those in leadership roles are responsible for the spiritual well-being, care, and nurturing of the congregation.

The First-Century Church focused on smaller, more manageable gatherings in homes and increased personal attention for their followers. Following Jesus's and his apostles' examples, improving the spiritual quality of people's lives should be the primary goal of Christian ministers. Through a careful exegesis of selected passages from the New Testament, the possibility of a more advanced model for leadership emerges, which may prove more adept at ministering to Christians. Presented herein are the network positions/offices or roles that served the public body of the First-Century Church, including how they functioned and trained others, which may be adapted by modern Christian churches. This study conceptualizes eight specific titles that signified positions that comprised the leadership body of the First-Century Church, formulating the proposed stratified leadership model, which could potentially invigorate congregations of today.

The First-Century Church accomplished a phenomenon recorded in Acts 19:10, which crossed cultures and boundaries but has not been repeated since; those believers took the gospel of Christ and spread it throughout Asia Minor in approximately two years and three months. Such a feat does not happen without an organized and orderly body of leadership guiding the way. This study theorized that the stratified leadership model presented herein was the structure for that organization. There is no specific passage of Scripture, like the Ten Commandments, which details the order and organization of the church's leaders in the first century AD. Instead, this research assembled the stratified leadership model from many Scriptures across the NT. In some ways, the efforts of this research are similar to a study concerning "The Mystery" that the apostle Paul wrote about in several passages across his letters but never assembled in a single chapter, requiring the biblical researcher to collect all the pieces of the puzzle before understanding the subject's full scope.

The studies of many other scholars were included in this work, for many of their efforts influenced and contributed to it. The study aimed to refine and unify all available evidential components into a singular operational model. Where previous scholarship focused its effort upon bishops, deacons, and elders, *Synonyms of the New Testament* by Richard C. Trench, raised the possibility for other service roles. The appeal that the believer should not be ignorant of God's purpose for leadership in his household (Rom 1:8–13) and closer examination of Eph 2:20 resulted in the conclusion that the traditional hierarchical structure resident in Christianity was not how the First-Century Church operated. Instead, the hierarchical pyramid with the most distinguished and venerable leader standing atop all others had been inverted through Jesus' proclamation: "Whosoever will be great among you, let him be your minister; and whosoever will be chief among you, let him be your servant" (Matt 20:26–27). The preeminent leader, the utmost servant, was to take the bottommost position serving and supporting all others, and each successive class of authority stood on top of the other until the lowliest level of the average believer was atop them all—layer after layer like the strata of the earth's crust. Jesus' teachings and example of selfless service became the *modus operandi*, while the illustration of the ancient Near Eastern household provided the structure with which this study assembled the positions of the stratified leadership model.

## The Model of the First-Century Church

The stratified leadership model of the First-Century Church is as follows: Jesus, God's *therápōn*, who is the cornerstone of the household of God, is first, and all others look to his example. The charismatic gift ministries of apostles, prophets, evangelists, pastors, and teachers, together with the Lord Jesus Christ, form the household's foundation. Upon them stand the *episkopoi*—overseers responsible for supervising all others, teaching, and setting the pace for the church. The overseers were the most spiritually mature and experientially seasoned of the ordained leadership roles. Yet, they were to excel in humility to the church's needs, the wisdom of the elders, and each other. The overseers previously served the church as successful ministers and household church managers, for their families were to be exemplary. Making up the next stratum are the *diakonoi*—ministers, more numerous than and answering to the overseers; they served the household, carried out church business, and attended to the needs of others, bringing the body of believers to spiritual maturity in Christ.

The church's respected elders—*presbuteroi* served as wise counselors for all levels of believers while working hand-in-hand with the overseers and ministers. They provided wisdom in negotiating sociopolitical situations and guided younger, more youthful believers, teaching them the conventions of proper conduct that would bring respect and honor to the church. Perhaps they might serve as marriage counselors or assist in child care, teaching, and rearing (Titus 2:4–5). The elders who had experience as overseers, ministers, and church managers, though they had graduated to an emeritus stage of service, could be called upon to assist and fill in where the church might need more support in those roles. Elders were relied upon as sage advisors for ordination rites and practices and for selecting individuals to lead newly founded home churches (Acts 15:6–23; 1 Tim 4:14).[1] The church elders were an invaluable resource for

---

1. Young, "On ΕΠΙΣΚΟΠΟΣ AND ΠΠΕΣΒΥΤΕΠΟΣ," 146–48.

managing and negotiating social pitfalls of culture, both internal to the church and external.

The successive stratum of leadership, supported by the strength of the more spiritually mature ones, were the church household managers—*oikonomoi* the stewards who cared for and tended to the in-home services, which were the beating heart of the First-Century Church. These managers received teaching and direction from the overseers and ministers; they accessed the elders' guidance and admonitions, nurturing the believers they welcomed into their homes and preaching the gospel of Christ to all in attendance. As household managers grew in spiritual maturity, respect, reputation, and attendance increased, they were promoted to ministers; likewise, ministers became overseers. The image of the household of God receives one of its most fabulous reflections in a faithful Christian family in action; another is in the fully functioning in-home church.

Next, the level of assistants and apprentices within the church stands on the shoulders of all the preceding leaders. The dedicated assistants—*hypēresia* received assignments attaching themselves to specific leaders: gift ministries, overseers, ministers, or church managers. The assistant's role consisted of a twofold purpose: attending to the needs of their assigned leader and leaning through instruction and imitating the function they performed in the household so that the assistant might become the leader's successor. The assistant could act as an envoy for their patron, and they would receive the due respect from the church for their effectual service.

The church servants—*douloi* were the first to volunteer for tasks benefiting the church. In the first century, they acted as messengers between churches and leaders, ran errands, and made themselves available for whatever the situation required (Phil 2:25; Col 4:7–9).[2] Their role in the church was the most flexible; they were the doers of the church, lending assistance and service without reservation. Logically, a leader might observe a *doulos* over time and select him to become a dedicated assistant. A flourishing in-home church might have several *douloi* among its attendees. An individual, known for their discipleship, inward focus, and application of teachings, previously a recipient of the other believer's care and attention upon maturing, would naturally ferment a desire to give

---

2. Kgatle, "Diakonos and Doulos," 79.

back. This natural progression of internal growth to external application allowed the church's disciples to become its *douloi*.

Lastly, the position of the doorkeeper—*thyrōros* is still needed and has a vital role in a flourishing in-home church. The doorkeeper, possibly not as active and dynamic as a *doulos*, was lower than an in-home church manager's assistant but still dedicated to a particular in-home church. The manager's assistant presumably was a doorkeeper first, who stepped into greater responsibility through maturation. The doorkeeper first earned the manager's and his assistant's trust because one of their responsibilities was gathering up any offerings the attendees presented for distribution amongst members or in support of the overseers and ministers. The doorkeeper took a roll call of all who attended and exercised the manager's authority, preventing the entry of any unwanted and unwelcome elements and keeping the house of the Lord holy.

Beginning with Jesus as the primus, pacesetter, forerunner, author, and finisher of the faith, each subsequent stratum added an increased degree of service and ministering to the one after it. From overseers to ministers and from overseers, ministers, and elders to the church managers. Then, those four strata rendered service to the needs of the assistants, the *douloi*, and the doorkeepers, which, in turn, benefited the leaders they worked closely with. Whenever possible, in a city, town, and home environment, the churches implemented these leadership roles, each group of faithful believers striving together to replicate the examples described in the epistles (Rom 12:16; 15:6; 2 Cor 13:11; Phil 1:27; 2:2; 1 Pet 3:8). Finally, in unison, all these roles, positions, and authorities ministered, served, taught, and nurtured the disciples, saints, and believers who attended their services. Together, all formed the household of God in the first century and successfully spread the gospel of Christ across Asia Minor.

## Theoretical Application

By applying the theory of the stratified leadership model of the early church to their congregations, modern Christian leaders stand to increase the unity of the body of believers and increase the quality of spiritual care delivered to their people. Because no Scripture declares "Thou shalt . . ." churches are free to adapt the model to fit their network of people best. The goal should be the service of others through the most efficient means available. One should never ignore the importance of evangelism to the growth of a church body, not merely from a numerical position but also a vantage of spiritual growth. Every believer is called to be an ambassador for Christ, spreading his gospel for all to hear (2 Cor 5:20). There is tremendous learning and wisdom found when one recounts the gospel message to another: the lives of the giver and the receiver are enriched. Car washes, oil changes, bake sales, and spaghetti dinners may help attract the attention of new people, but these activities should always be secondary to the preeminence of God's Word.

The concern for this study lies in answering the question "How can a church effectively minister to the spiritual needs of its people, both those who are established in the congregation and those newly won?" The leadership positions presented herein aim to eliminate the marginalization of attendees and deliver to all members with effectual ministering. Recall the statements from the first chapter of this study, which points out that because of the increased potential for personal attention, people across North America are drawn to smaller social groups and that effective pastoral leadership is necessary for a church to exceed two hundred members.[3] Utilizing the stratified leadership model, a church of two hundred members could have the pastor as the overseer, a council of six to twelve elders, two ministers, and somewhere between six to twenty household fellowship managers. These numbers only account for the adult members of the church as children and young people should accompany their parents, though the church could offer activities for them in addition to the side. One does not want to break up the nucleus of the Christian family but, in every available practical instance, keep them together.

This application of the model divides up as follows: a single household fellowship could be as small as three to five families, therefore six to ten adults, with the possibility of some single adults in attendance. Depending on the size and accommodations of the home, that number could rise to between fifteen to thirty adults. Six groups of fifteen members per group result in a minimum of ninety members, while twenty home fellowships of fifteen adults per each grows the church membership to three hundred, not counting children and teenagers. The home fellowship, or perhaps the church refers to that level as a Bible study, would probably reach maximum capacity for service to its members between twenty to thirty adults and should be planning to become two groups

---

3. Wagner, *Everychurch Guide to Growth*, 36, 100–103.

of attendees. Within each home fellowship, there would be the manager (and wife), possibly an elder (and his wife), an assistant who is in training to become a manager, a doorkeeper, and perhaps a *doulos* (or a few). If they had an elder and spouse in attendance, that in-home fellowship would receive direct representation in the church council. If one of the church's ministers (plus spouse) led an in-home group, the presence of an elder may or may not be needed. The in-home groups would rally around a central church building, where the overseer would lead the entire congregation. The leaders, ministers, and elders would assist and submit to the leadership of an overseer responsible for the community. The leaders, ministers, and elders should be divided so that all the in-home groups (as contrasted with an actual church edifice) receive attention, guidance, and strengthening.

In this proposed application, the two ministers would be responsible for their own in-home group and two to nine other in-home fellowships. The managers of those two to nine other home fellowships would report regularly and meet with their minister, and potentially, one of those managers could act as the minister's assistant. In addition, the elders of the church council would be dispersed among the home groups, bringing additional oversight and attention. A minister with five to nine home groups under his care should work with the overseer and the council to groom another up-and-coming minister. The in-home groups could meet on various weekday nights for short sessions, perhaps gather for a meal, or conduct a game night together. Then, the whole congregation would gather for a more significant, extended Sunday event, possibly including an afternoon meal. Following a pattern similar to this description, one overseer is not overburdened with attending to the individual needs of two hundred to three hundred members but receives assistance from a diffuse network of other trained, experienced, and capable members. These numbers and ratios should be adjusted according to the needs of the church's membership so that every person can mature spiritually.

The principles within the leadership model presented in this study need not be restricted to churches and realms of religious movements. The business arena of modern life stands to benefit from the lessons and concepts from the ancient world. Many people in the corporate, manufacturing, data processing, educational, and service-industry fields of employment complain of similar problems to those observed in the introduction of this study, such as feeling ignored, devalued, and marginalized, which can result in oppression, depression, and low self-worth.

Any company should recognize that without its workforce, there would be a void within, and its profits would suffer. It would do well to consider restructuring its model to take care of its lowest members. Many companies have enacted programs emphasizing care and concern for employees' needs and well-being, bolstering their infrastructure. Biblical principles generate efficacious results regardless of whether or not one is a Christian. Positive actions fueled by positive principles produce a profitable outcome.

## CONCLUSION

This dissertation began with an observation of a communal problem in modern Christianity: the decline of attendance in church membership. A closer look into the situation revealed that those who had departed expressed disinterest in traditional church practices and politics, detachment from bloated assemblies that resulted in the marginalization of members, and overall negligence by those in leadership. The belief that the Scriptures of the Bible hold all the answers to life and living prompted the search within its pages for a solution. Discovering in Rom 1 that believers should not be ignorant of leadership's purpose in the church, which is to see that the people mature in Christ and their lives bear spiritual fruit, was the start of the research quest of this discourse. A paradigm shift was observed in the practices of the members of the First-Century Church, starting with the book the Acts of the Apostles, which steered them away from the hierarchical format of the temple at Jerusalem and into the homes of the ordinary people. This observation spurred the research endeavoring to discover how the First-Century Church accomplished its successes.

This study discovered seven specific service-oriented leadership positions in operation with the early church: some dominant, overt, and others more supportive. The eighth position, the *therápōn*, was theoretically possible, though not directly applied to anyone in the First-Century Church, and appeared to be utilized more as a visionary goal or a posthumous accolade. The research of the eight roles and how they interacted produced the body of this work. This study argued for and demonstrated from selected New Testament scriptures that God's design of leadership, which was in operation in the early church, was a stratified model, different and superior to the hierarchical models of the temple cult and synagogue of the Second Temple era, which could adapt to suit any size congregation without sacrificing the personal attention needed by its followers. Then, this study presented a hypothetical pattern for how a modern Christian church could implement the model from the early church. That proposed pattern held the potential for growth that most churches desire but without risking losing the quality of oversight that Christian members desire and deserve. This dissertation displays that the First-Century Church conducted itself differently than the traditional religious structure, which Christianity should return to operate. This dissertation promotes that the First-Century Church's stratified leadership model could potentially revitalize church memberships for modern Christianity. The research developed and presented herein promotes a practical service-focused leadership model that gives prominence to the organization's members. The attestation of the New Testament proved the model successful in the First-Century Church. While the stratified leadership model benefits and improves Christian churches worldwide, it should be considered a pragmatic blueprint that any organization, not only religious ones, could potentially adapt and replicate for developing effective leadership in other categories of life.

# Bibliography

Albertz, Rainer, and Rüdiger Schmitt. *Family and Household Religion in Ancient Israel and the Levant*. University Park, PA: Pennsylvania State University Press, 2012.

Arcari, Luca, ed. *Beyond Conflicts: Cultural and Religious Cohabitations in Alexandria and Egypt Between the 1st and the 6th Century CE*. Tübingen: Mohr Siebeck, 2017.

Baker, Warren, and Eugene Carpenter. *The Complete Word Study Dictionary Old Testament*. Chattanooga, TN: AMG, 2003.

Bailey, Sarah Pulliam. "Church Membership in the U.S. Has Fallen Below the Majority for the First Time in Nearly a Century." *Washington Post*, Mar. 29, 2021. https://www.washingtonpost.com/religion/2021/03/29/church-membership-fallen-below-majority.

Balcer, Jack Martin. "The Athenian Episkopos and the Achaemenid 'King's Eye.'" *AJP* 98.3 (1977) 252–63.

Baldovin, John F. "Hippolytus and the Apostolic Tradition: Recent Research and Commentary." *TS* 64.3 (Sep. 2003) 520–42.

Bartlett, David L. "1 Peter." In *Hebrews, the General Epistles, and Revelation: Fortress Commentary on the Bible Study Edition*, edited by Margaret Aymer et al, 667–84. Minneapolis: Fortress and 1517 Media, 2016.

Beard, Mary, John North, and S. R. F. Price. *Religions of Rome*. Cambridge: Cambridge University Press, 1999.

Belleville, Linda. "Ιουνιαν . . . Επισημοι Εν Τοις Αποστολοις: A Re-Examination of Romans 16.7 in Light of Primary Source Materials." *NTS* 51.2 (2005) 231–49.

———. "Lexical Fallacies in Rendering Αὐθεντεῖν in 1 Timothy 2:12: BDAG in Light of Greek Literary and Nonliterary Usage." *BBR* 29.3 (2019) 317–41.

Bradshaw, Paul F. *Rites of Ordination: Their History and Theology*. Collegeville, MN: Liturgical, 2013.

Brenton, Lancelot C. L. *The Septuagint with Apocrypha: Greek and English*. 8th printing. Peabody, MA: Hendrickson, 1999.

Britannica, Editors of Encyclopedia. "Saint Titus." Encyclopedia Britannica. https://www.britannica.com/biography/Saint-Titus.

———. "Mishna." Encyclopedia Britannica. https://www.britannica.com/topic/Mishna.

Brown, Francis, et. al. *The New Brown-Driver-Briggs-Gesenius Hebrew and English Lexicon with Appendix Containing the Biblical Aramaic*. Peabody, MA: Hendrickson, 1979.

Bullinger, E. W. *How to Enjoy the Bible*. Grand Rapids: Kregel, 1990.

———. *Number in Scripture*. Grand Rapids: Kregel, 1998.

———. *Figures of Speech Used in the Bible*. Grand Rapids: Baker, 2003.

Burtchaell, James Tunstead. *From Synagogue to Church*. New York: Cambridge University Press, 2004.

Butcher, Louis A, Jr. "The Decline in Church Attendance in Lancaster County, Pennsylvania and What Can Be Done to Reverse the Trend." PhD dissertation, Lancaster Theological Seminary, 2015. Ann Arbor: UMI, 2015. https://www.worldcat.org/title/decline-in-church-attendance-in-lancaster-county-pennsylvania-and-what-can-be-done-to-reverse-the-trend/oclc/930150015.

Campbell, R. Alastair. "The Elders of the Jerusalem Church." *JTS* 44.2 (Oct. 1993) 511–28.

———. "The Elders: Seniority in Earliest Christianity." *TynBul* 44.1 (1993) 183–87.

———. "*The Elder and the Overseer: One Office in the Early Church*, by Benjamin L. Merkle." *EvQ* 77.3 (2005) 281–83.

Cataclesia. "Death by a Thousand Cuts: Examining Biblical Hapax Legomena One Word at a Time." Oct. 24, 2022. https://cateclesia.com/2022/10/24/death-by-a-thousand-cuts-examining-biblical-hapax-legomena-one-word-at-a-time/.

*Cheers*. "Where Everybody Knows Your Name." Performed by Gary Portnoy. Written by Gary Portnoy and Judy Hart Angelo. NBC Broadcasting 1982.

Chrysostom, John. *Homilies on Galatians, Ephesians, Philippians, Colossians, Thessalonians, Timothy, Titus and Philemon, vol. XII: Nicene and Post-Nicene Fathers*. Edited by Philip Schaff. Grand Rapids: Eerdmans, 1979.

Collins, John N. "Re-thinking 'Eyewitnesses' in the Light of 'Servants of the Word' (Luke 1:2)." *ExpTim* 121.9 (2010) 447–52.

———. "Deacons." In *Diakonia: Re-Interpreting the Ancient Sources* (2009; online edition, Oxford Academic, Oct. 3, 2011) 235–244. https://doi.org/10.1093/acprof:oso/9780195396027.003.0014.

Condon, Kevin. "Church Offices by the Time of the Pastoral Epistles." *Proceedings of the Irish Biblical Association* 2 (1977) 74–94.

Cook, Johann. "The Septuagint as a Holy Text—The First 'Bible' of the Early Church." *HvTSt* 76.4 (2020) 1–9.

Coogan, Michael David, et. al. *The New Oxford Annotated Bible*. College edition. 3rd ed. Oxford: Oxford University Press, 2001.

Daly, Peter. "What Would Christ Say If He Could See The Church Today?" *National Catholic Reporter*, Mar. 11, 2013. https://www.ncronline.org/blogs/parish-diary/what-would-christ-say-if-he-could-see-church-today/.

Danker, Frederick William. *The Concise Greek-English Lexicon of the New Testament*. Chicago: University of Chicago Press, 2009.

Duvall, J. Scott, and J. Daniel Hays. *Grasping God's Word: A Hands-on Approach to Reading, Interpreting, and Applying the Bible*. 3rd ed. Grand Rapids: Zondervan, 2012.

Edmondson, Stephen. *Calvin's Christology*. Cambridge: Cambridge University Press, 2004.

Elliott, John H. "Elders as Leaders in 1 Peter and the Early Church." *HvTSt* 64.2 (2008) 681–95.

Ehrman, Bart D. *After the New Testament, 100–300 C.E.: A Reader in Early Christianity*. 2nd ed. New York: Oxford University Press, 2015.

Eusebius. *The History of the Church*. Translated by G. A. Williamson. New York: Dorset, 1984.

Ferguson, Everett. *Backgrounds of Early Christianity*. 3rd ed. Grand Rapids: Eerdmans, 2003.
Fraser, Richard. "Office of Deacon." *Presb* 11.1 (1985) 13–19.
Freeman, James M. *Manners and Customs of the Bible*. Plainfield, NJ: Logos International, 1972.
Frend, W. H. C. *The Rise of Christianity*. Philadelphia: Fortress Press, 1984.
Goldhill, Simon. *The Temple of Jerusalem*. Cambridge: Harvard University Press, 2005.
Goodrich, John K. "Erastus of Corinth (Romans 16.23): Responding to Recent Proposals on His Rank, Status, and Faith." *NTS* 57.4 (Oct. 2011) 583–93.
———. "Overseers as Stewards and the Qualifications for Leadership in the Pastoral Epistles." *ZNW* 104.1 (2013) 77–97.
Goppelt, Leonhard. *Apostolic and Post-Apostolic Times*. London: Black, 1970.
Grabbe, Lester L. *A History of the Jews and Judaism in the Second Temple Period, Volume 2: The Coming of the Greeks: The Early Hellenistic Period (335–175 BCE)*. London: Bloomsbury, 2011.
Grant, Michael, and Rachel Kitzinger. *Civilization of the Ancient Mediterranean: Greece and Rome*. New York: Scribner's, 1988.
Green, Christopher. *The Message of the Church*. Downers Grove, IL: InterVarsity, 2014.
Green, Sr, Jay, ed. *The Interlinear Bible*. 2nd ed. Peabody, MA: Hendrickson, 1986.
Green, Joel B, and Lee Martin McDonald. *The World of the New Testament: Cultural, Social, and Historical Contexts*. Grand Rapids: Baker Academic, 2013.
———. *The World of the New Testament: Cultural, Social, and Historical Contexts*. Grand Rapids: Baker Academic, 2017.
Greenhalgh, P. A. L. "The Homeric Therapon and 'Opaon' and Their Historical Implications." *BICS* 29 (1982) 81–90.
Grenfell, Bernard P, Arthur S. Hunt, and Edgar J. Goodspeed, eds. *The Tebtunis Papyri*. Vol. 2. London: Oxford University Press, 1907.
Grenz, Stanley J, and Denise Muir Kjesbo. *Women in the Church: A Biblical Theology of Women in Ministry*. Downers Grove, IL: InterVarsity, 1995.
Harris, Edward. "Part I—Professionals and Professional Identity in Greece and Rome." In *Skilled Labour and Professionalism in Ancient Greece and Rome*, edited by Edmund Stewart, Edward Harris, and David Lewis, 27–126. Cambridge: Cambridge University Press, 2020. https://doi.org/10.1017/9781108878135.
Hartmann, Andrea. "Junia—A Woman Lost in Translation: The Name IOYNIAN in Romans 16:7 and its History of Interpretation." *Open Theology* 6.1 (2020) 646–60.
Holmes, Michael W, ed. *The Apostolic Fathers in English*. Grand Rapids: Baker Academic, 2006.
Hübner, Jamin. "Revisiting the Clarity of Scripture in 1 Timothy 2:12." *JETS* 59.1 (2016):99–117.
Jordan, Borimir. "The Meaning of the Technical Term 'Hyperesia' in Naval Contexts of the Fifth and Fourth Centuries B.C." *California Studies in Classical Antiquity* 2 (1969) 183–207.
Josephus, Flavius, and William Whiston. *The Works of Flavius Josephus: Complete and Unabridged*. Translated by William Whiston, A.M. Peabody, MA: Hendrickson, 1996.
Kgatle, Mookgo Solomon. "Diakonos and Doulos as Concepts of True Discipleship in Mark 10.43–44: A Social Scientific Reading." *JPT* 28.1 (Jan. 2019) 71–83.

Knight, George W. "The Number and Functions of the Permanent Offices in the New Testament Church." *Presb* 1.2 (Fall 1975) 111–16.

———. "Two Offices (Elders/Bishops and Deacons) and Two Orders of Elders (Preaching/Teaching Elders and Ruling Elders): A New Testament Study." Presb 11.1 (Spring 1985) 1–12.

Köstenberger, Andreas J, and Richard D. Patterson. *Invitation to Theological Studies Series: Invitation to Biblical Interpretation: Exploring the Hermeneutical Triad of History, Literature, and Theology*. Grand Rapids: Kregel, 2018.

———, and Thomas R. Scheiner. *Women in the Church: An Interpretation and Application of 1 Timothy 2:9–15*, ed. Andreas J. Köstenberger and Thomas R. Scheiner, 3rd ed. Wheaton, IL: Crossway, 2016.

Lawler, Magdalen. *Well of Living Water: Jesus and the Samaritan Woman*. Havertown, PA: Messenger, 2019.

Leustean, Lucian N. "Eastern Orthodoxy, Geopolitics and the 2016 'Holy and Great Synod of the Orthodox Church.'" *Geopolitics* 23.1 (2018) 201–16.

Lightfoot, J. B. *St. Paul's Epistle to the Philippians*. London: Macmillan, 1881.

———. *The Apostolic Fathers*. Edited by J. R. Harmer. Grand Rapids: Christian Classics Ethereal Library, 2012.

———, and Edward D. Andrews. *The Apostolic Fathers: What Did They Teach?* Cambridge: Christian, 2016.

Lockyer, Herbert. *All the Apostles of the Bible: Studies in the Characters of the Apostles, the Men Jesus Chose, and the Message They Proclaimed*. Grand Rapids: Zondervan, 1972.

Louw, Johannes P. and Eugene A. Nida. *Greek-English Lexicon of the New Testament: Based on Semantic Domains*. 2nd ed. New York: United Bible Societies, 1989.

MacDonald, Margaret Y. *The Pauline Churches a Socio-Historical Study of Institutionalization in the Pauline and Deutero-Pauline Writings*. Cambridge: Cambridge University Press, 1988.

MacMullen, Ramsay. "Perceptible." In *Paganism in the Roman Empire*, 1–48. New Haven: Yale University Press, 1981.

Mather, P. Boyd. "Paul in Acts as 'Servant' and 'Witness.'" *BR* 30 (1985) 23–44.

May, David M. "Servant and Steward of the Mystery: Colossians 1:26–27; 2:2; 4:3." *RevExp* 116.4 (2019) 469–74.

McDowell, Sean. *The Fate of the Apostles: Examining the Martyrdom Accounts of the Closest Followers of Jesus*. Burlington, VT: Routledge, 2015.

McLaren, James S. *Power and Politics in Palestine: The Jews and the Governing of Their Land, 100 BC–AD 70*. London: Bloomsbury, 2015.

Merkle, Benjamin L. *The Elder and Overseer: One Office in the Early Church*. StBibLit New York: Peter Lang, 2003.

———. "Are the Qualifications for Elders or Overseers Negotiable?" *BSac* 171.682 (Apr. 2014) 172–88.

———. "The Authority of Deacons in Pauline Churches." *JETS* 64.2 (June 2021) 309–25.

———, and Thomas R. Schreiner, eds. *Shepherding God's Flock: Biblical Leadership in the New Testament and Beyond*. Grand Rapids: Kregel, 2014.

Metzger, Bruce Manning, and Michael David Coogan. *The Oxford Companion to the Bible*. New York: Oxford University Press, 1993.

Miller, David W. "The Uniqueness of New Testament Church Eldership." *Grace Theological Journal* 6.2 (1985) 315–27.

Millgram, Rabbi Abraham. "Minyan: The Congregational Quorum." https://www.myjewishlearning.com/article/minyan-the-congregational-quorum/.

Morrison, J. S. "Hyperesia in Naval Contexts in the Fifth and Fourth Centuries BC." *JHS* 104 (1984) 48–59.

Mounce, William D. *Basics of Biblical Greek*. Grand Rapids: Zondervan, 1993.

———, and Robert H. Mounce. *The Zondervan Greek and English Interlinear New Testament (NASB/NIV)*. 2nd ed. Grand Rapids: Zondervan, 2011.

Mowry, Lucetta. "The Early Circulation of Paul's Letters." *JBL* 63.2 (1944) 73–86.

Nagy, Gregory. "Achilles and Patroklos as Models for the Twinning of Identity." Nov. 2, 2020. *The Center for Hellenic Studies*, Harvard University. https://chs.harvard.edu/curated-article/gregory-nagy-achilles-and-patroklos-as-models-for-the-twinning-of-identity.

Neusner, Jacob. ""Pharisaic-Rabbinic" Judaism: A Clarification." *HR* 12.3 (1973) 250–70.

Newman, Hillel, and Ruth M. Ludlam. *Proximity to Power and Jewish Sectarian Groups of the Ancient Period: A Review of Lifestyle, Values, and Halakhah in the Pharisees, Sadducees, Essenes, and Qumran*. Leiden: Brill, 2006.

Novakovic, Lidija. "Jews and Samaritans." *The World of the New Testament: Cultural, Social, and Historical Contexts*. Grand Rapids: Baker Academic, 2013.

Optatus. *The Work of St. Optatus, Bishop of Milevis, Against the Donatists, with Appendix*. London: Longmans, Green, 1917.

Osborne, Grant R. *Ephesians: Verse by Verse*. Bellingham, WA: Lexham Press, 2017.

Orthodox Observer News. "His Eminence Archbishop Elpidophoros Elevates Dean of Holy Cross School of Theology to Economos of Archdiocese." Feb 8, 2022. https://www.goarch.org/-/archbishop-elpidophoros-elevates-dean-parsenios-holy-cross-2022.

Orthodox Times. "Archdiocese of Thyateira: Symeon Mene Ordained to the Holy Diaconate." Jul. 18, 2022. https://orthodoxtimes.com/archdiocese-of-thyateira-symeon-mene-ordained-to-the-holy-diaconate/.

Page, Sydney H. T. "Whose Ministry? A Re-Appraisal of Ephesians 4:12." *NovT* 47.1 (2005) 26–46.

Pascoe, David. "Living as God's Stewards: Exploring some Theological Foundations." *ACR* 90.1 (2013) 22–33.

Paley, Frederick Apthorp, ed. "Supplices." In *Euripides: With an English Commentary*, 367–442. Cambridge Library Collection—Classics. Cambridge: Cambridge University Press, 2010.

Payne, Philip B. "1 Tim 2:12 and the Use of οὐδέ to Combine Two Elements to Express a Single Idea." *NTS* 54.2 (2008) 245–46.

Peterson, Paul Silas. *The Decline of Established Christianity in the Western World: Interpretations and Responses*. London, New York: Routledge, Taylor & Francis, 2017.

Pew Research Center. Religion & Public Life Project. "America's Changing Religious Landscape." May 12, 2015. https://www.pewforum.org/2015/05/12/americas-changing-religious-landscape.

———, "In U.S, Decline of Christianity Continues at Rapid Pace." Oct. 17, 2019. https://www.pewresearch.org/religion/2019/10/17/in-u-s-decline-of-christianity-continues-at-rapid-pace/.

Purpura, Ashley M. *God, Hierarchy, and Power: Orthodox Theologies of Authority from Byzantium*. New York: Fordham University Press, 2018.

Rajak, Tessa, and David Noy. "Archisynagogoi: Office, Title and Social Status in the Greco-Jewish Synagogue." *JRS* 83 (1993) 75–93.

Rayburn, Robert S. "Three Offices: Minister, Elder, Deacon." *Presb* 12.2 (1986) 105–14.

Regev, Eyal. "The Sadducees, the Pharisees, and the Sacred: Meaning and Ideology in the Halakhic Controversies Between the Sadducees and Pharisees." *Review of Rabbinic Judaism* 9.1–2 (2006) 126–40.

Rhodes, Peter J. (Durham), and Markschies, Christoph (Berlin). "Episkopos, Episkopoi." In *Brill's New Pauly*, edited by Hubert Cancik, et al. https://doi.org/10.1163/1574-9347_bnp_e333250.

Richardson, Peter, and Amy Marie Fisher. *Herod: King of the Jews and Friend of the Romans*. 2nd ed. London: Taylor and Francis, 2017.

Robertson, A. T. *Word Pictures in the New Testament: Concise Edition*. Nashville: Holman, 2000.

Sanders, E. P. *Judaism: Practice and Belief, 63 BCE–66 CE*. Minneapolis: 1517 Media, 2016.

Senior, Roger. *The Contextualisation of Leadership in Paul Applied to English-Speaking Methodist Churches in Peninsular Malaysia*. Oxford: Regnum Books International, 2017.

Simmons, L. M. "The Talmudical Law of Agency." *JQR* 8.4 (1896) 614–31.

Smith, William. *Smith's Bible Dictionary*. New Jersey: Fleming H. Revel, 1975.

Steinsaltz, Rabbi Adin. *The William Davidson Talmud* (Koren–Steinsalz). Sefaria. https://www.sefaria.org/Berakhot.6b.2?ven=William_Davidson_Edition_-_English&lang=bi.

Stephenson, Paul. *Constantine Roman Emperor, Christian Victor*. New York: Peter Mayer, 2009.

Stevenson, Angus, ed. *Oxford Dictionary of English*. 3rd ed. Oxford, New York: Oxford University Press, 2010.

Stewart, Edmund, Edward Harris, and David Lewis. *Skilled Labour and Professionalism in Ancient Greece and Rome*. Edited by Edmund Stewart, Edward Harris, and David Lewis. Cambridge: Cambridge University Press, 2020.

Stewart-Sykes, Alistair. *The Didascalia Apostolorum: An English Version with Introduction and Annotation*. Turnhout: Brepols, 2009.

Strauch, Alexander. *Paul's Vision for the Deacons: Assisting the Elders with the Care of God's Church*. Littleton, CO: Lewis & Roth Publishers, 2017.

Strong, James. *Strong's Exhaustive Concordance of the Bible*. Nashville: Thomas Nelson, 2010.

Swanson, Robert N. "Apostolic Successors: Priests and Priesthood, Bishops, and Episcopacy in Medieval Western Europe," In *A Companion to Priesthood and Holy Orders in the Middle Ages*, edited by G. Peters and C. C. Anderson, 4–42. Leiden: Brill, 2015. https://brill.com/edcollbook/title/22194.

Thayer, Joseph H. *Thayer's Greek-English Lexicon of the New Testament*. Peabody, MA: Hendrickson, 2009.

Trench, Richard Chenevix. *Synonyms of The New Testament*. 9th ed. Grand Rapids: Eerdmans, 1948.

van Haeperen, Françoise. "Des pontifes païens aux pontifes chrétiens." *RBPH* 81.1 (2003) 137–59.

van Opstall, Emilie M, ed. *Sacred Thresholds: The Door to the Sanctuary in Late Antiquity*. Boston: Brill, 2018.

van Zyl, Hermie C. "The Evolution of Church Leadership in the New Testament—A New Consensus?" *Neot* 32.2 (1998) 585–604.
Wagner, C. Peter, Elmer L. Towns, and Thom S. Rainer. *The Everychurch Guide to Growth: How Any Plateaued Church Can Grow*. Nashville: Broadman & Holman, 1998.
Walsh, Michael. *Roman Catholicism: The Basics*. London: Taylor & Francis, 2016.
Wallace, Daniel B. *Greek Grammar Beyond the Basics*. Grand Rapids: Zondervan, 1996.
Wilshire, Leland. "The TLG Computer and Further Reference to ΑΥΘΕΝΤΕΩ in 1 Timothy 2:12." *NTS* 34 (1988) 120–34.
Young, Frances M. "On ΕΠΙΣΚΟΠΟΣ AND ΠΠΕΣΒΥΤΕΠΟΣ." *JTS* 45.1 (1994) 142–48.

# Scripture Index

## OLD TESTAMENT / HEBREW BIBLE

### Genesis
| | |
|---|---|
| 20:7 | 76 |

### Exodus
| | |
|---|---|
| 1:5 | 112 |
| 3:18 | 112 |
| 15:20–21 | 78 |
| 18:13–20 | 59 |
| 21:2–6 | 125 |
| 24:1–9 | 112 |
| 33:17–23 | 133 |

### Leviticus
| | |
|---|---|
| 16 | 33 |
| 21:10 | 40 |

### Numbers
| | |
|---|---|
| 4:16 | 102 |
| 11:16 | 40 |
| 12:7 | 133, 134 |
| 12:8 | 133 |
| 35:25 | 40 |

### Deuteronomy
| | |
|---|---|
| 18:15–18 | 134 |
| 18:25 | 77 |

### Judges
| | |
|---|---|
| 4:4 | 78 |

### 1 Samuel
| | |
|---|---|
| 17:34–36 | 83 |

### 2 Samuel
| | |
|---|---|
| 15:24–29 | 35 |

### 1 Kings
| | |
|---|---|
| 1:39–40 | 54 |

### 1 Chronicles
| | |
|---|---|
| 9:17–18 | 130 |
| 9:22 | 130 |
| 9:24 | 129 |
| 15:18 | 130 |
| 18:16 | 32 |
| 24:31 | 32 |
| 26:30 | 102 |

### 2 Chronicles
| | |
|---|---|
| 7:19–22 | 54 |
| 31:14 | 130 |
| 36:23 | 104 |

### Ezra
| | |
|---|---|
| 1:1–8 | 104 |
| 3:10 | 32 |
| 5:5 | 113 |

## Ezra (continued)

| | |
|---|---|
| 6:7–14 | 113 |
| 7:7 | 32, 125 |

## Nehemiah

| | |
|---|---|
| 11:9 | 105 |

## Job

| | |
|---|---|
| 10:12 | 102 |

## Psalms

| | |
|---|---|
| 23 | 51, 83, 184 |
| 68:18 | 87 |
| 84:10 | 130 |
| 107:20 | 164 |
| 109:8 | 102 |
| 119:1–11 | 54 |

## Proverbs

| | |
|---|---|
| 1:5 | 67 |
| 11:14 | 67 |
| 12:5 | 67 |
| 24:6 | 67 |
| 29:18 | 137 |

## Song of Solomon

| | |
|---|---|
| 5:10 | 134 |

## Isaiah

| | |
|---|---|
| 8:14 | 141 |
| 18:16 | 141 |
| 41:8 | 133 |
| 42:1 | 135 |
| 42:6–7 | 135 |
| 44:28 | 104 |
| 45:1 | 104 |
| 52:13–15 | 135 |
| 53:10–11 | 135 |
| 55:1 | 54 |

## Jeremiah

| | |
|---|---|
| 1:7–8 | 77 |
| 7:11 | 55 |
| 49:14 | 71 |

## Micah

| | |
|---|---|
| 6:4 | 78 |

# APOCRYPHA

## Wisdom of Solomon

| | |
|---|---|
| 12:6 | 167, 170 |

## 1 Maccabees

| | |
|---|---|
| 12:1–3 | 7 |
| 16:1–26 | 7 |

# NEW TESTAMENT

## Matthew

| | |
|---|---|
| 4:23 | 46 |
| 4:25 | 46 |
| 5:25 | 16 |
| 5:48 | 138 |
| 8 | 46 |
| 9:7 | 56 |
| 9:10 | 48 |
| 9:23 | 48 |
| 9:28 | 48 |
| 9:36–37 | 83 |
| 9:36 | 52 |
| 10:1–14 | 48 |
| 10:2–4 | 71 |
| 10:5–6 | 71 |
| 10:40 | 71 |
| 11:10–11 | 77 |
| 11:28–29 | 7 |
| 15:1–9 | 36 |
| 15:24 | 52 |
| 16:1 | 35 |
| 16:6–12 | 53 |
| 16:6 | 35 |
| 16:11–12 | 35 |
| 16:18–19 | 57 |
| 16:18 | 4, 41, 55 |
| 16:19 | 131, 139 |
| 16:24–25 | 50 |

| | | | | | |
|---|---|---|---|---|---|
| 17:2 | 139 | 3:2 | 34, 35 | | |
| 17:24–27 | 45 | 4:15 | 46 | | |
| 20:20 | 49 | 4:17 | 110 | | |
| 20:25–27 | 49 | 4:18–19 | 46 | | |
| 20:25–26 | 174 | 4:20 | 37 | | |
| 20:26–27 | 194 | 5:17 | 35 | | |
| 20:26 | 51 | 6:13–16 | 71 | | |
| 20:28 | 46 | 6:13 | 72 | | |
| 22:13 | 46 | 7:16 | 77 | | |
| 22:15–22 | 45 | 7:36–46 | 48 | | |
| 22:23 | 36 | 9:1–6 | 48 | | |
| 22:34 | 36 | 10:1–9 | 48 | | |
| 23: 8–12 | 50 | 10:7–10 | 131 | | |
| 23:11 | 51 | 10:16 | 71 | | |
| 23:13–27 | 36 | 11:24 | 56 | | |
| 23:23–28 | 54 | 12:37–40 | 142 | | |
| 24:1–2 | 77 | 12:48 | 91 | | |
| 24:42–44 | 142 | 12:58 | 16 | | |
| 25:43 | 104 | 16:1–8 | 116 | | |
| 28:19 | 3 | 16:1–3 | 117 | | |
| | | 16:10 | 111 | | |
| **Mark** | | 17:11 | 81 | | |
| 1:1 | 79 | 19:30–38 | 54 | | |
| 1:21 | 46 | 19:40–41 | 55 | | |
| 2:15 | 47 | 19:44 | 103 | | |
| 3:6 | 54 | 19:45–47 | 55 | | |
| 3:14–19 | 48 | 20:1 | 54 | | |
| 5:38 | 37 | 20:19–40 | 84 | | |
| 6:34 | 52, 83 | 20:26 | 172 | | |
| 9:2 | 139 | 21:5–6 | 77 | | |
| 9:35 | 51 | 22:66 | 159 | | |
| 9:37 | 71 | | | | |
| 10:42–44 | 125 | **John** | | | |
| 10:42–45 | 7 | 1:1–17 | 134 | | |
| 10:43 | 51 | 2:5 | 51 | | |
| 10:45 | 126 | 2:9 | 51 | | |
| 12:13 | 36, 54 | 4:3–4 | 47 | | |
| 13:1–2 | 77 | 4:5 | 81 | | |
| 13:1 | 55 | 4:9 | 47 | | |
| 13:2 | 55 | 4:20 | 47 | | |
| 13:34 | 130 | 4:35 | 53 | | |
| | | 5:36 | 71 | | |
| **Luke** | | 7:53 | 56 | | |
| 1:8–9 | 34 | 10:1–5 | 84 | | |
| 2:30–32 | 135 | 10:11–13 | 84 | | |
| 2:36–38 | 78, 165 | 10:2–12 | 83 | | |
| | | 10:2–4 | 51 | | |

## John (continued)

| | |
|---|---|
| 10:3–4 | 184 |
| 10:3 | 184 |
| 10:7–9 | 52 |
| 10:11–18 | 52 |
| 10:11 | 3, 186 |
| 10:14 | 3, 186 |
| 12:26 | 51 |
| 13:3–10 | 7 |
| 13:4–16 | 72 |
| 13:5 | 49 |
| 13:15–17 | 49 |
| 14:6 | 186, 191 |
| 15:1–2 | 53 |
| 15:2 | 53 |
| 15:5 | 53 |
| 15:6 | 53 |
| 15:8–10 | 53 |
| 15:19 | 141 |
| 18:13 | 34 |
| 18:16–17 | 130, 131 |
| 18:24 | 34 |
| 19:28–30 | 71 |
| 21:15–17 | 139 |
| 21:15–19 | 52 |
| 21:19 | 139 |

## Acts

| | |
|---|---|
| 1:5 | 57 |
| 1:6–11 | 146 |
| 1:8 | 57 |
| 1:12–15 | 57 |
| 1:15 | 41, 110 |
| 1:17 | 59 |
| 1:20 | 100, 102, 105 |
| 1:23–26 | 57, 89 |
| 1:24–26 | 151 |
| 1:25–26 | 73 |
| 1:25 | 16, 17, 71, 100 |
| 2:16 | 78 |
| 2:17 | 41 |
| 2:18 | 125 |
| 2:25–30 | 78 |
| 2:38 | 78 |
| 2:41 | 41 |
| 2:42–47 | 41 |
| 2:42–45 | 117 |
| 2:42 | 41 |
| 2:46 | 117 |
| 3:21 | 78 |
| 3:22 | 77 |
| 4:5 | 112 |
| 4:6 | 34, 35 |
| 4:8 | 112 |
| 4:11 | 56 |
| 4:23 | 96, 112 |
| 4:24–31 | 106 |
| 5:34 | 35, 142 |
| 5:42 | 117 |
| 6:1–6 | 111, 151 |
| 6:1 | 58, 110, 158 |
| 6:2 | 107 |
| 6:3–6 | 89 |
| 6:3–4 | 59 |
| 6:5 | 80, 81 |
| 6:6 | 108 |
| 6:7 | 6, 110 |
| 6:12 | 96, 112 |
| 7:37 | 77 |
| 8:3–4 | 142 |
| 8:5–6 | 81, 103 |
| 8:14 | 103 |
| 8:26 | 81 |
| 8:31 | 109 |
| 9:1–6 | 142 |
| 9:1–2 | 142 |
| 9:1 | 110 |
| 9:19–22 | 85 |
| 9:19–20 | 110 |
| 9:19 | 110 |
| 9:25 | 110 |
| 9:27 | 142 |
| 9:39–41 | 158 |
| 10:1–11:18 | 114 |
| 10:7 | 119 |
| 10:25–37 | 41 |
| 10:34 | 166 |
| 11:25–30 | 143 |
| 11:29–30 | 96 |
| 11:30 | 59 |
| 12:13 | 111, 131 |
| 13:1–13 | 85 |
| 13:1–2 | 89, 143 |
| 13:1 | 79, 85 |
| 13:2–3 | 108 |

# SCRIPTURE INDEX

| | |
|---|---|
| 13:2 | 73 |
| 13:3 | 152 |
| 13:5 | 73, 123 |
| 13:14 | 65 |
| 14:1 | 65 |
| 14:11 | 137 |
| 14:14 | 73, 143 |
| 14:19 | 143 |
| 14:21–27 | 73 |
| 14:23 | 59, 113, 151, 158 |
| 15:2–29 | 112 |
| 15:6–23 | 195 |
| 15:22 | 70 |
| 15:23 | 97 |
| 15:32 | 79 |
| 15:36 | 95, 103 |
| 16:1–6 | 149 |
| 16:1 | 128, 149 |
| 16:4 | 97 |
| 16:11–15 | 114 |
| 16:25–34 | 114 |
| 17:1 | 65 |
| 17:14–15 | 128 |
| 17:23 | 38 |
| 18:20 | 101 |
| 18:1–11 | 114 |
| 18:1–2 | 120 |
| 18:1 | 74 |
| 18:5 | 128 |
| 18:6 | 143 |
| 18:20 | 101 |
| 18:24–28 | 164 |
| 18:24–27 | 120 |
| 19:10 | 8, 143, 194 |
| 19:22 | 118, 128 |
| 19:31 | 70 |
| 19:39 | 4 |
| 20:4 | 128 |
| 20:17 | 96, 97 |
| 20:20 | 6 |
| 20:28 | 96, 97, 101, 105 |
| 21:8–11 | 165 |
| 21:8–9 | 79 |
| 21:8 | 80 |
| 21:10–11 | 79 |
| 21:20 | 142 |
| 22:3 | 85, 142 |
| 22:5 | 159 |
| 22:28 | 126 |
| 23:6 | 35, 64, 142 |
| 23:7 | 36 |
| 26:4–12 | 64 |
| 26:5 | 142 |
| 26:16 | 123, 142 |
| 27:11 | 67 |

## Romans

| | |
|---|---|
| 1:1–2 | 126 |
| 1:1 | 64, 126 |
| 1:8–13 | 194 |
| 1:10–13 | 95 |
| 1:13 | xiii, 3, 6, 162 |
| 1:16 | 64, 79 |
| 2:11 | 166 |
| 6:22 | 161 |
| 10:15 | 80 |
| 11:13 | 16, 17, 143 |
| 12:2 | 138 |
| 12:3 | 17, 69 |
| 12:4 | 69 |
| 12:6–7 | 69 |
| 12:6 | 17 |
| 12:16 | 111, 197 |
| 13:4 | 46 |
| 15:6 | 111, 197 |
| 15:24 | 8 |
| 16:1 | 108, 157 |
| 16:3–5 | 120 |
| 16:5 | 6 |
| 16:7 | 74, 75 |
| 16:21 | 128, 150 |
| 16:23 | 26, 118 |

## 1 Corinthians

| | |
|---|---|
| 1:11 | 6 |
| 1:17 | 81 |
| 3:5 | 108 |
| 3:6 | 163 |
| 3:9 | 163 |
| 4:1–2 | 120, 163 |
| 4:1 | 118, 123, 143, 162 |
| 4:16 | 144 |
| 4:17 | 150, 161 |
| 7 | 126, 165 |

## 1 Corinthians (continued)

| | |
|---|---|
| 7:8 | 158 |
| 7:23 | 161 |
| 9:5–6 | 73 |
| 9:24–26 | 137 |
| 10:1–14 | 65 |
| 11:1 | 81, 144 |
| 11:7–11 | 174 |
| 12:4–6 | 70 |
| 12:14–27 | 147 |
| 12:27–28 | 66, 67, 144, 174, 190 |
| 12:28 | 12, 65, 68, 70, 84 |
| 14:32–35 | 172 |
| 14:34 | 164, 166 |
| 15:10 | 143 |
| 15:51–52 | 88 |
| 16:5 | 95 |
| 16:10 | 128, 150 |
| 16:14 | 174 |
| 16:15–19 | 6 |
| 16:16 | 174 |
| 16:19 | 74, 119 |

## 2 Corinthians

| | |
|---|---|
| 1:1 | 128 |
| 2:13 | 176 |
| 3:1–4 | 128 |
| 3:2–3 | 91 |
| 3:6 | 109 |
| 3:18 | 88 |
| 4:5 | 64, 126, 161 |
| 5:17–21 | 109 |
| 5:20 | 198 |
| 8:7 | 180 |
| 8:19 | 151 |
| 8:23 | 73, 176 |
| 10:4 | 148 |
| 11:7 | 81 |
| 13:11 | 111, 197 |

## Galatians

| | |
|---|---|
| 1:8 | 81 |
| 1:10 | 64, 126 |
| 1:14 | 142 |
| 1:19 | 74 |
| 2:1 | 176 |
| 2:7 | 143 |
| 2:20 | 144 |
| 3:28 | 166 |
| 6:7–8 | 163 |
| 6:9–10 | 163 |
| 6:10 | 121, 152 |

## Ephesians

| | |
|---|---|
| 2:5–6 | 181 |
| 2:19–21 | 56 |
| 2:19–20 | 68 |
| 2:19 | 118, 121, 144, 152, 177, 190 |
| 2:20 | 91, 194 |
| 3:2 | 86 |
| 3:8 | 20, 143 |
| 3:15 | 152 |
| 4:3 | 111 |
| 4:6–13 | 86 |
| 4:11–13b | 69, 70 |
| 4:11–12 | 88 |
| 4:11 | 70, 80, 81, 84, 86, 87, 88 |
| 4:12 | 82 |
| 4:13 | 88, 111 |
| 5 | 165 |
| 5:21 | 172, 179 |
| 5:22–24 | 157, 166 |
| 5:22 | 174 |
| 6:10–18 | 148 |
| 6:12 | 149 |
| 6:21 | 109 |

## Philippians

| | |
|---|---|
| 1:1 | 46, 62, 99, 101, 106, 108, 126, 128, 150 |
| 1:13 | 143 |
| 1:27 | 106, 111, 197 |
| 2:2 | 111, 197 |
| 2:5 | 138, 144 |
| 2:5–11 | 106 |
| 2:6 | 137 |
| 2:7–8 | 50 |
| 2:19–22 | 161 |
| 2:25–30 | 106 |
| 2:25 | 74, 128, 196 |

| | |
|---|---|
| 3:5 | 64, 142 |
| 3:14 | 105 |
| 3:21 | 88 |
| 4:9 | 106, 163 |
| 4:18 | 128 |
| 4:23 | 106 |

## Colossians

| | |
|---|---|
| 1:7 | 109 |
| 1:25 | 108, 143 |
| 1:28 | 138 |
| 3:16 | 109, 164 |
| 3:18 | 174 |
| 3:21 | 157 |
| 3:25 | 166 |
| 4:7–9 | 128, 196 |
| 4:7 | 109 |
| 4:12 | 128 |
| 4:15 | 6 |
| 4:16 | 95, 178 |
| 4:17 | 120 |

## 1 Thessalonians

| | |
|---|---|
| 1:1 | 150 |
| 2:6–7 | 74 |
| 2:6 | 150 |
| 3:2 | 109, 150 |
| 4:15–18 | 146 |
| 4:17 | 181 |
| 5:2 | 142 |
| 5:12–13 | 18 |

## 2 Thessalonians

| | |
|---|---|
| 1:1 | 150 |
| 3:7–8 | 173 |

## 1 Timothy

| | |
|---|---|
| 1:1–3 | 148 |
| 1:3 | 64, 105, 148, 150 |
| 1:18 | 148 |
| 2:5–7 | 85 |
| 2:5 | 77, 99, 131 |
| 2:7 | 85, 108, 143 |
| 2:8–11 | 165 |
| 2:8 | 165 |
| 2:9 | 165 |
| 2:11 | 171 |
| 2:12 | 164, 165, 166, 167, 168, 169, 170, 171, 172, 173, 174, 175, 187, 192 |
| 2:13–15 | 172 |
| 2:13–14 | 173, 174 |
| 3 | 62, 93, 99, 165 |
| 3:1–7 | 97, 153 |
| 3:1 | 16, 101, 102, 153 |
| 3:2–7 | 17 |
| 3:2–3 | 180 |
| 3:2 | 93, 94, 95, 97, 101, 106, 153, 179, 180, 181, 182, 183 |
| 3:3 | 153, 181, 186 |
| 3:4–5 | 153, 155, 156, 180 |
| 3:4 | 94, 160 |
| 3:5 | 111, 153, 160 |
| 3:8–9 | 154 |
| 3:8 | 46, 120, 180, 181, 186 |
| 3:10 | 16, 111, 155, 179 |
| 3:11 | 155, 156, 158, 180 |
| 3:12–13 | 156 |
| 3:12 | 46, 155, 156, 160, 180, 181 |
| 3:13 | 16, 180 |
| 3:15 | 56, 156, 161, 177 |
| 4:7 | 174 |
| 4:12 | 152 |
| 4:14 | 108, 152, 159, 195 |
| 5 | 62, 93 |
| 5:1–8 | 181 |
| 5:1–3 | 160 |
| 5:1–2 | 152, 160 |
| 5:2 | 114 |
| 5:3 | 158 |
| 5:7 | 179 |
| 5:11 | 158 |
| 5:16 | 158 |
| 5:1–17 | 97 |
| 5:17 | 93, 94, 95, 97, 160, 180, 183 |

## 2 Timothy

| | |
|---|---|
| 1:6 | 152 |

## 2 Timothy (continued)

| | |
|---|---:|
| 1:11 | 85, 143 |
| 2:2 | 85, 147, 163 |
| 2:3-4 | 161 |
| 2:3 | 149 |
| 2:6 | 161, 162 |
| 2:7 | 148 |
| 2:15 | 92, 161, 171, 187 |
| 2:16-17 | 161 |
| 2:20-21 | 161 |
| 2:22 | 161 |
| 2:24 | 161, 180 |
| 3:6-7 | 174 |
| 3:16-17 | 9, 167, 187 |
| 3:16 | 171 |
| 4:5 | 80 |
| 4:7 | 137, 144 |
| 4:8 | 137 |
| 4:13 | 178 |
| 4:20 | 118 |

## Titus

| | |
|---|---:|
| 1:1 | 64, 126, 176 |
| 1:5-8 | 181 |
| 1:5-7 | 96, 180, 181 |
| 1:5 | 64, 89, 105, 112, 113, 115, 176, 183 |
| 1:6-9 | 17 |
| 1:6 | 177, 179, 180 |
| 1:7 | 95, 101, 106, 115, 118, 121, 177, 179, 182, 186 |
| 1:8-9 | 177 |
| 1:8 | 183 |
| 1:9 | 93, 94, 97, 180 |
| 2:2-6 | 177 |
| 2:4-5 | 177, 195 |
| 2:7-8 | 177 |
| 5:17 | 113 |

## Philemon

| | |
|---|---:|
| 1:1-2 | 120 |
| 1:16 | 128 |

## Hebrews

| | |
|---|---:|
| 3:1-6 | 133 |
| 3:2 | 134 |
| 3:5 | 132, 134 |
| 4:15 | 40 |
| 8:6 | 99 |
| 9:7 | 33 |
| 9:15 | 99 |
| 12:1 | 137 |
| 12:2 | 192 |
| 12:5-11 | 103 |
| 12:15 | 103 |
| 12:24 | 99 |
| 13:20-21 | 13 |
| 13:20 | 83, 184 |
| 13:23 | 149 |

## James

| | |
|---|---:|
| 1:1 | 181 |
| 1:21 | 171 |
| 1:22 | 91 |
| 1:27 | 158 |
| 2:14-17 | 128 |
| 5:14 | 115 |

## 1 Peter

| | |
|---|---:|
| 1:1 | 140 |
| 1:2-5 | 140 |
| 1:3-4 | 141 |
| 1:7 | 140 |
| 1:12 | 80 |
| 1:13 | 140 |
| 1:18-23 | 182 |
| 1:20-21 | 167 |
| 1:24-25 | 182 |
| 2:1-5 | 182 |
| 2:4-5 | 141 |
| 2:5 | 182 |
| 2:6-7 | 56 |
| 2:9 | 182 |
| 2:11 | 140 |
| 2:12 | 103 |
| 2:20-21 | 141 |
| 2:21 | 182, 185 |
| 2:25 | 83, 101, 107, 141, 182, 183, 193 |
| 3:1-7 | 172 |
| 3:8 | 197 |

| | |
|---|---|
| 3:18–22 | 141 |
| 4:7–11 | 183 |
| 4:8–10 | 193 |
| 4:9 | 182 |
| 4:10 | 110, 120, 183, 190 |
| 4:11 | 183 |
| 4:17 | 56 |
| 5:1–4 | 185 |
| 5:1–3 | 183 |
| 5:1 | 94, 98, 140, 141 |
| 5:2–3 | 141 |
| 5:2 | 103, 185 |
| 5:3 | 174 |
| 5:4 | 83 |
| 5:5 | 115, 183 |
| 5:5–7 | 20 |
| 5:13 | 8 |

## 2 Peter

| | |
|---|---|
| 1:1 | 141 |
| 1:2–8 | 141 |
| 1:14–15 | 141 |
| 1:20–21 | 9, 133 |
| 1:20 | 171 |
| 2:1–3 | 141 |
| 3:1–8 | 141 |
| 3:10 | 141 |
| 3:13 | 142 |
| 3:14 | 142 |
| 3:15–16 | 142 |
| 3:18 | 142 |

## Revelation

| | |
|---|---|
| 1:1 | 125 |
| 3:7 | 131 |
| 3:8 | 131 |
| 18:17 | 67 |

www.ingramcontent.com/pod-product-compliance
Lightning Source LLC
Chambersburg PA
CBHW070251230426
43664CB00014B/2484